Siúil, a Rún
The Girl from the Other Side

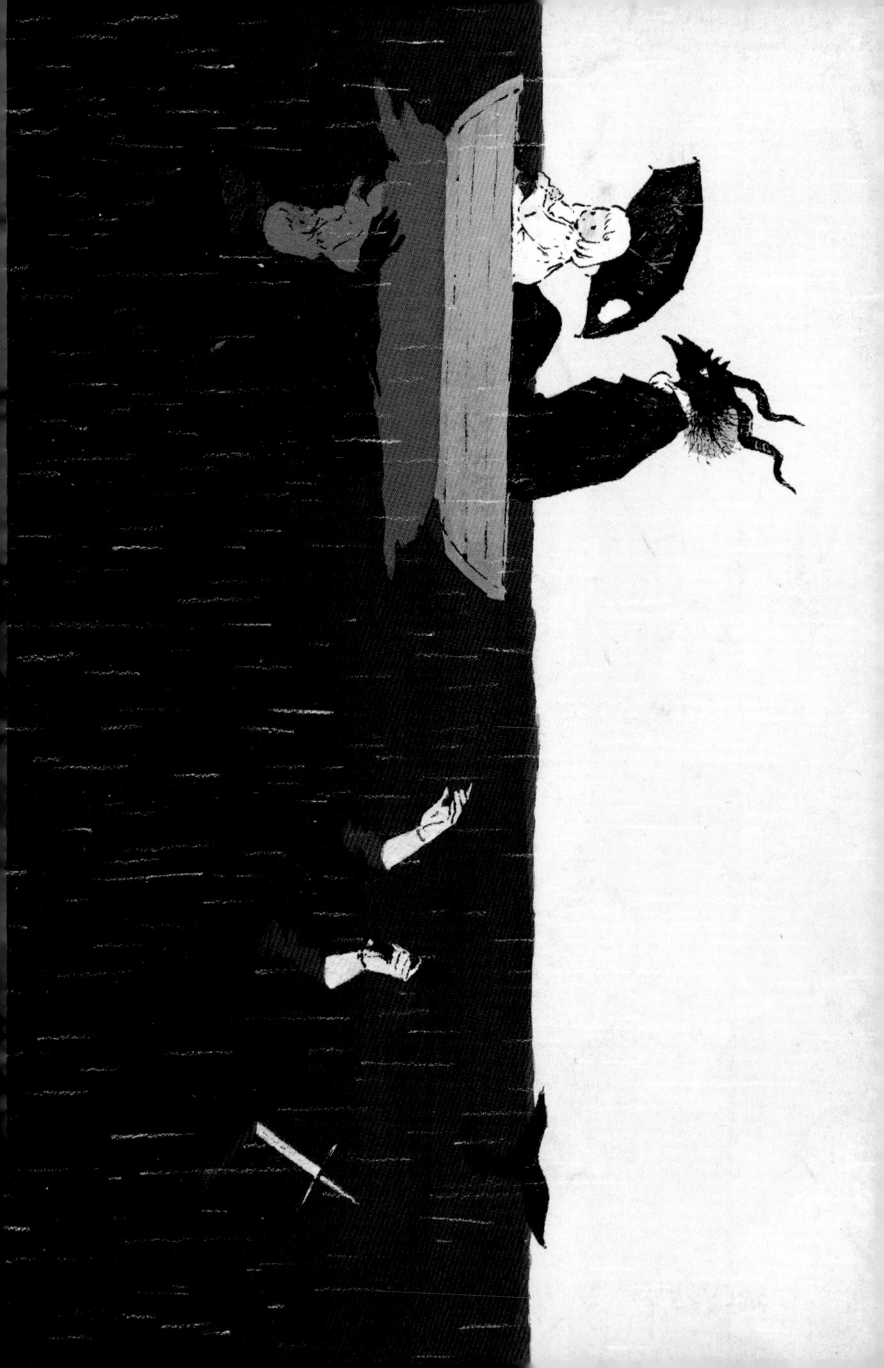

Chapter 21

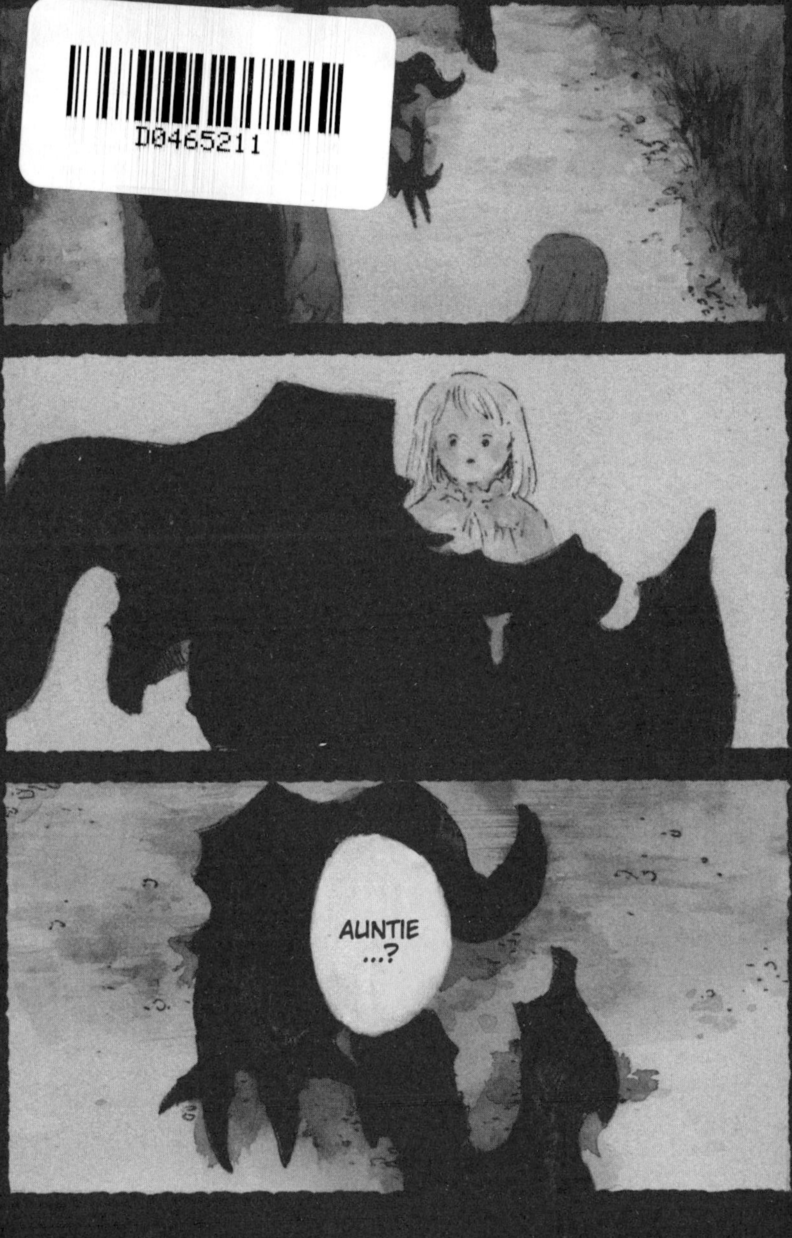
AUNTIE ...?

Chapter 21

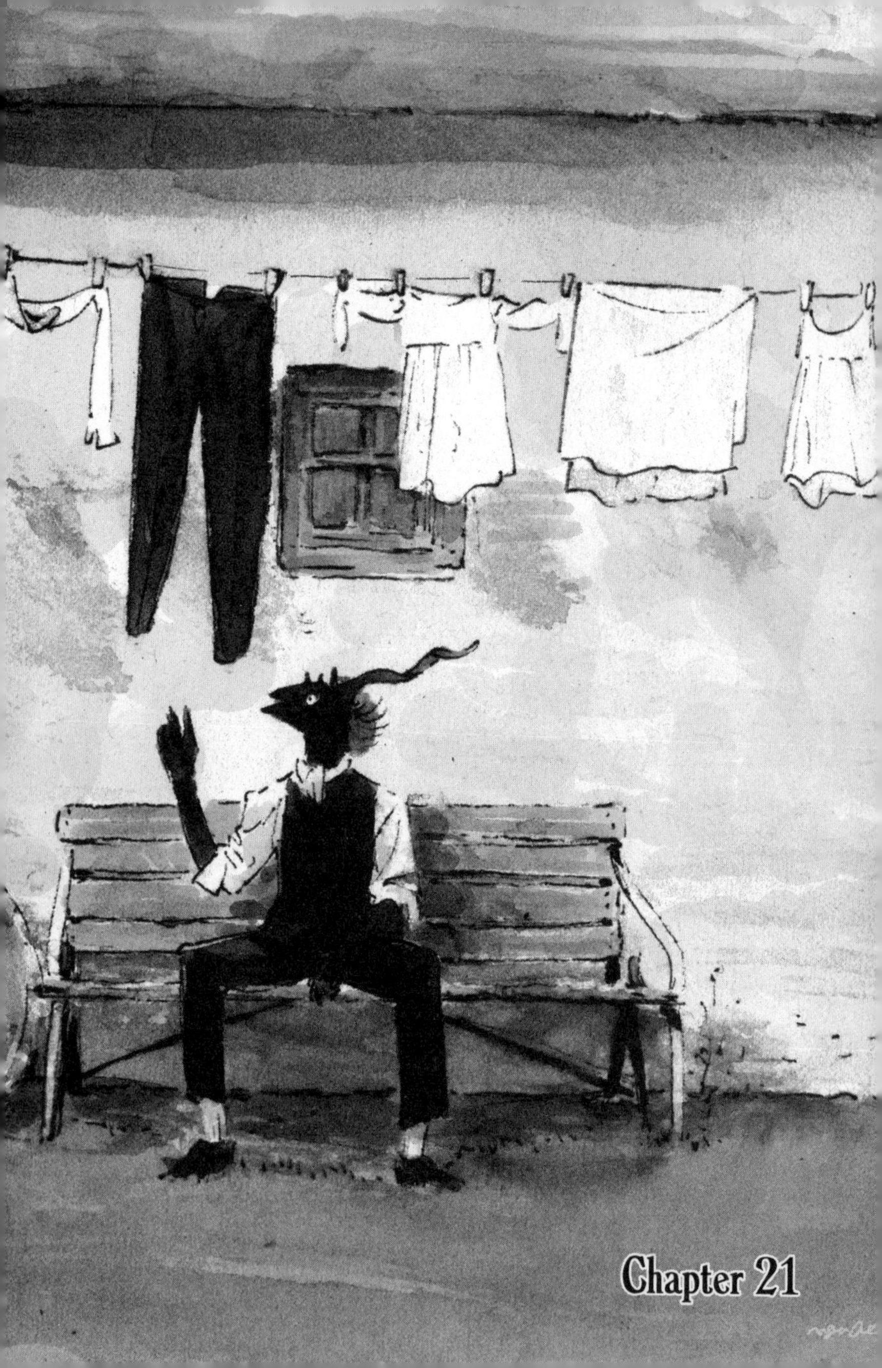

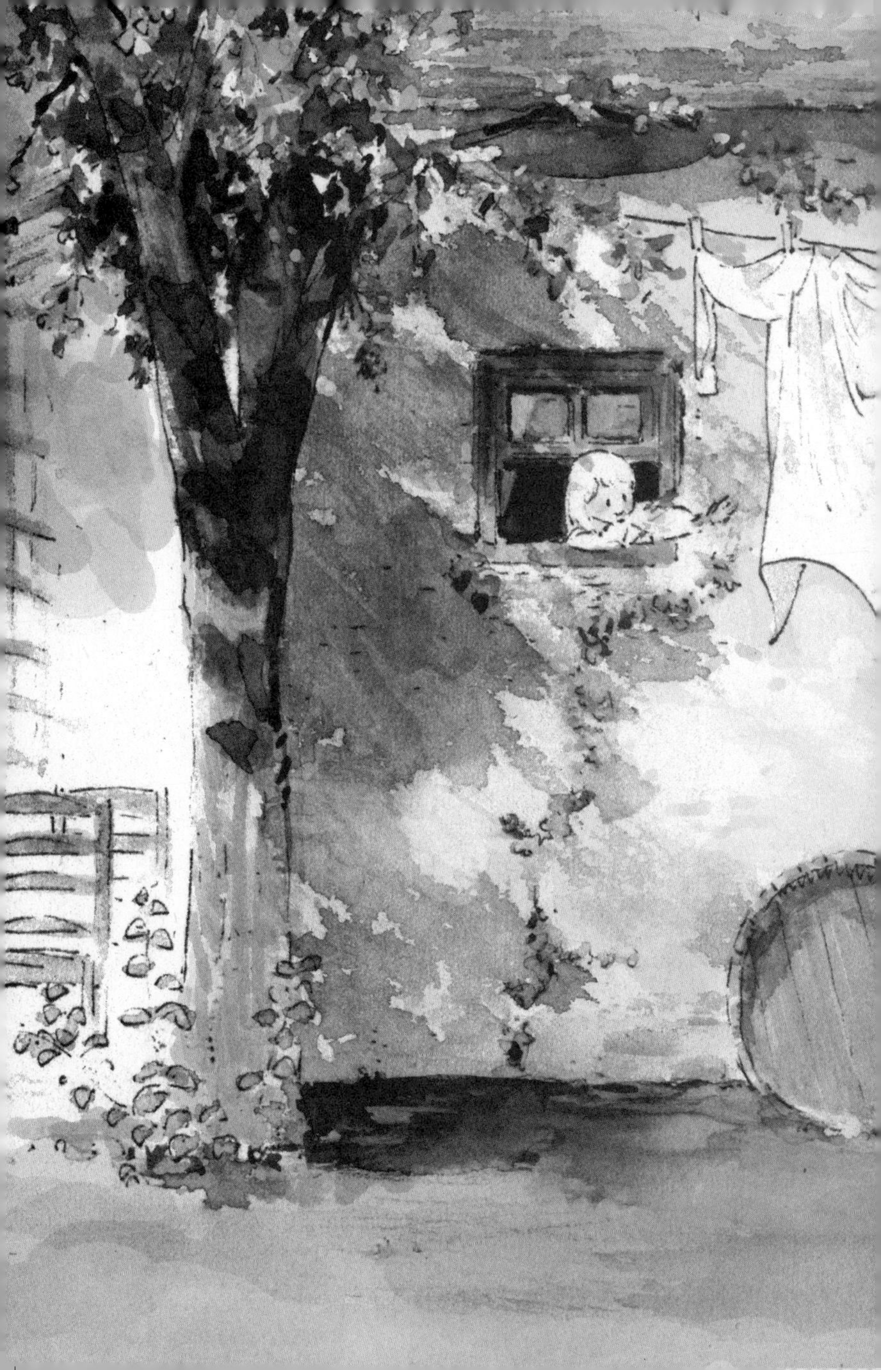

Siúil, a Rún
The Girl from the Other Side

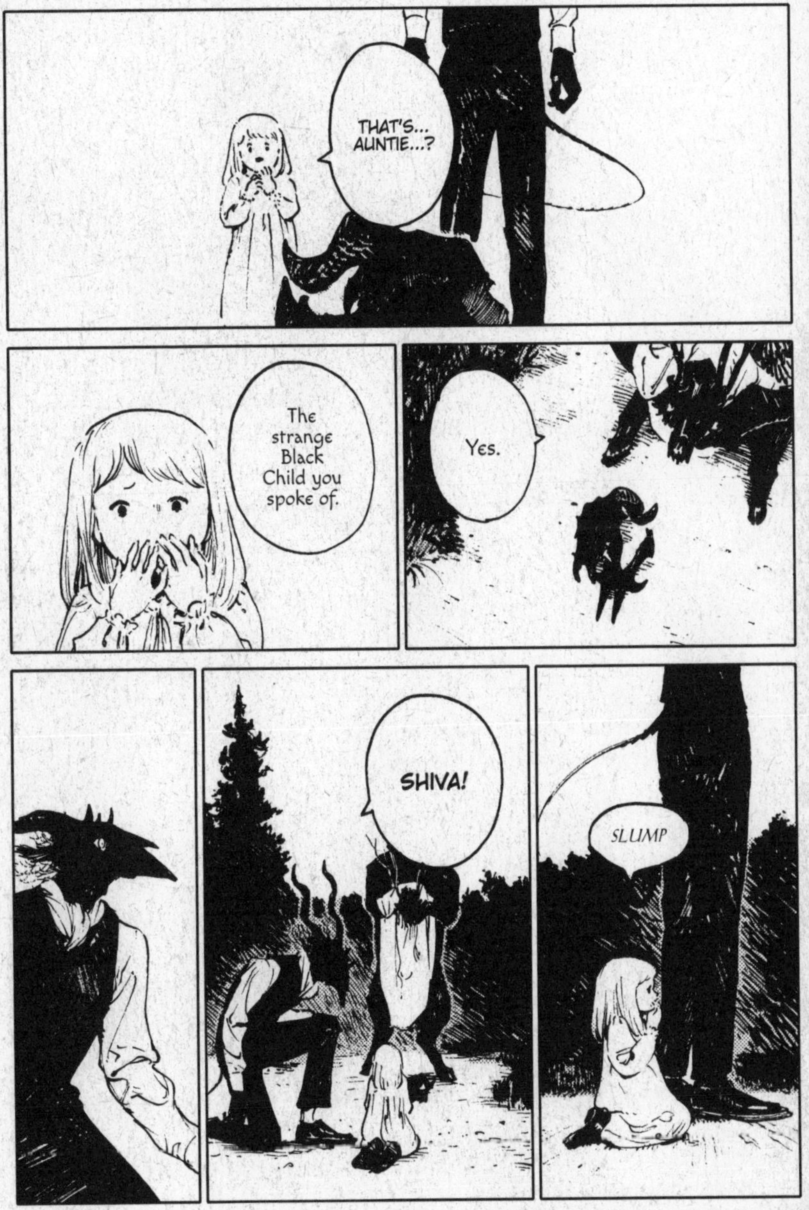
THAT'S... AUNTIE...?
Yes.
The strange Black Child you spoke of.
SLUMP
SHIVA!

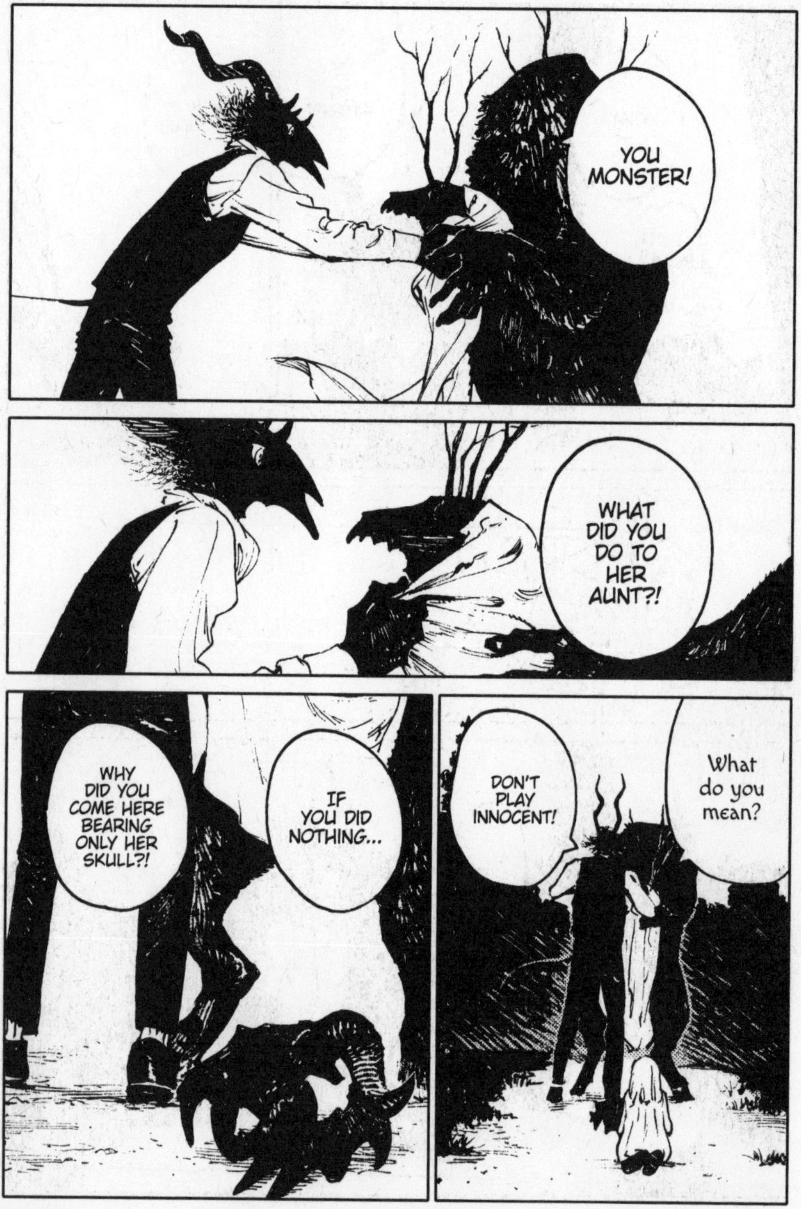
YOU MONSTER!
WHAT DID YOU DO TO HER AUNT?!
What do you mean?
DON'T PLAY INNOCENT!
IF YOU DID NOTHING...
WHY DID YOU COME HERE BEARING ONLY HER SKULL?!

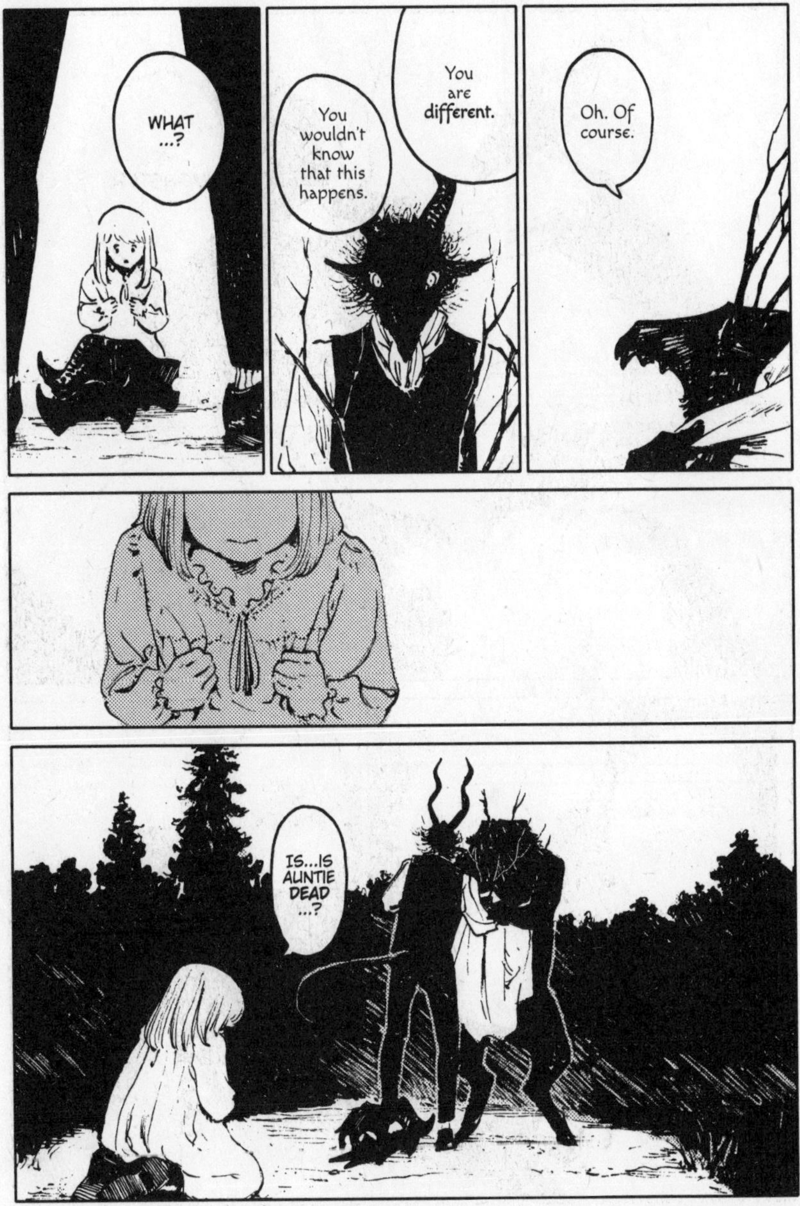
Oh. Of course.
You are different.
You wouldn't know that this happens.
WHAT ...?
IS...IS AUNTIE DEAD ...?

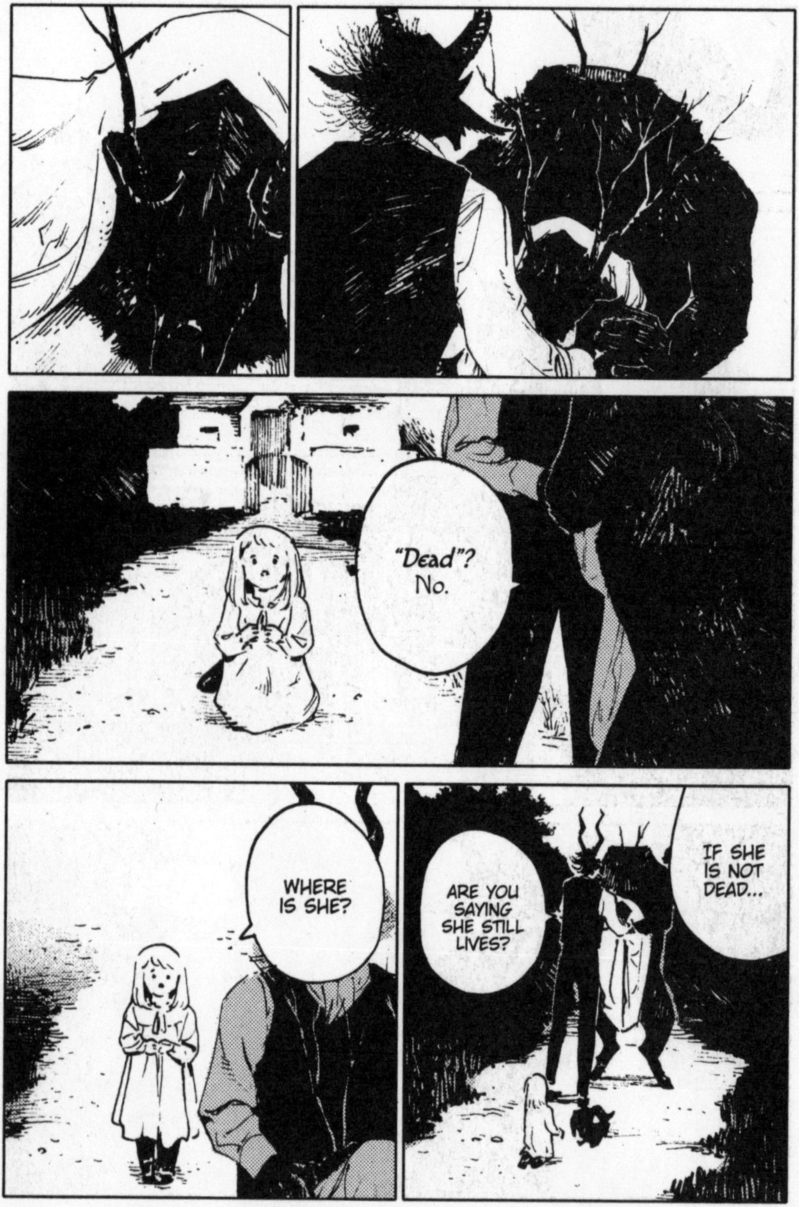
"Dead"? No.
IF SHE IS NOT DEAD...
ARE YOU SAYING SHE STILL LIVES?
WHERE IS SHE?

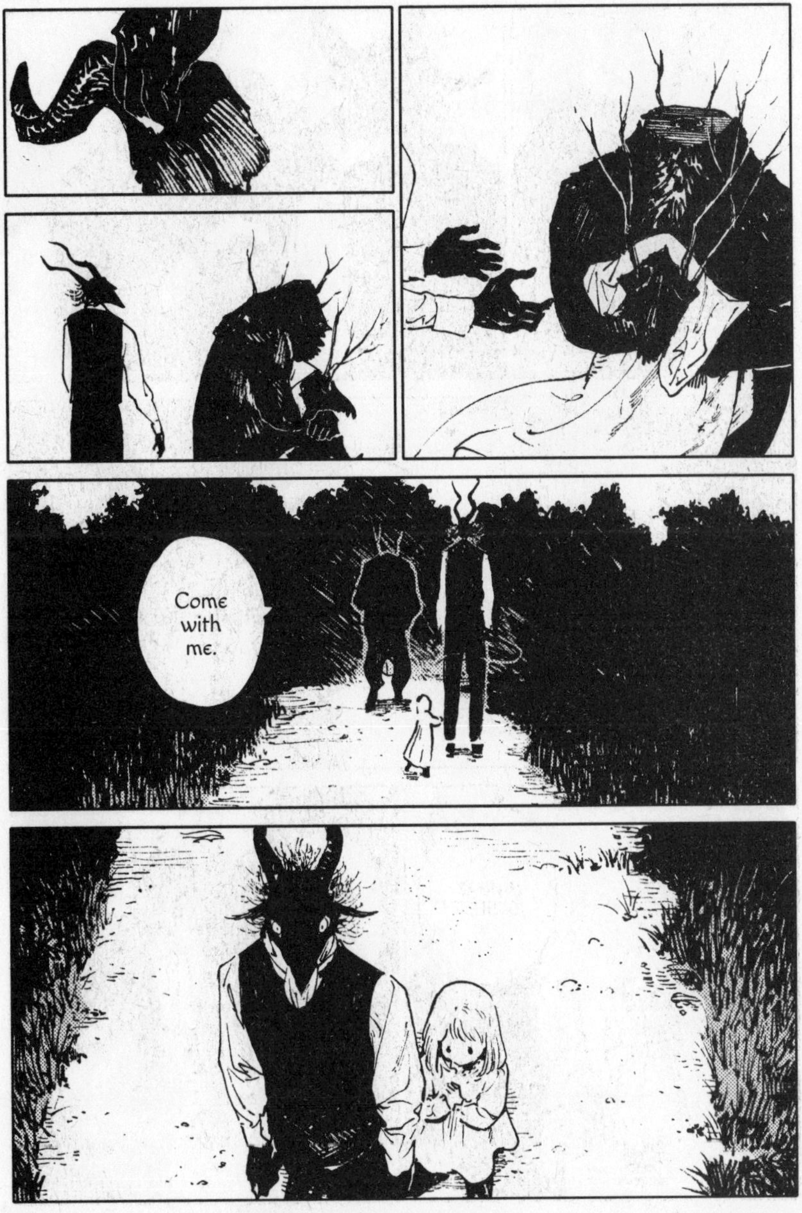
Come with me.

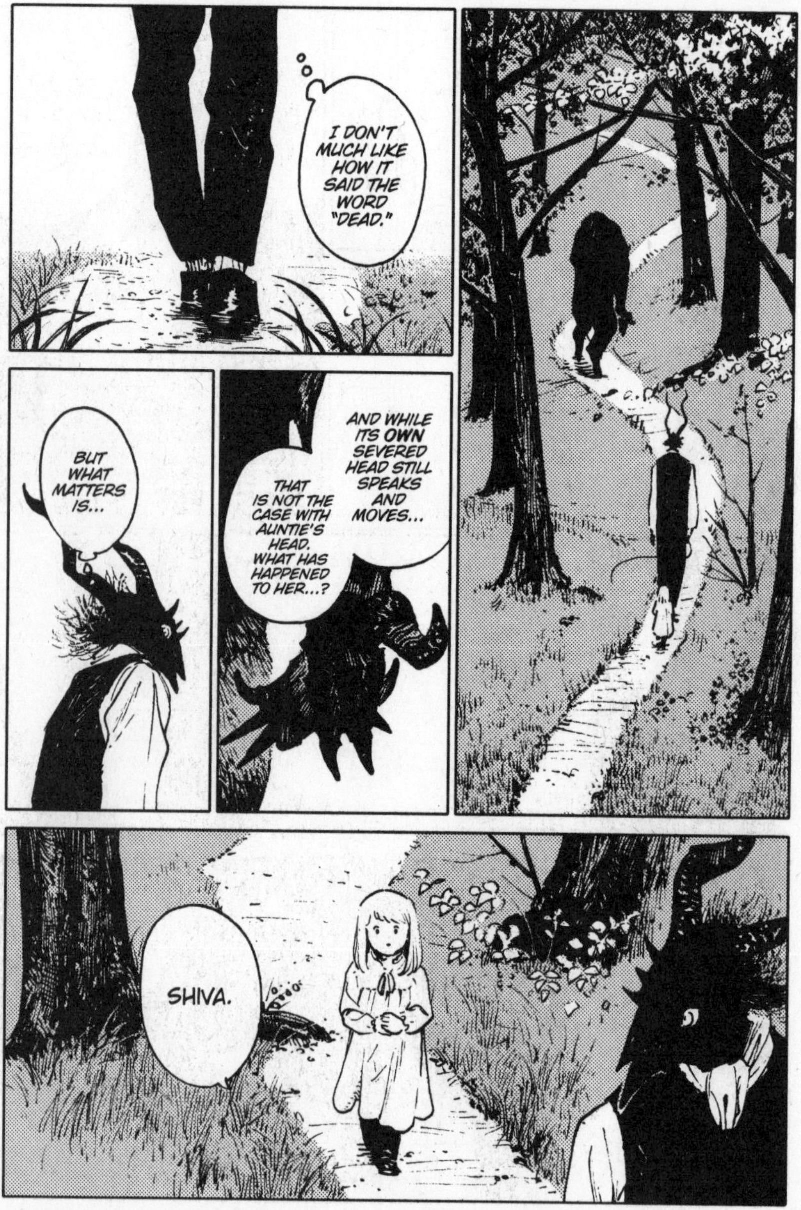
I DON'T MUCH LIKE HOW IT SAID THE WORD "DEAD."
AND WHILE ITS OWN SEVERED HEAD STILL SPEAKS AND MOVES...
THAT IS NOT THE CASE WITH AUNTIE'S HEAD. WHAT HAS HAPPENED TO HER...?
BUT WHAT MATTERS IS...
SHIVA.

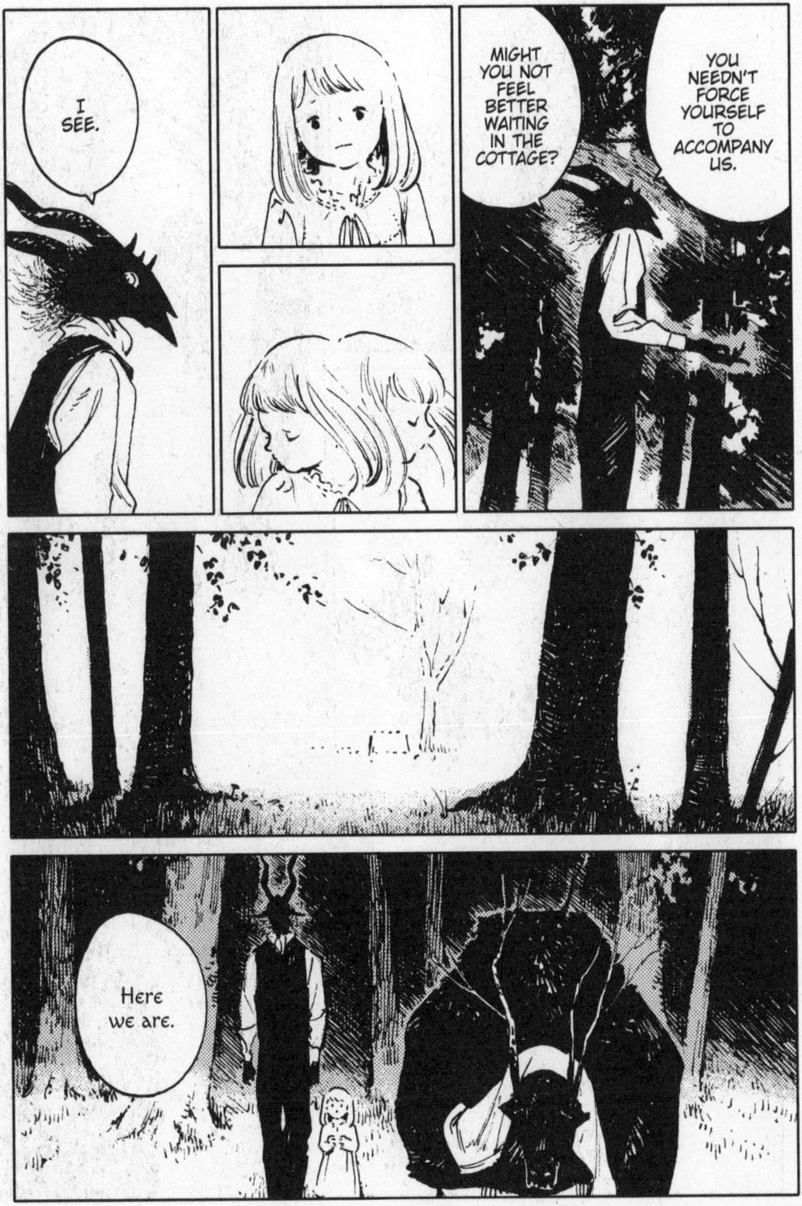
YOU NEEDN'T FORCE YOURSELF TO ACCOMPANY US.
MIGHT YOU NOT FEEL BETTER WAITING IN THE COTTAGE?
I SEE.
Here we are.

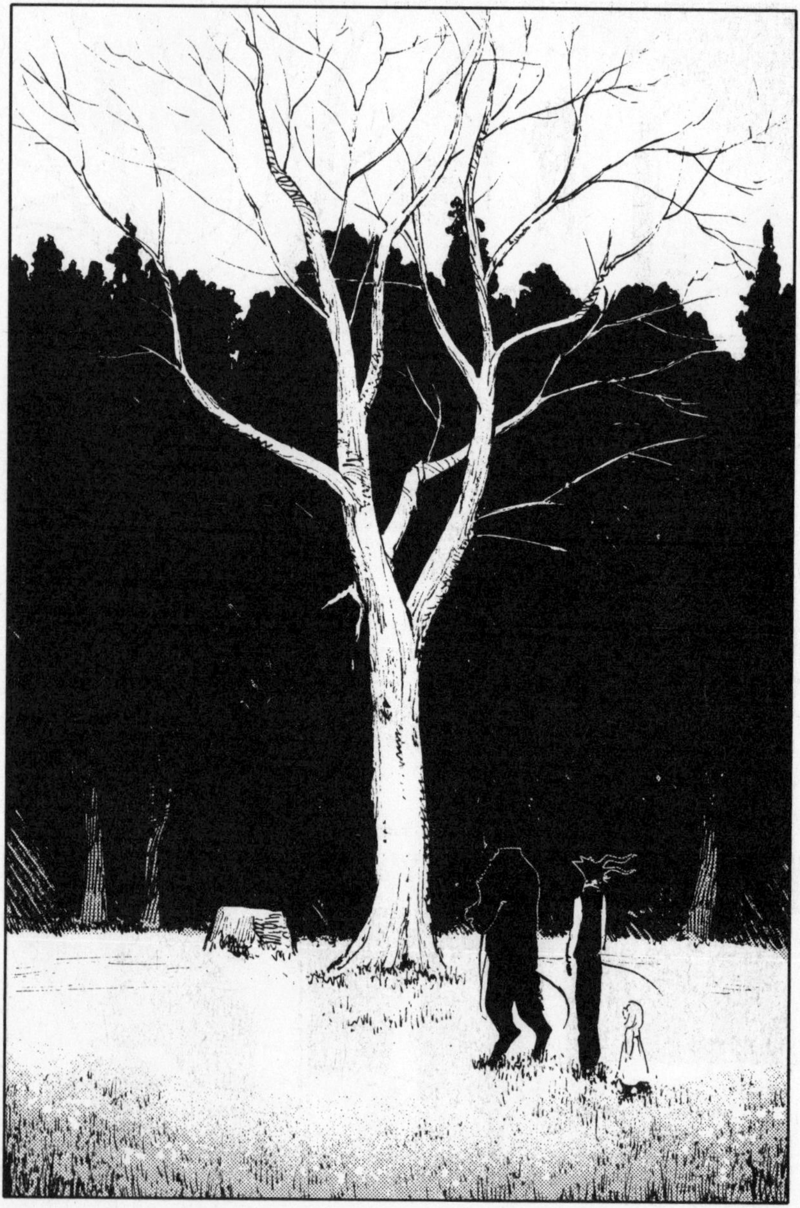

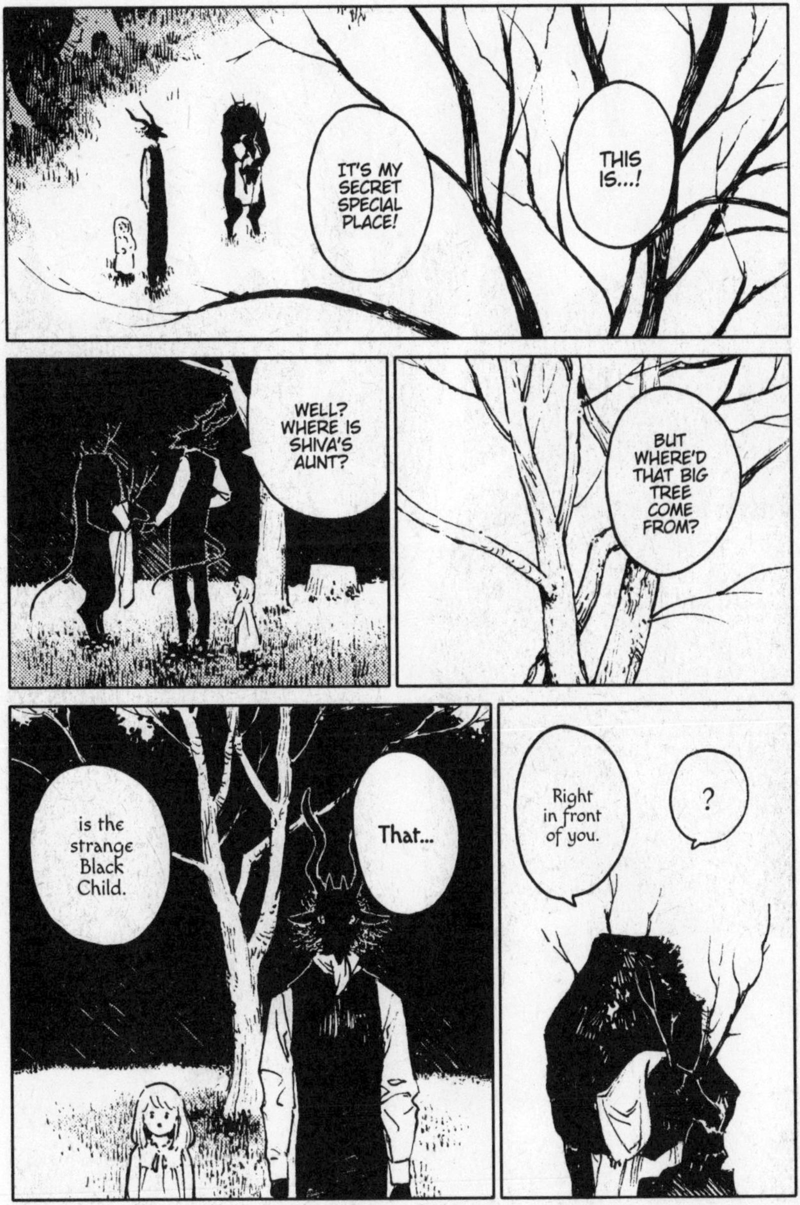
THIS IS...!
IT'S MY SECRET SPECIAL PLACE!
BUT WHERE'D THAT BIG TREE COME FROM?
WELL? WHERE IS SHIVA'S AUNT?
?
Right in front of you.
That...
is the strange Black Child.

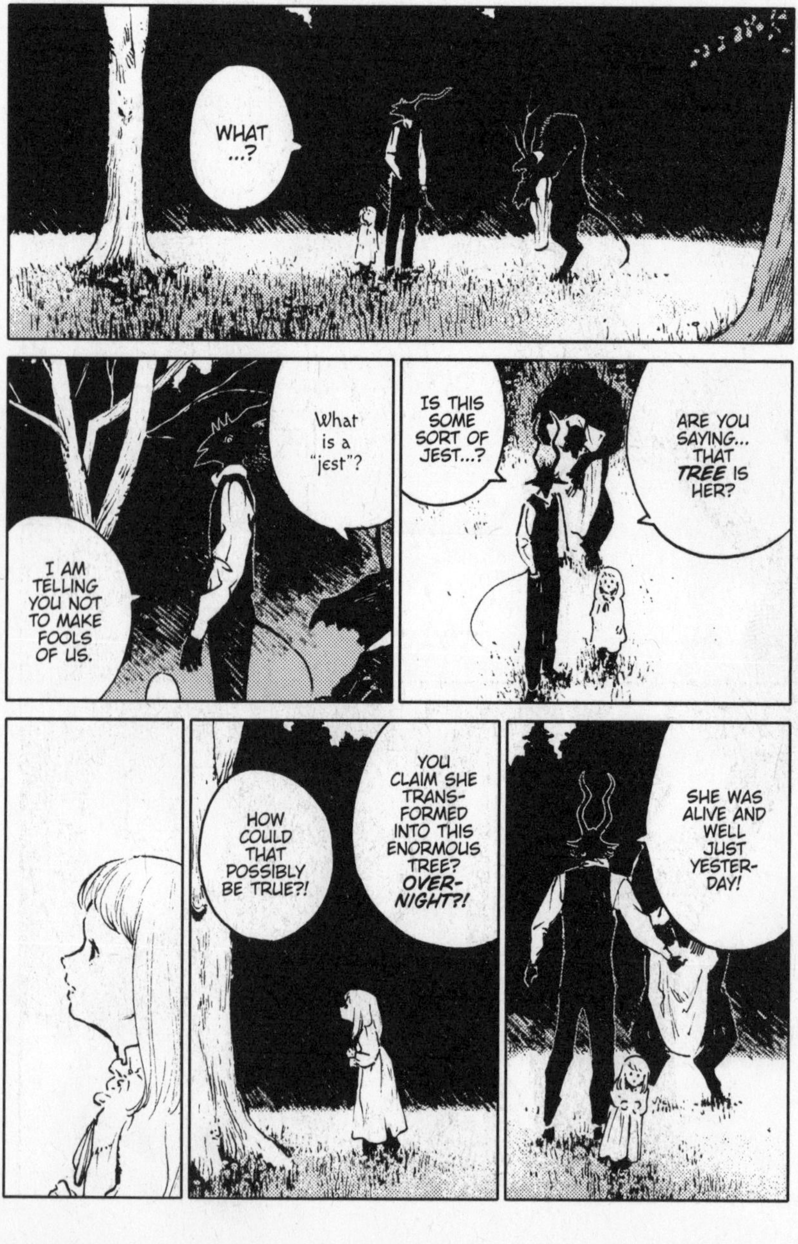
WHAT ...?
ARE YOU SAYING... THAT *TREE* IS HER?
IS THIS SOME SORT OF JEST...?
What is a "jest"?
I AM TELLING YOU NOT TO MAKE FOOLS OF US.
SHE WAS ALIVE AND WELL JUST YESTERDAY!
YOU CLAIM SHE TRANSFORMED INTO THIS ENORMOUS TREE? *OVERNIGHT?!*
HOW COULD THAT POSSIBLY BE TRUE?!

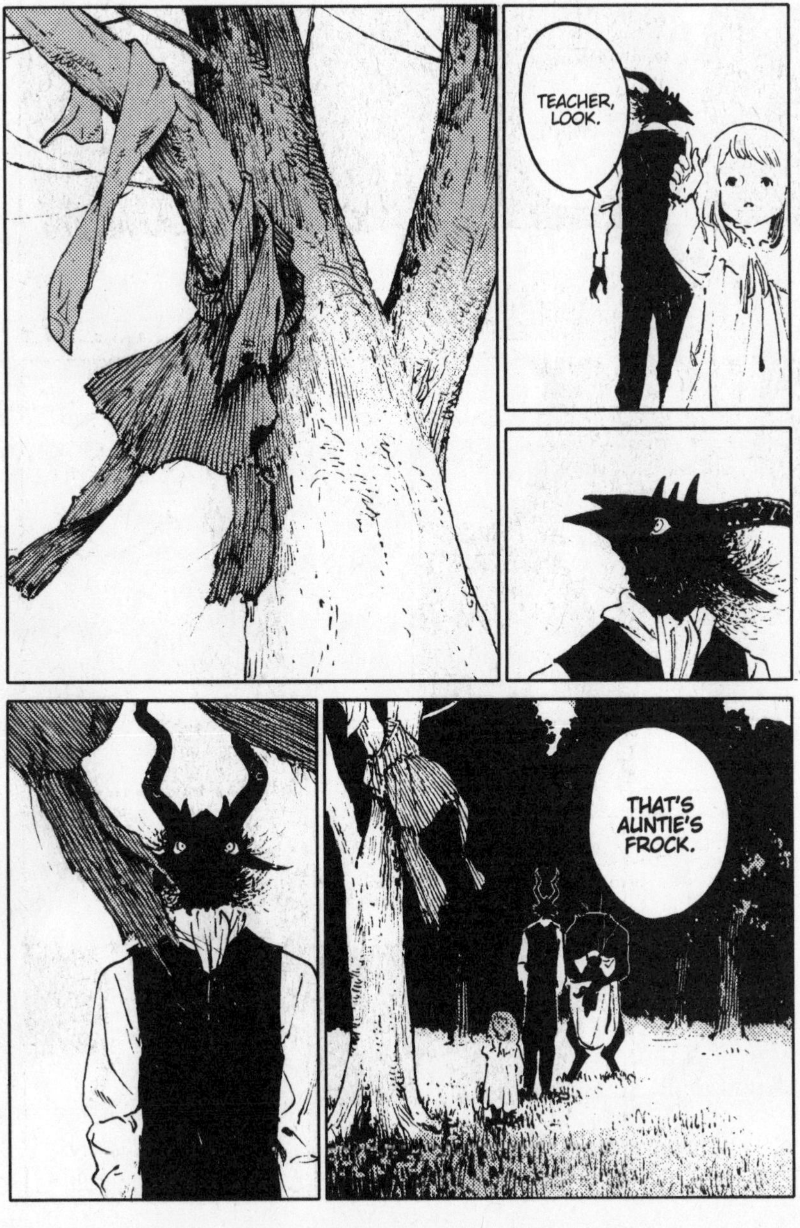
TEACHER, LOOK.
THAT'S AUNTIE'S FROCK.

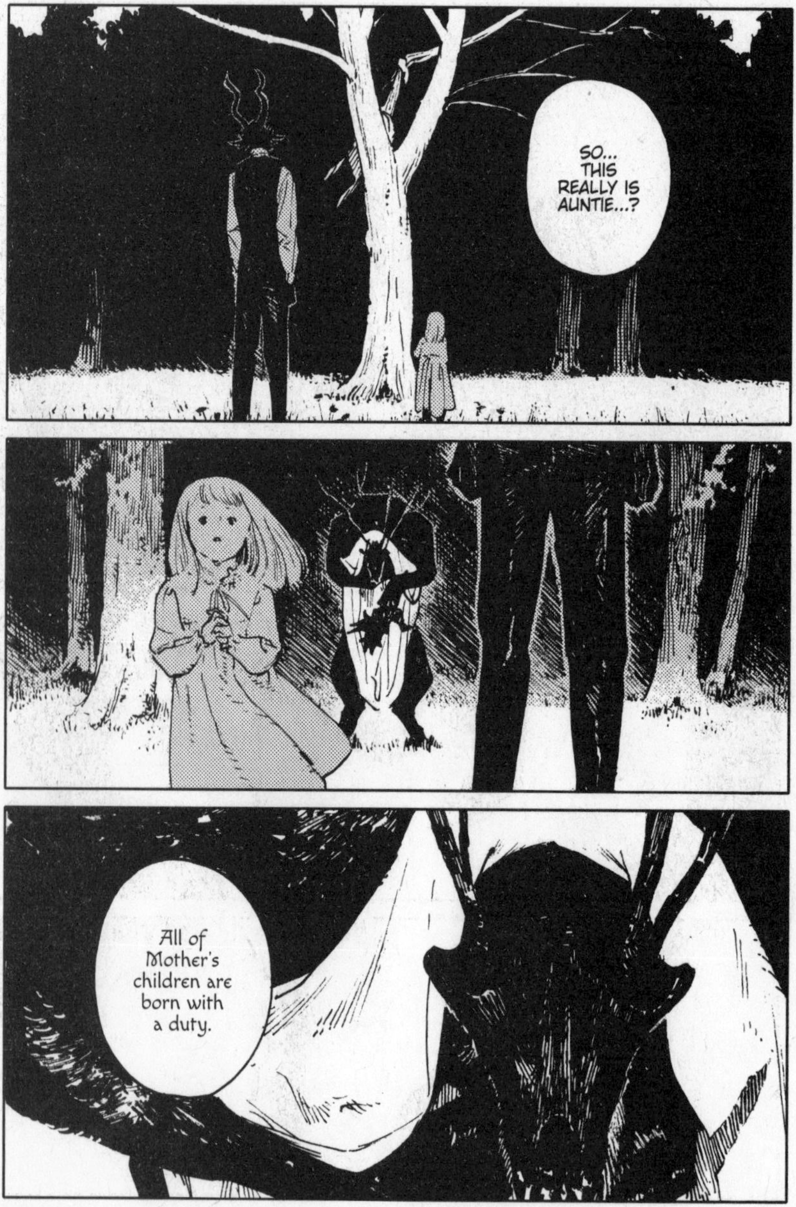
SO... THIS REALLY IS AUNTIE...?
All of Mother's children are born with a duty.

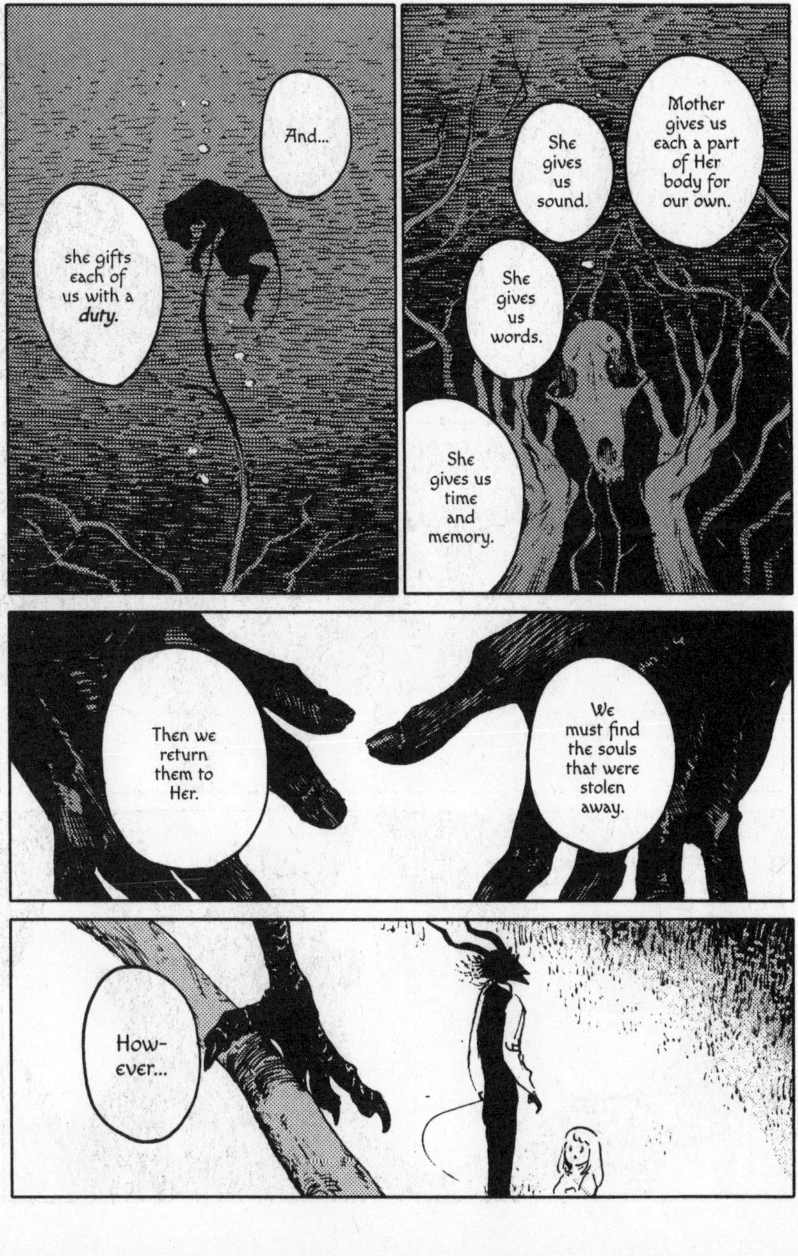
Mother gives us each a part of Her body for our own.
She gives us sound.
She gives us words.
She gives us time and memory.
And...
she gifts each of us with a *duty*.
We must find the souls that were stolen away.
Then we return them to Her.
How-ever...

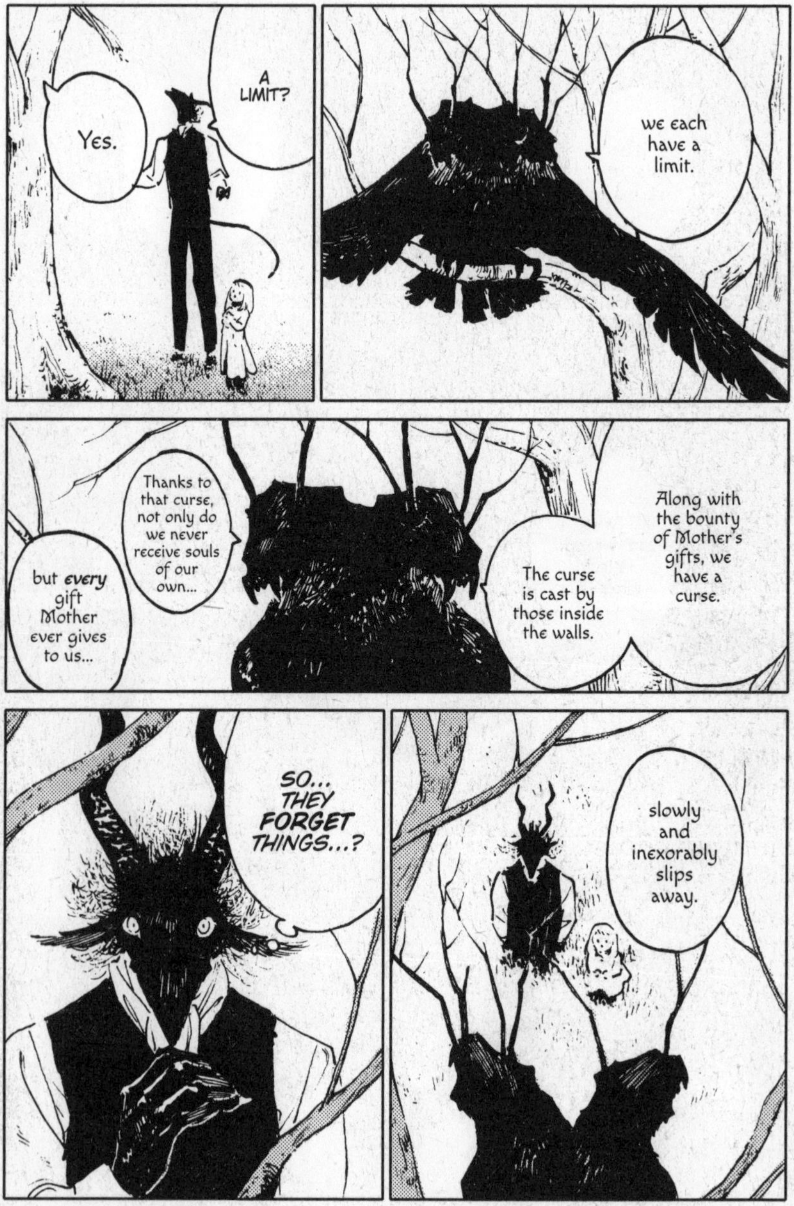
we each have a limit.
A LIMIT?
Yes.
Along with the bounty of Mother's gifts, we have a curse.
The curse is cast by those inside the walls.
Thanks to that curse, not only do we never receive souls of our own...
but *every* gift Mother ever gives to us...
slowly and inexorably slips away.
SO... THEY FORGET THINGS...?

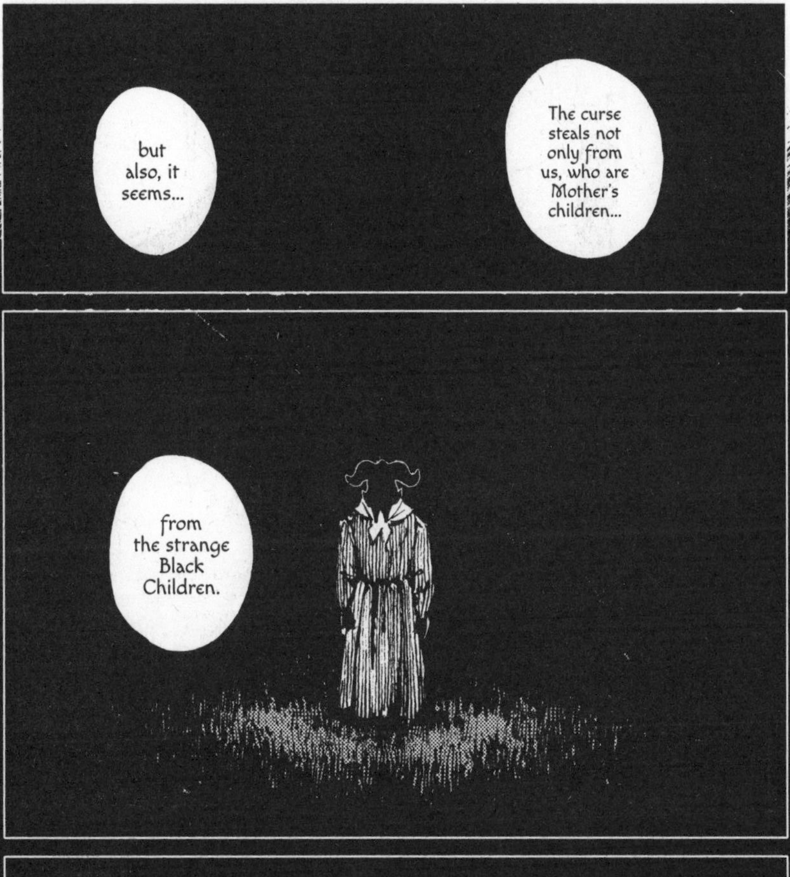
The curse steals not only from us, who are Mother's children...
but also, it seems...
from the strange Black Children.

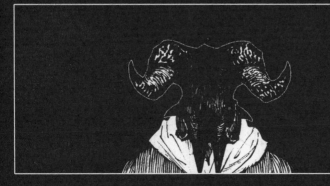

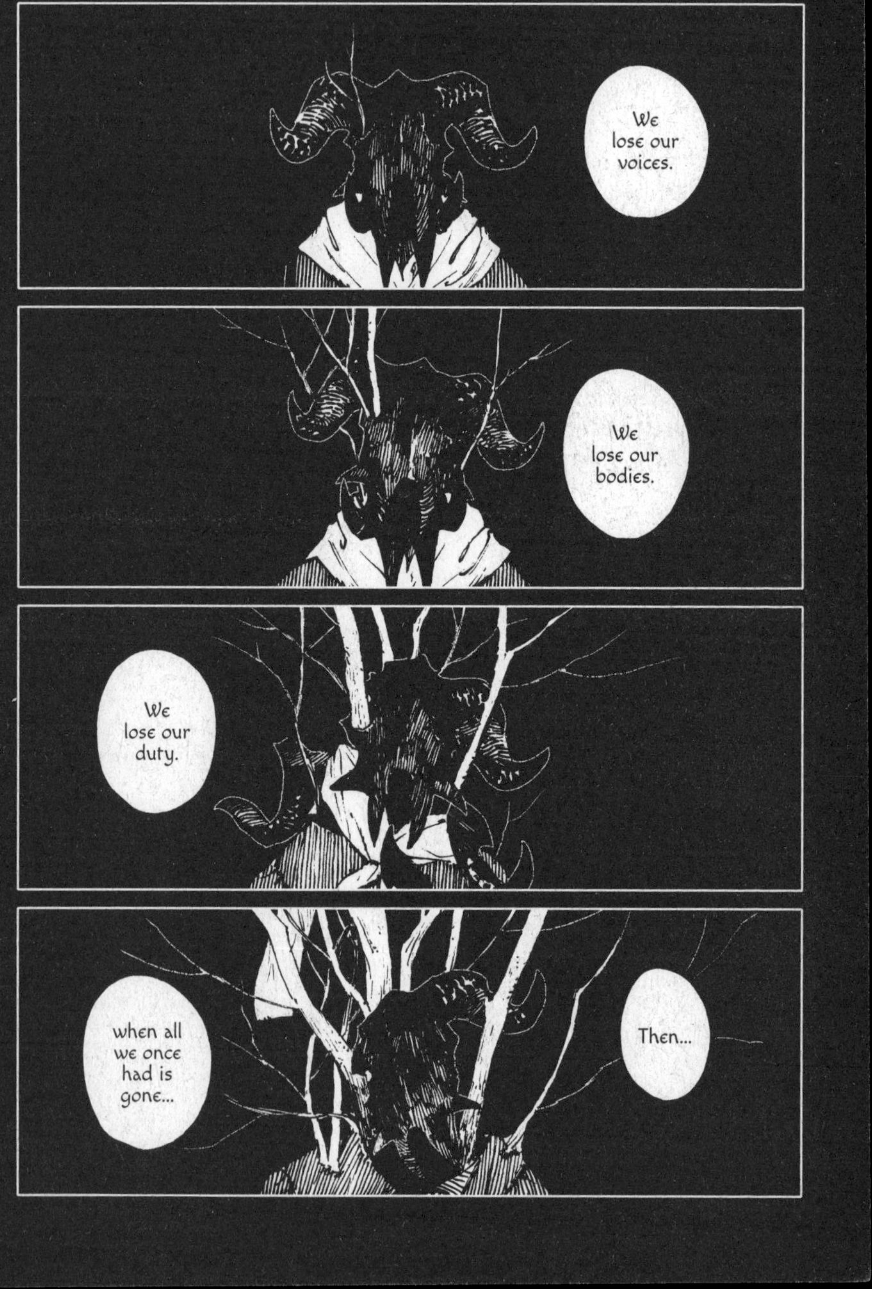
We lose our voices.
We lose our bodies.
We lose our duty.
Then...
when all we once had is gone...

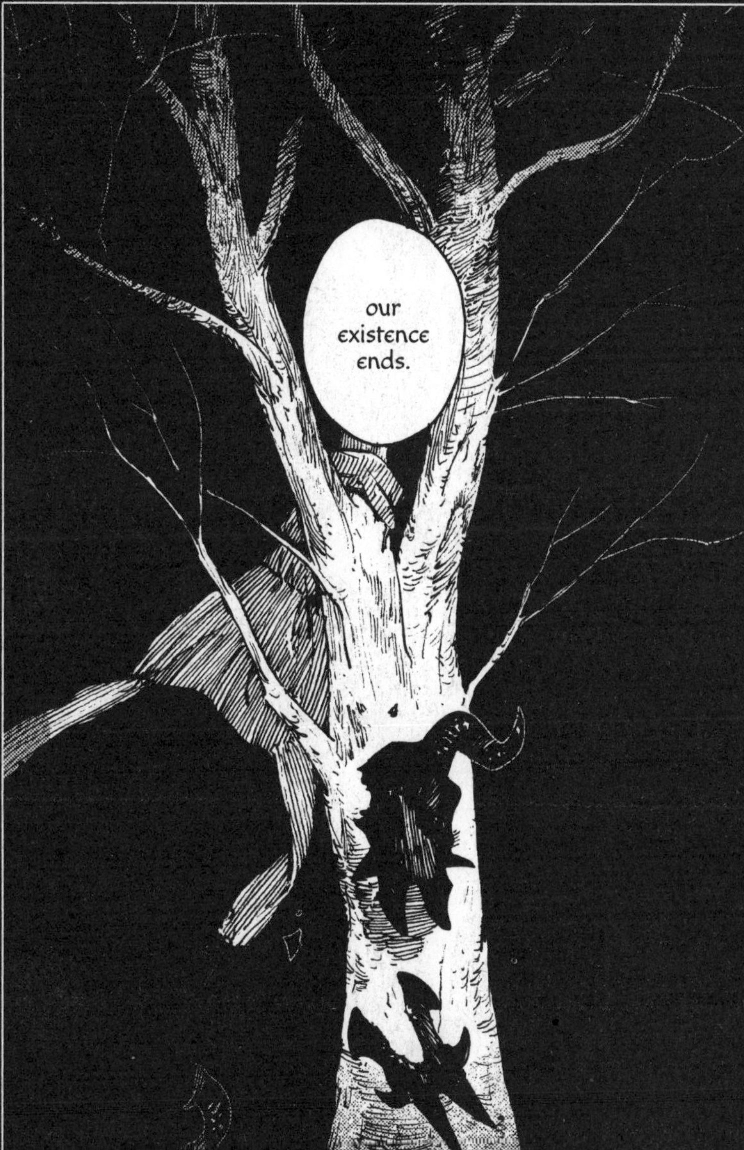
our existence ends.

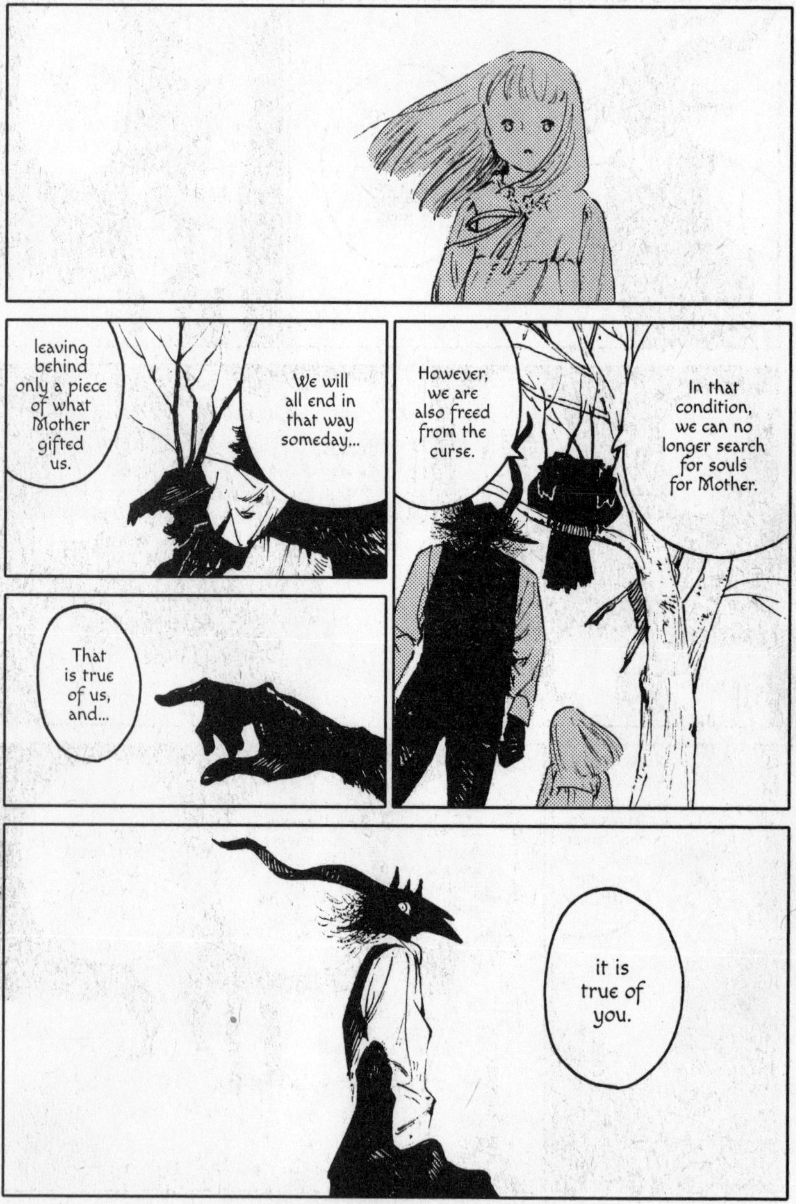
In that condition, we can no longer search for souls for Mother.
However, we are also freed from the curse.
We will all end in that way someday...
leaving behind only a piece of what Mother gifted us.
That is true of us, and...
it is true of you.

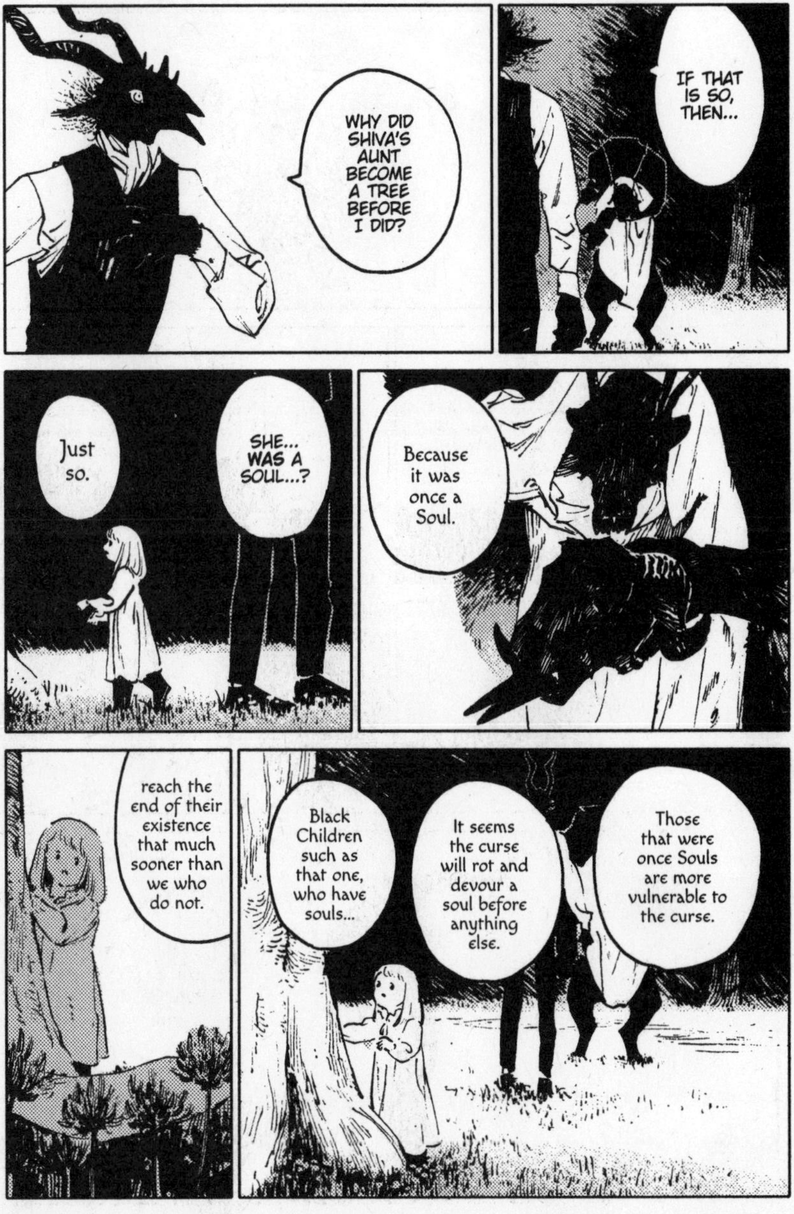
IF THAT IS SO, THEN...
WHY DID SHIVA'S AUNT BECOME A TREE BEFORE I DID?
Because it was once a Soul.
SHE... WAS A SOUL...?
Just so.
Those that were once Souls are more vulnerable to the curse.
It seems the curse will rot and devour a soul before anything else.
Black Children such as that one, who have souls...
reach the end of their existence that much sooner than we who do not.

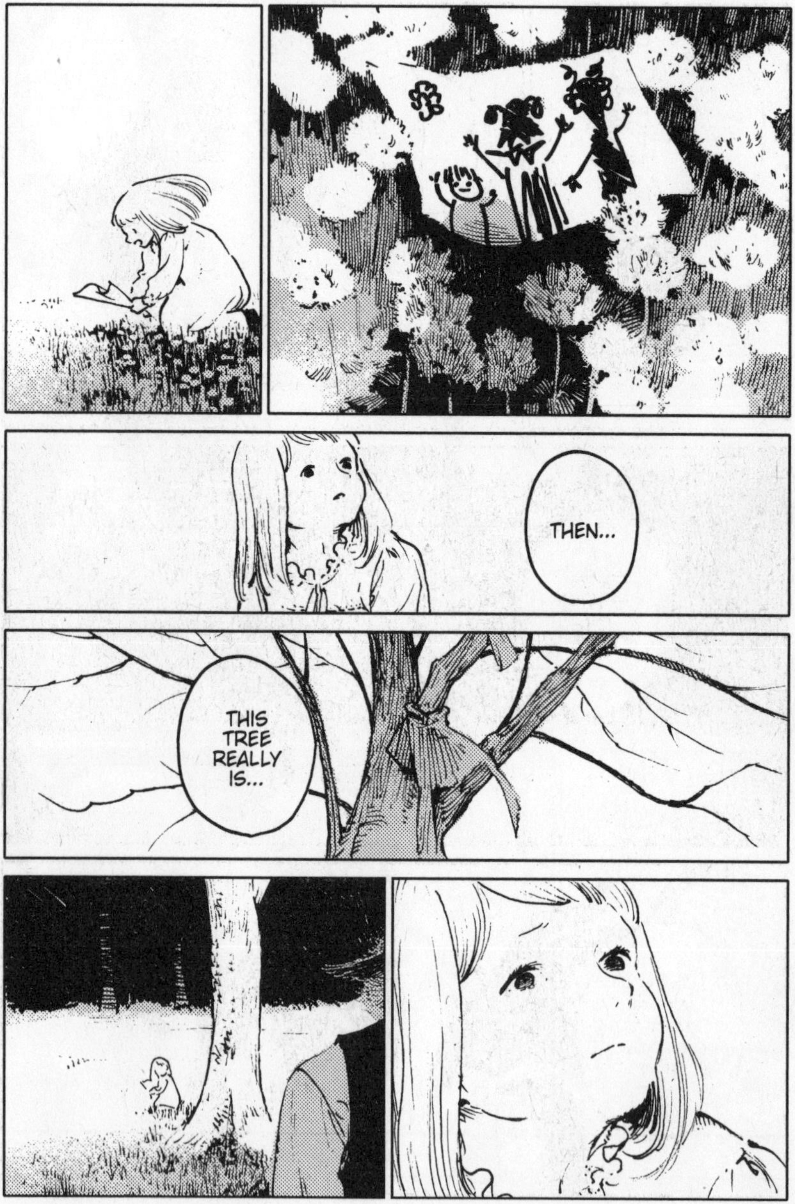
THEN...
THIS TREE REALLY IS...

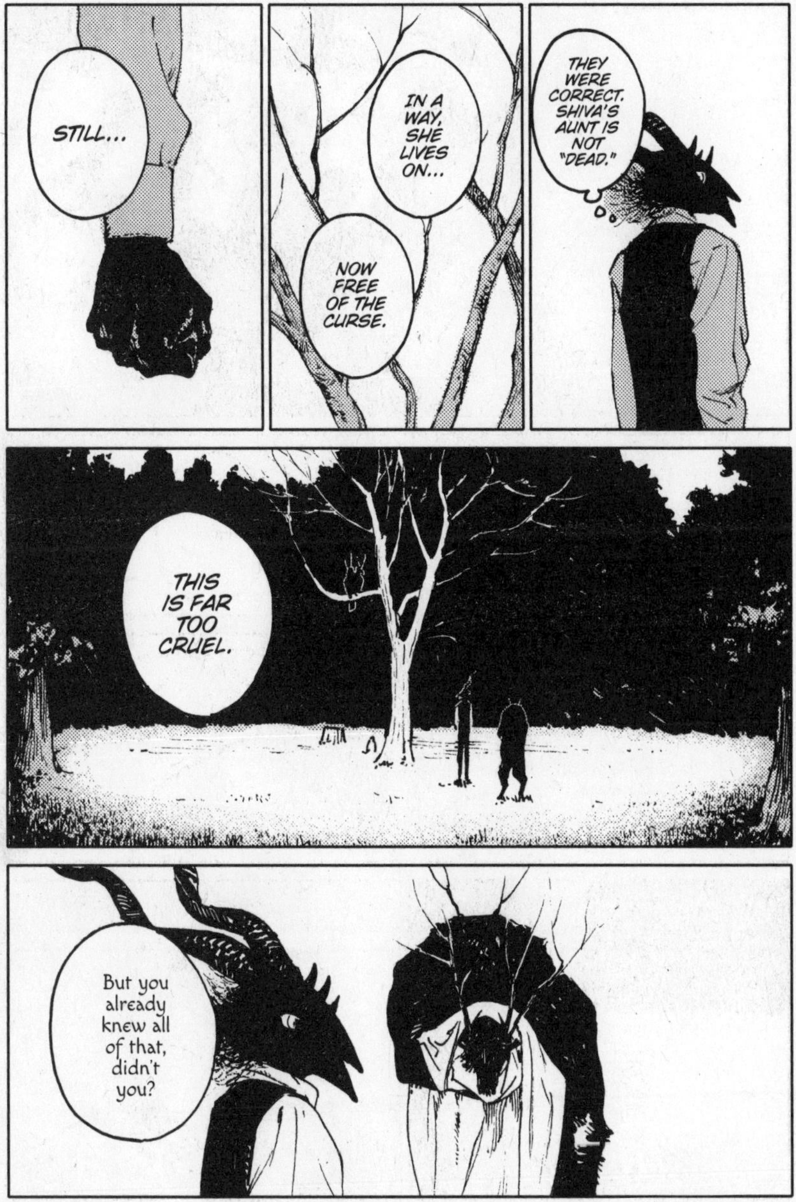
THEY WERE CORRECT. SHIVA'S AUNT IS NOT "DEAD."
IN A WAY, SHE LIVES ON...
NOW FREE OF THE CURSE.
STILL...
THIS IS FAR TOO CRUEL.
But you already knew all of that, didn't you?

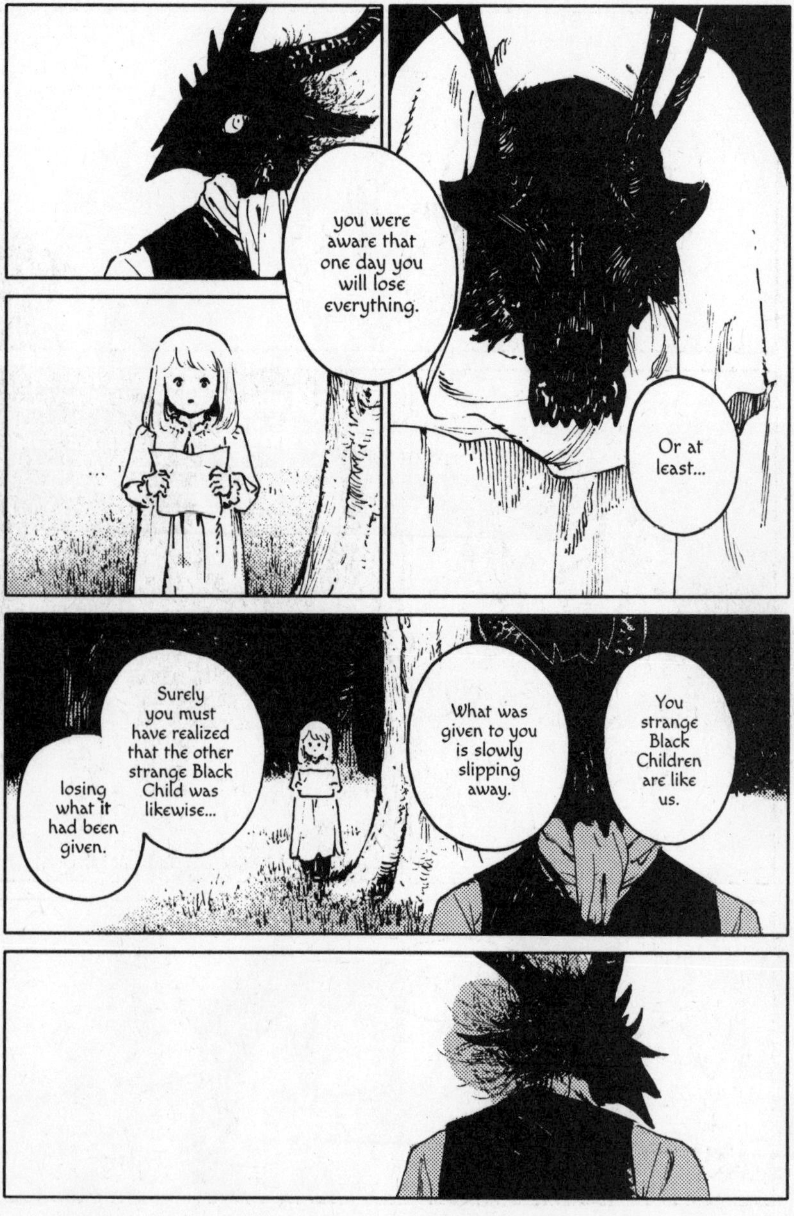
Or at least...
you were aware that one day you will lose everything.
...
You strange Black Children are like us.
What was given to you is slowly slipping away.
Surely you must have realized that the other strange Black Child was likewise...
losing what it had been given.

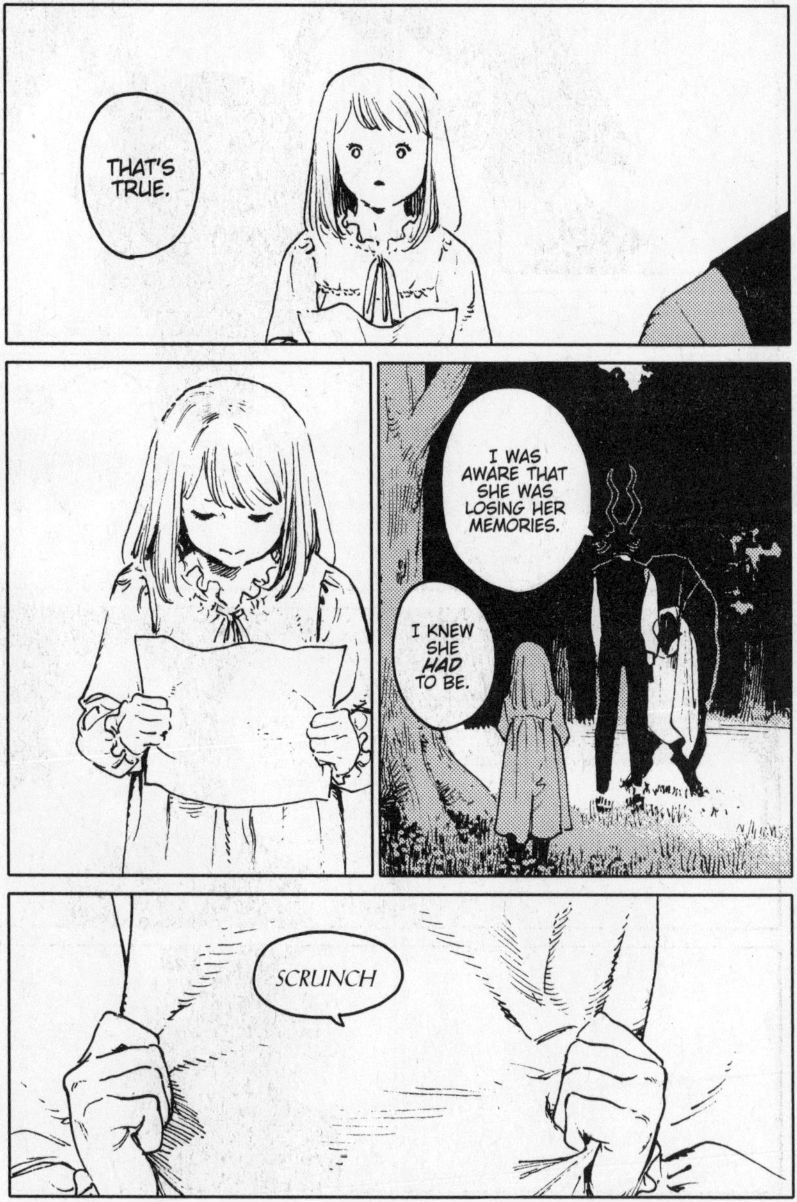
THAT'S TRUE.
I WAS AWARE THAT SHE WAS LOSING HER MEMORIES.
I KNEW SHE *HAD* TO BE.
SCRUNCH

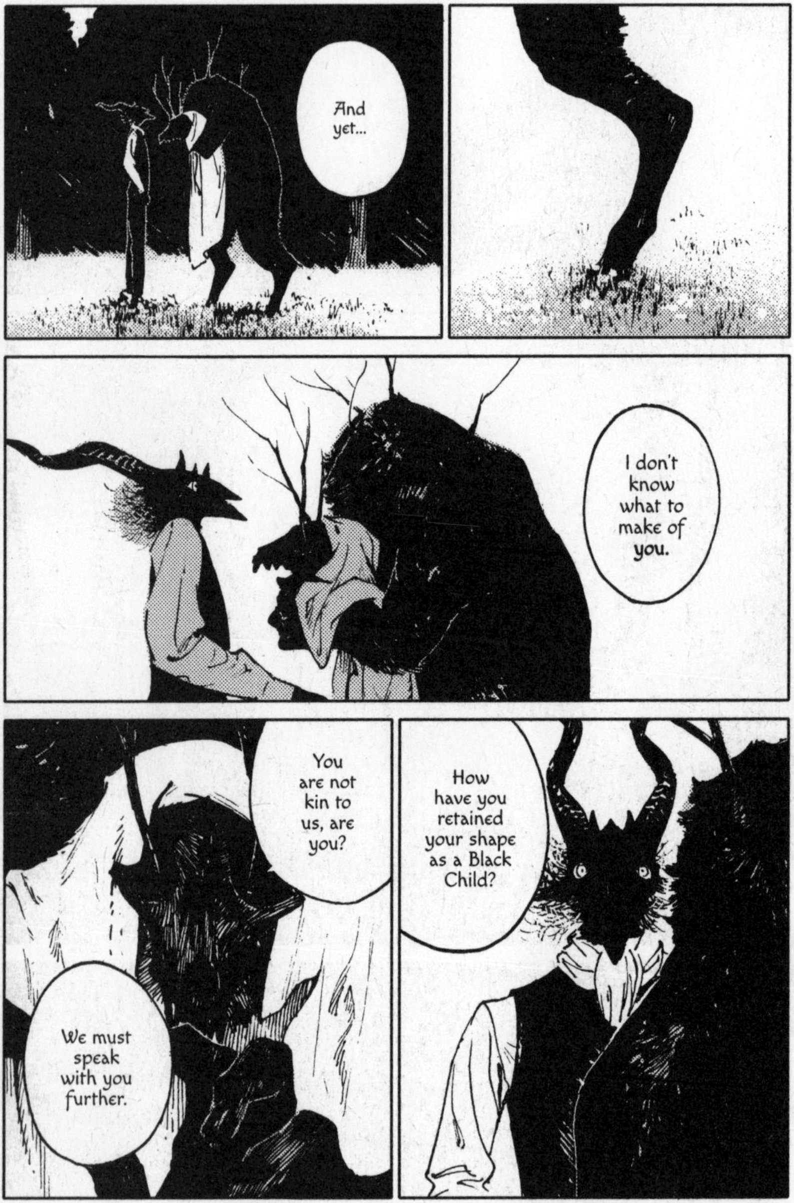
And yet...
I don't know what to make of you.
How have you retained your shape as a Black Child?
You are not kin to us, are you?
We must speak with you further.

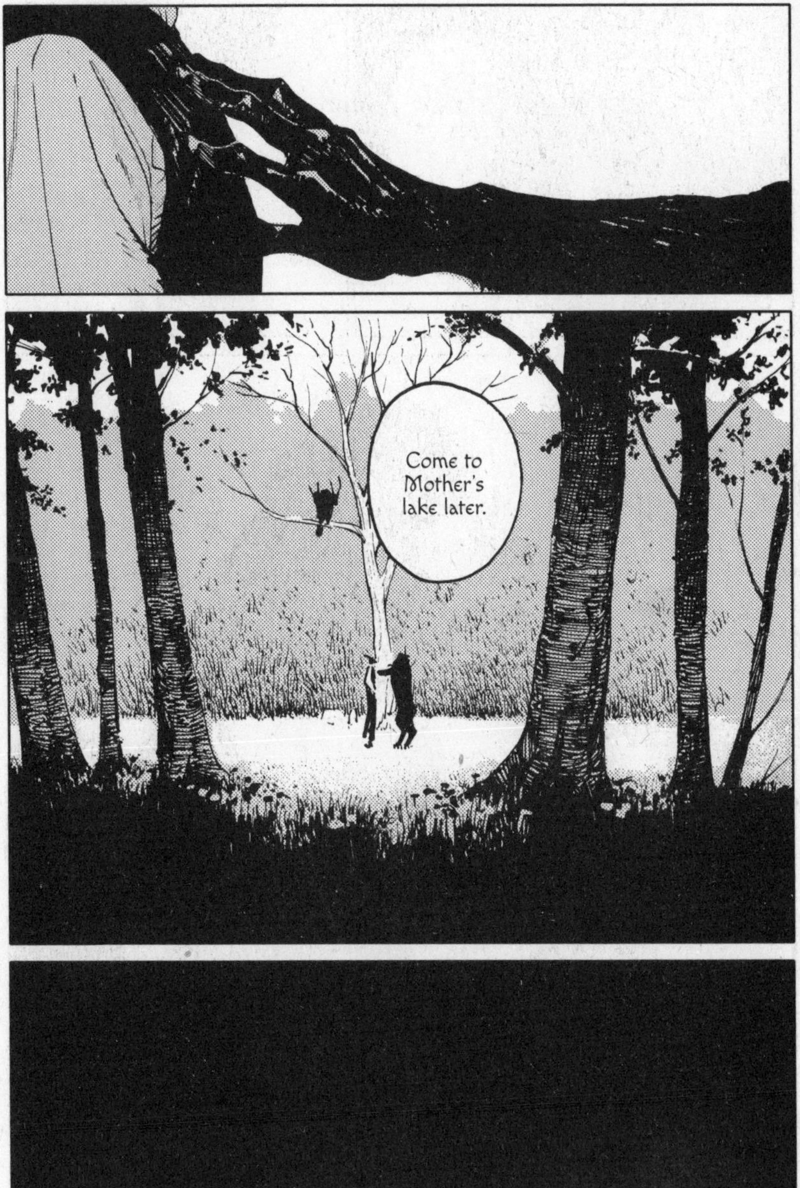
Come to Mother's lake later.

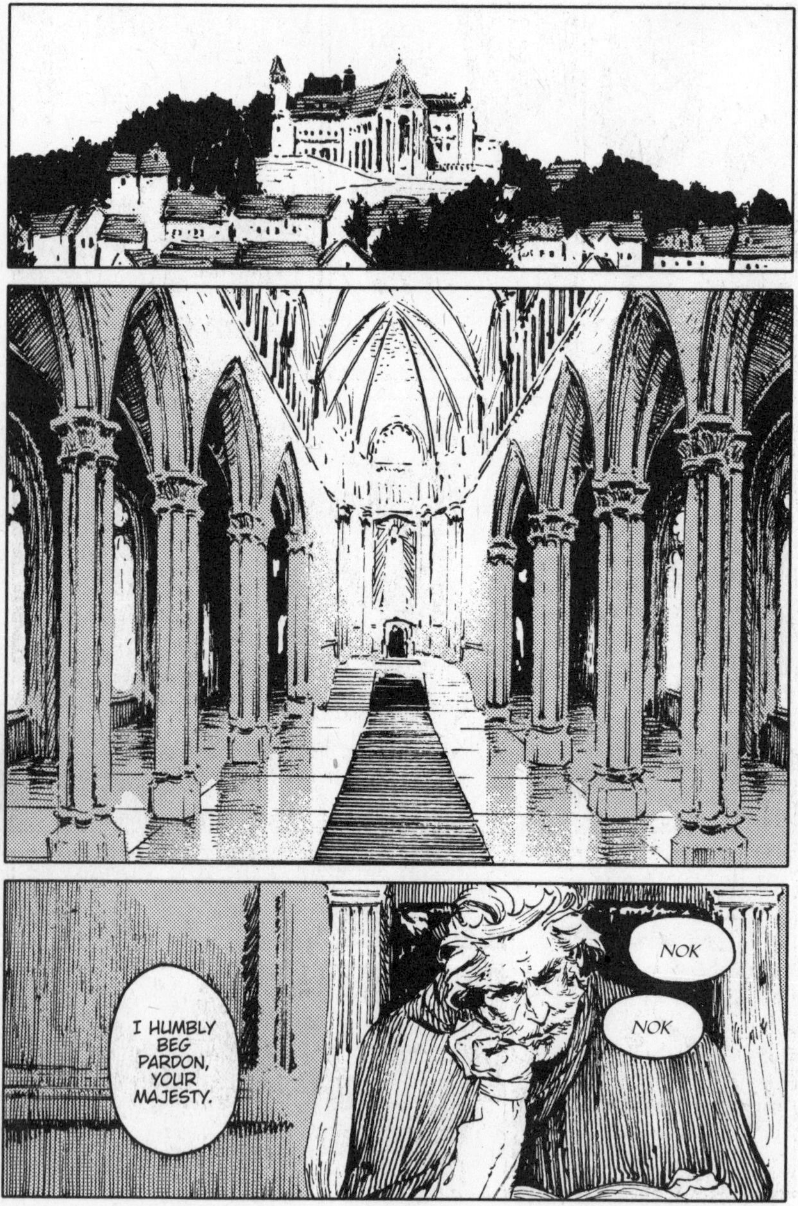
NOK
NOK
I HUMBLY BEG PARDON, YOUR MAJESTY.

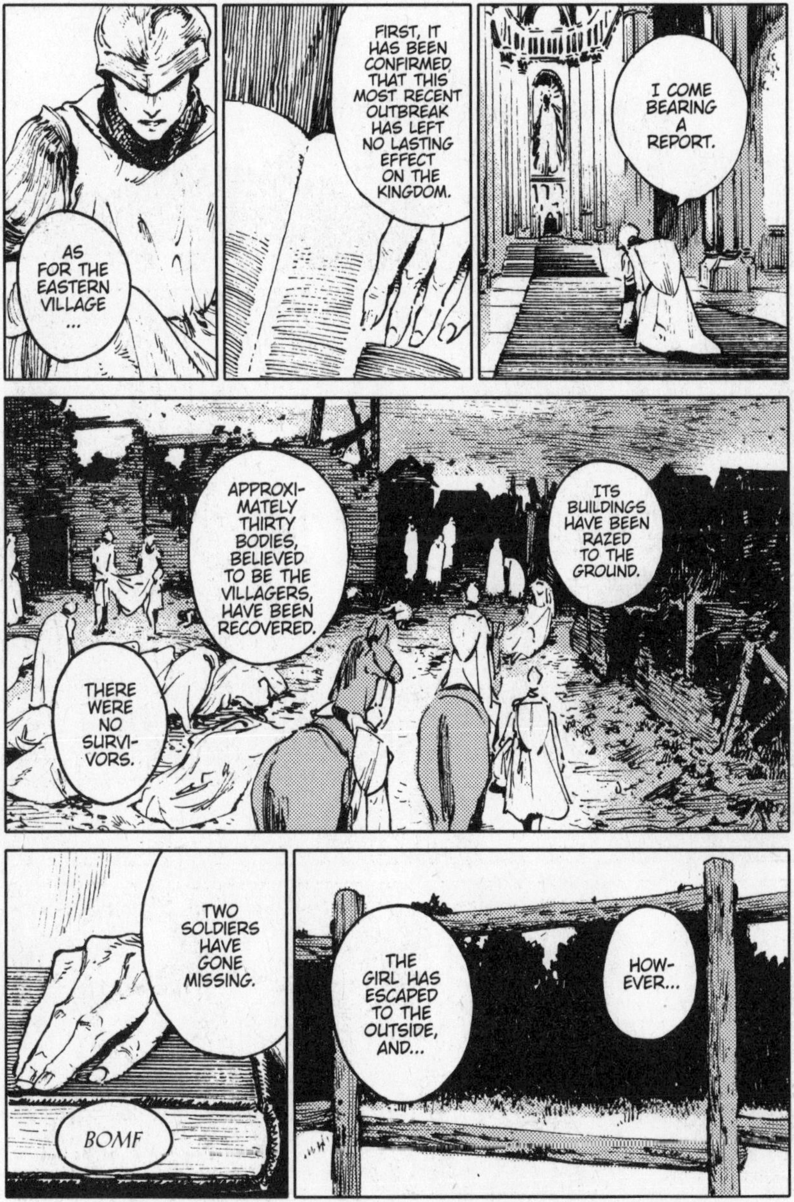
I COME BEARING A REPORT.
FIRST, IT HAS BEEN CONFIRMED THAT THIS MOST RECENT OUTBREAK HAS LEFT NO LASTING EFFECT ON THE KINGDOM.
AS FOR THE EASTERN VILLAGE...
ITS BUILDINGS HAVE BEEN RAZED TO THE GROUND.
APPROXIMATELY THIRTY BODIES, BELIEVED TO BE THE VILLAGERS, HAVE BEEN RECOVERED.
THERE WERE NO SURVIVORS.
HOWEVER...
THE GIRL HAS ESCAPED TO THE OUTSIDE, AND...
TWO SOLDIERS HAVE GONE MISSING.
BOMF

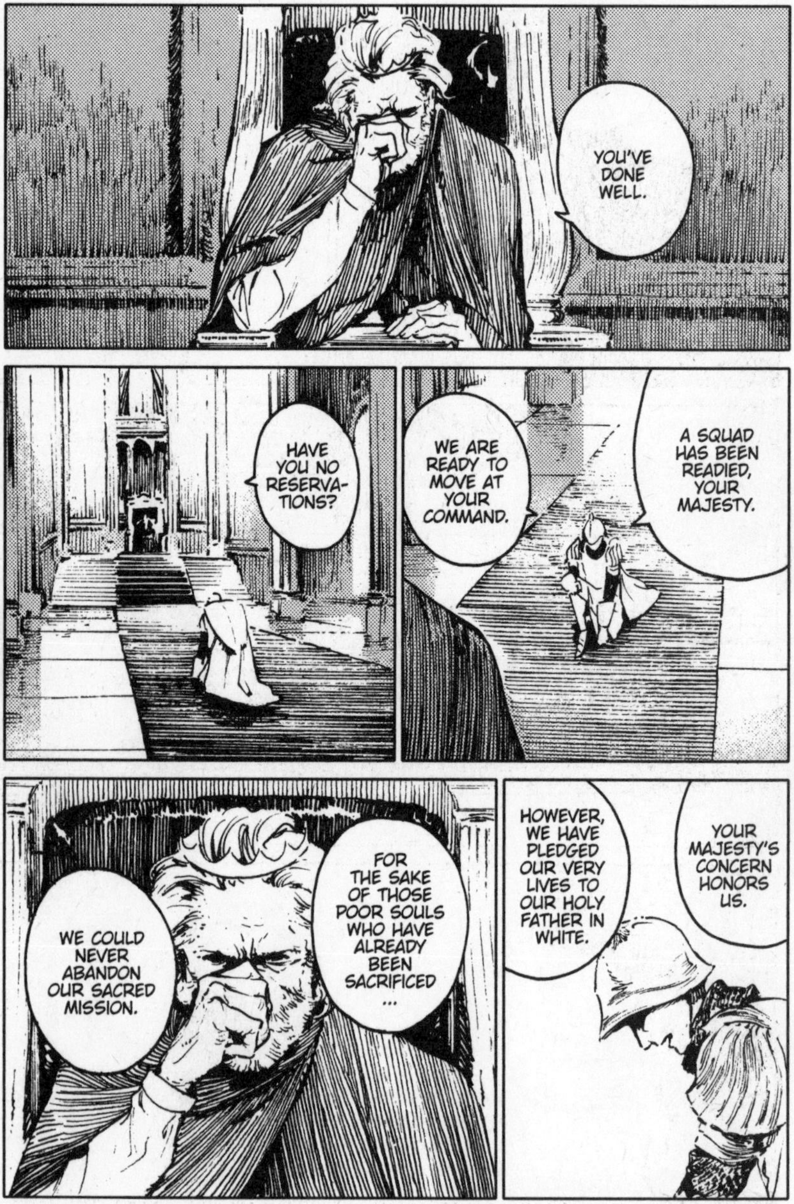
YOU'VE DONE WELL.
A SQUAD HAS BEEN READIED, YOUR MAJESTY.
WE ARE READY TO MOVE AT YOUR COMMAND.
HAVE YOU NO RESERVA-TIONS?
YOUR MAJESTY'S CONCERN HONORS US.
HOWEVER, WE HAVE PLEDGED OUR VERY LIVES TO OUR HOLY FATHER IN WHITE.
FOR THE SAKE OF THOSE POOR SOULS WHO HAVE ALREADY BEEN SACRIFICED ...
WE COULD NEVER ABANDON OUR SACRED MISSION.

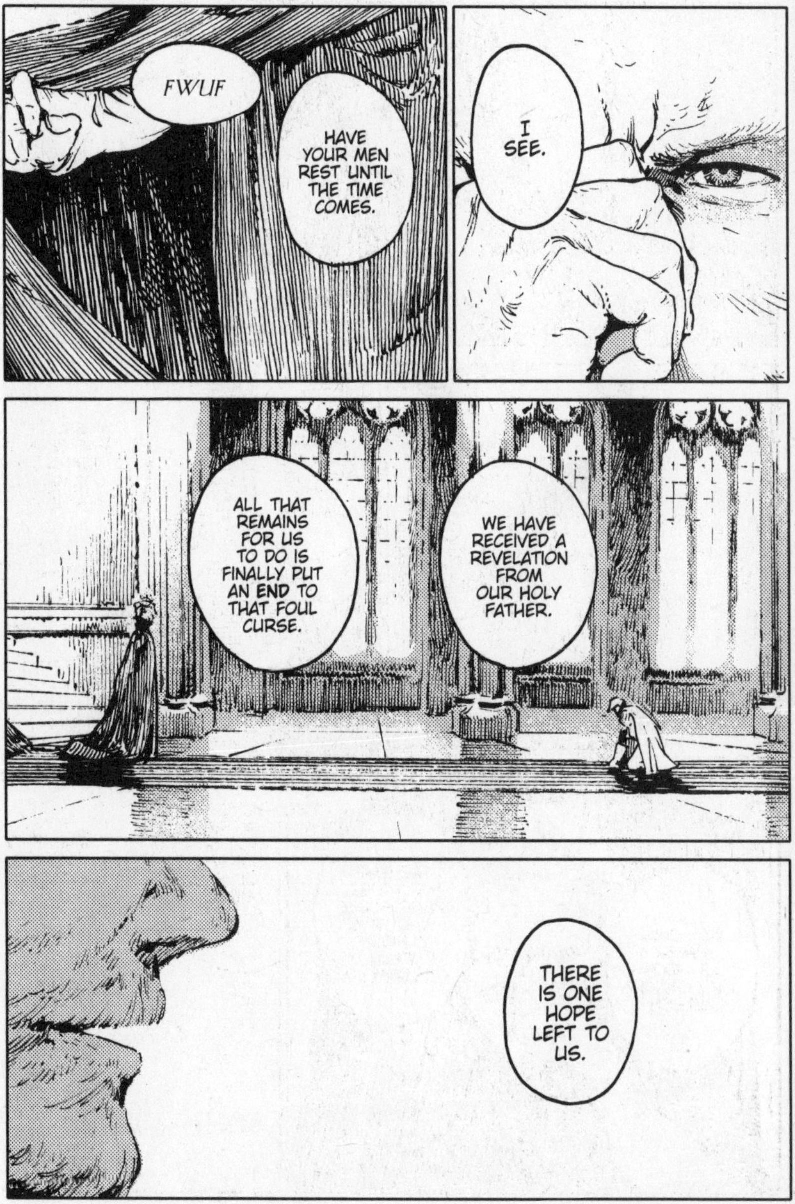
I SEE.
HAVE YOUR MEN REST UNTIL THE TIME COMES.
FWUF
WE HAVE RECEIVED A REVELATION FROM OUR HOLY FATHER.
ALL THAT REMAINS FOR US TO DO IS FINALLY PUT AN END TO THAT FOUL CURSE.
THERE IS ONE HOPE LEFT TO US.

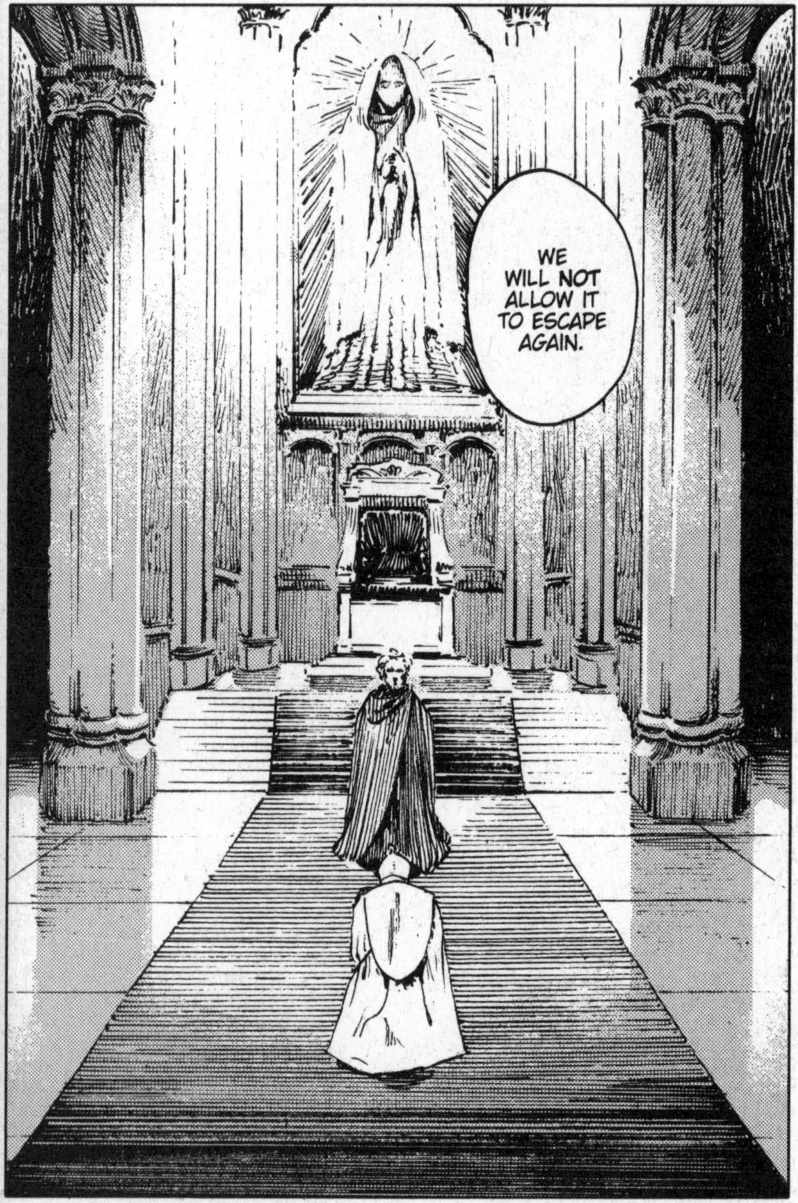
WE WILL NOT ALLOW IT TO ESCAPE AGAIN.

Siúil, a Rún
The Girl from the Other Side

Siúil, a Rún
The Girl from the Other Side

Chapter 22

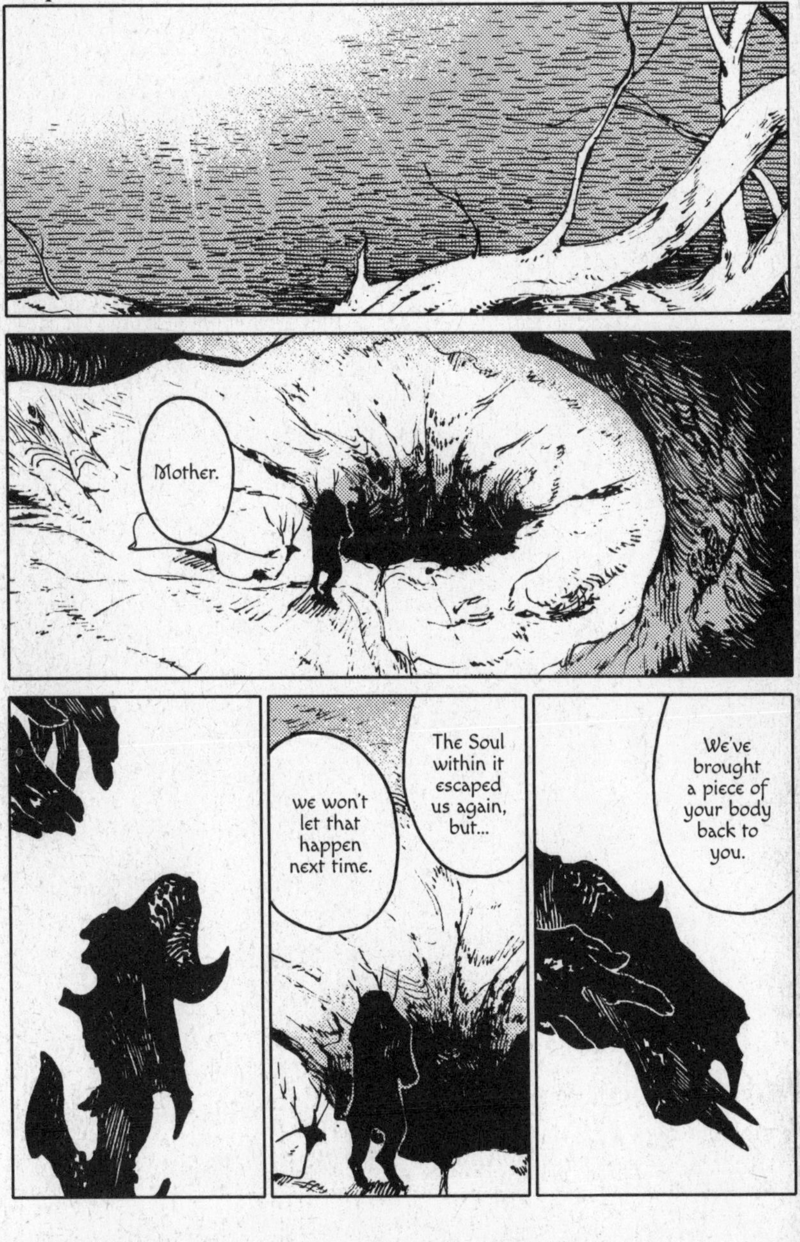
Mother.
We've brought a piece of your body back to you.
The Soul within it escaped us again, but...
we won't let that happen next time.

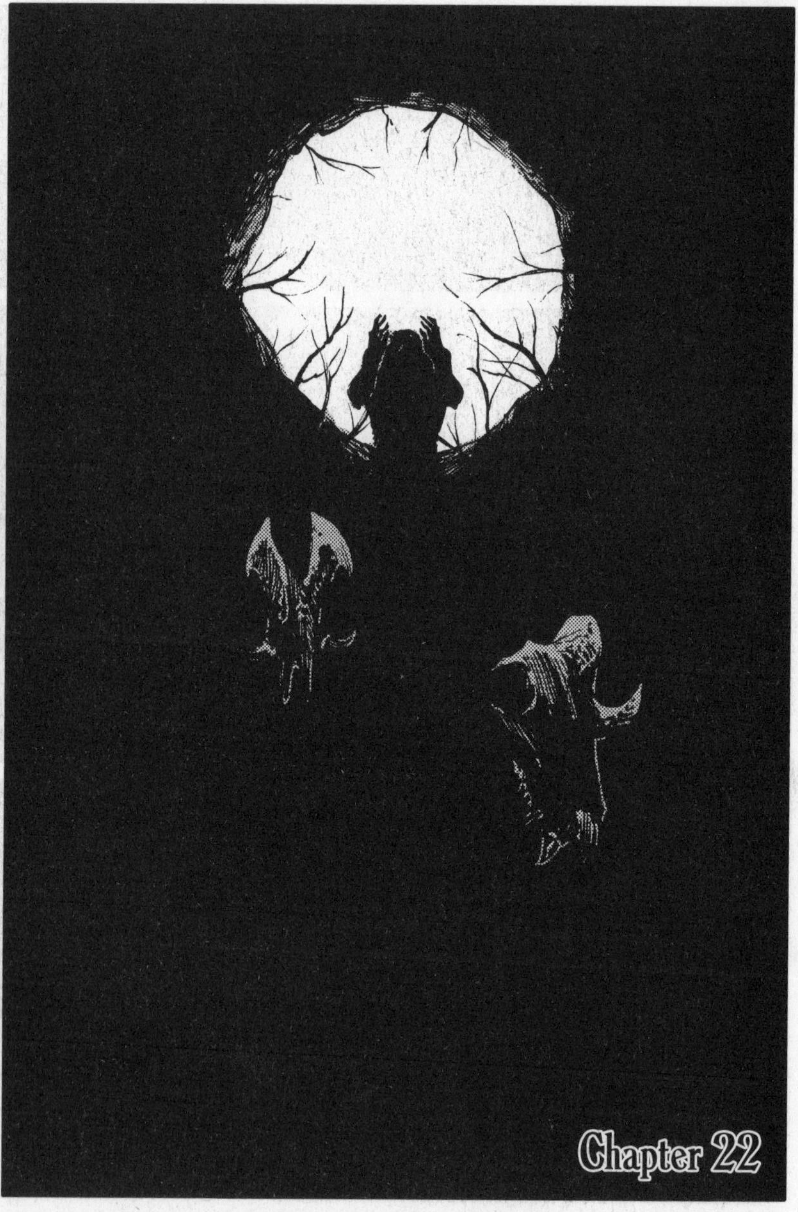
Chapter 22

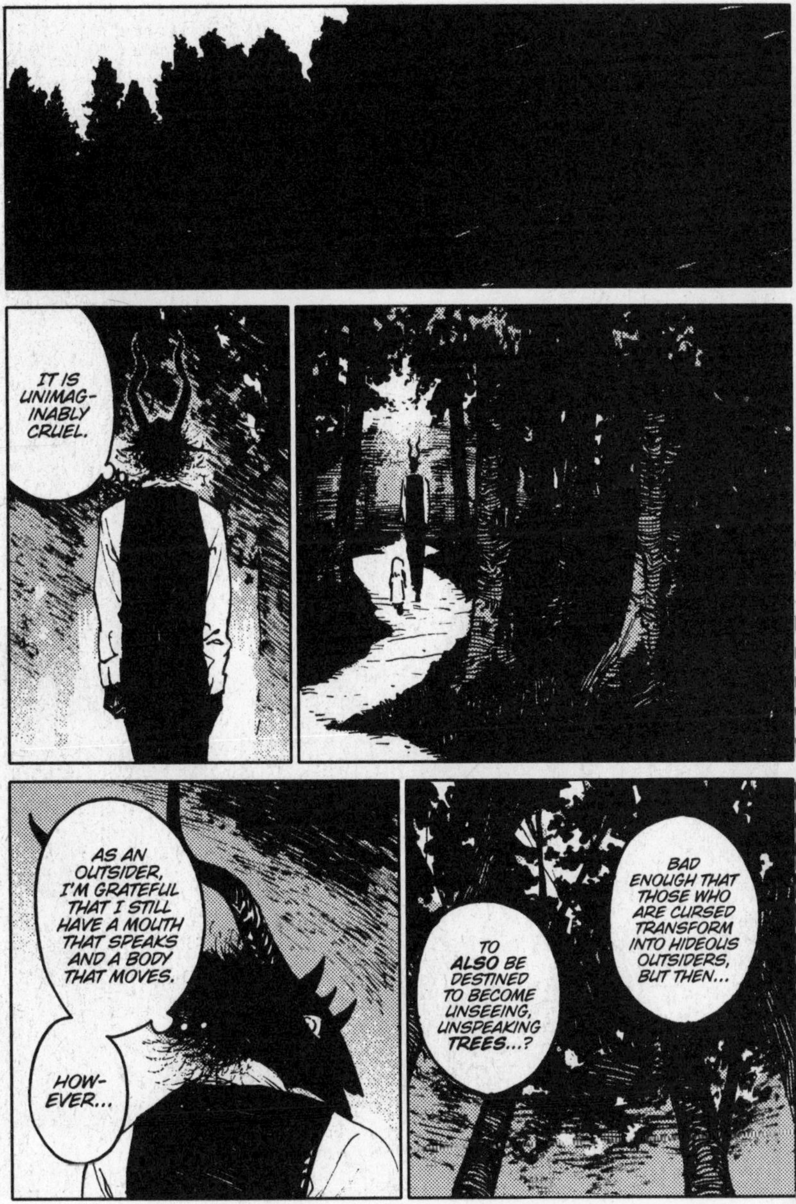
IT IS UNIMAGINABLY CRUEL.
BAD ENOUGH THAT THOSE WHO ARE CURSED TRANSFORM INTO HIDEOUS OUTSIDERS, BUT THEN...
TO **ALSO** BE DESTINED TO BECOME UNSEEING, UNSPEAKING **TREES...?**
AS AN OUTSIDER, I'M GRATEFUL THAT I STILL HAVE A MOUTH THAT SPEAKS AND A BODY THAT MOVES.
HOW-EVER...

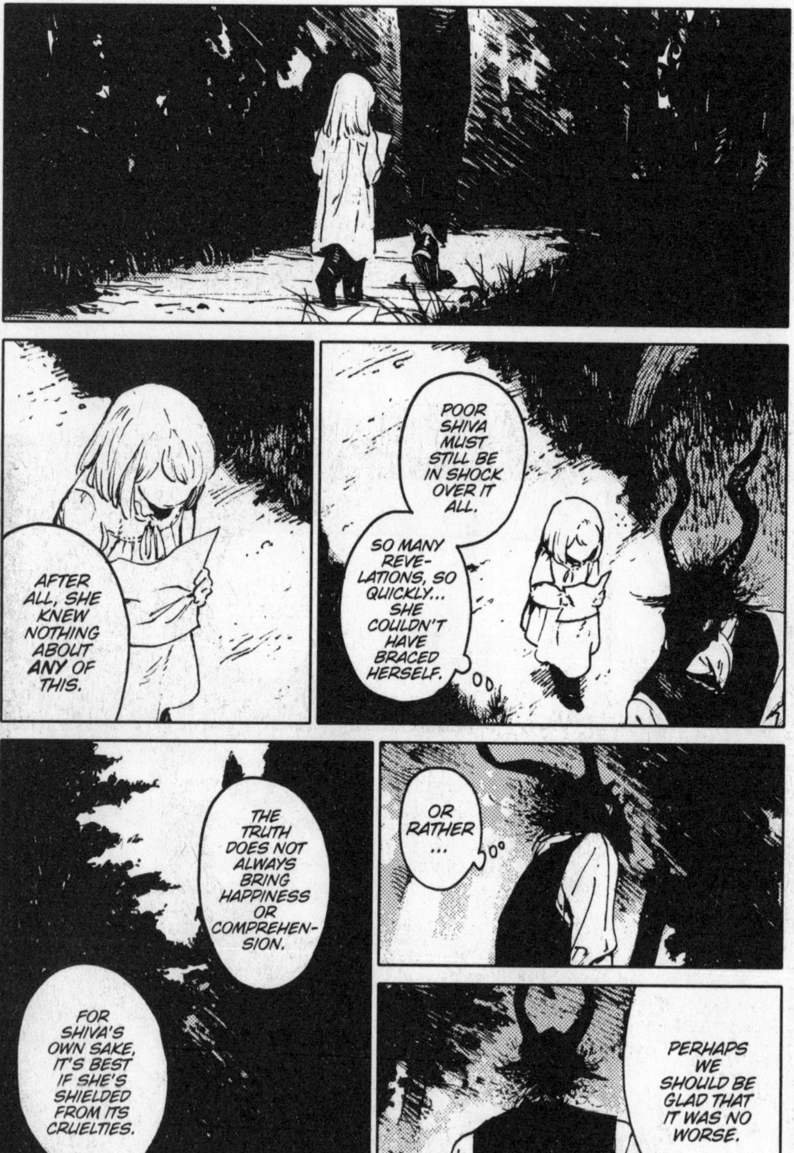
POOR SHIVA MUST STILL BE IN SHOCK OVER IT ALL.
SO MANY REVE-LATIONS, SO QUICKLY... SHE COULDN'T HAVE BRACED HERSELF.
AFTER ALL, SHE KNEW NOTHING ABOUT ANY OF THIS.
OR RATHER ...
PERHAPS WE SHOULD BE GLAD THAT IT WAS NO WORSE.
THE TRUTH DOES NOT ALWAYS BRING HAPPINESS OR COMPREHEN-SION.
FOR SHIVA'S OWN SAKE, IT'S BEST IF SHE'S SHIELDED FROM ITS CRUELTIES.

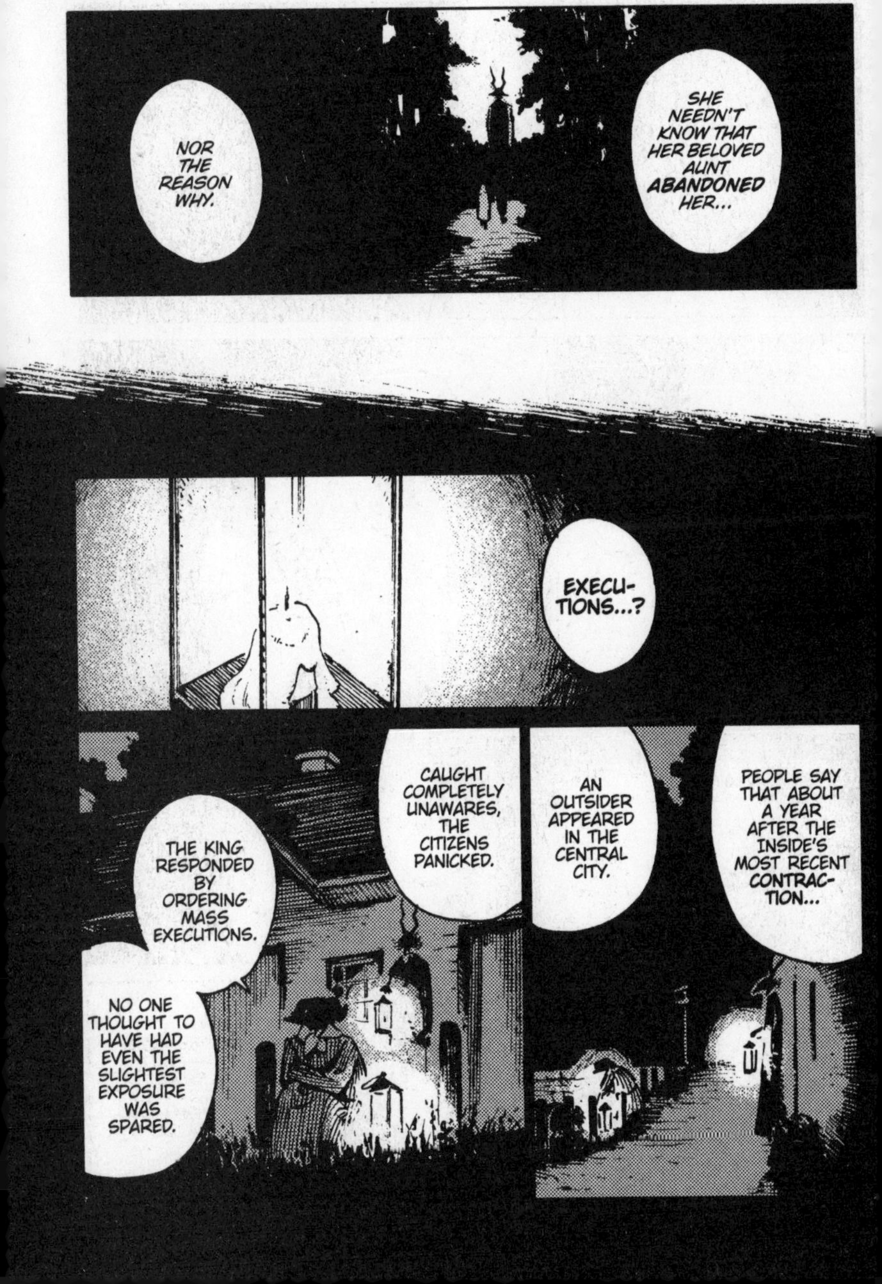
SHE NEEDN'T KNOW THAT HER BELOVED AUNT ABANDONED HER...
NOR THE REASON WHY.
EXECUTIONS...?
PEOPLE SAY THAT ABOUT A YEAR AFTER THE INSIDE'S MOST RECENT CONTRACTION...
AN OUTSIDER APPEARED IN THE CENTRAL CITY.
CAUGHT COMPLETELY UNAWARES, THE CITIZENS PANICKED.
THE KING RESPONDED BY ORDERING MASS EXECUTIONS.
NO ONE THOUGHT TO HAVE HAD EVEN THE SLIGHTEST EXPOSURE WAS SPARED.

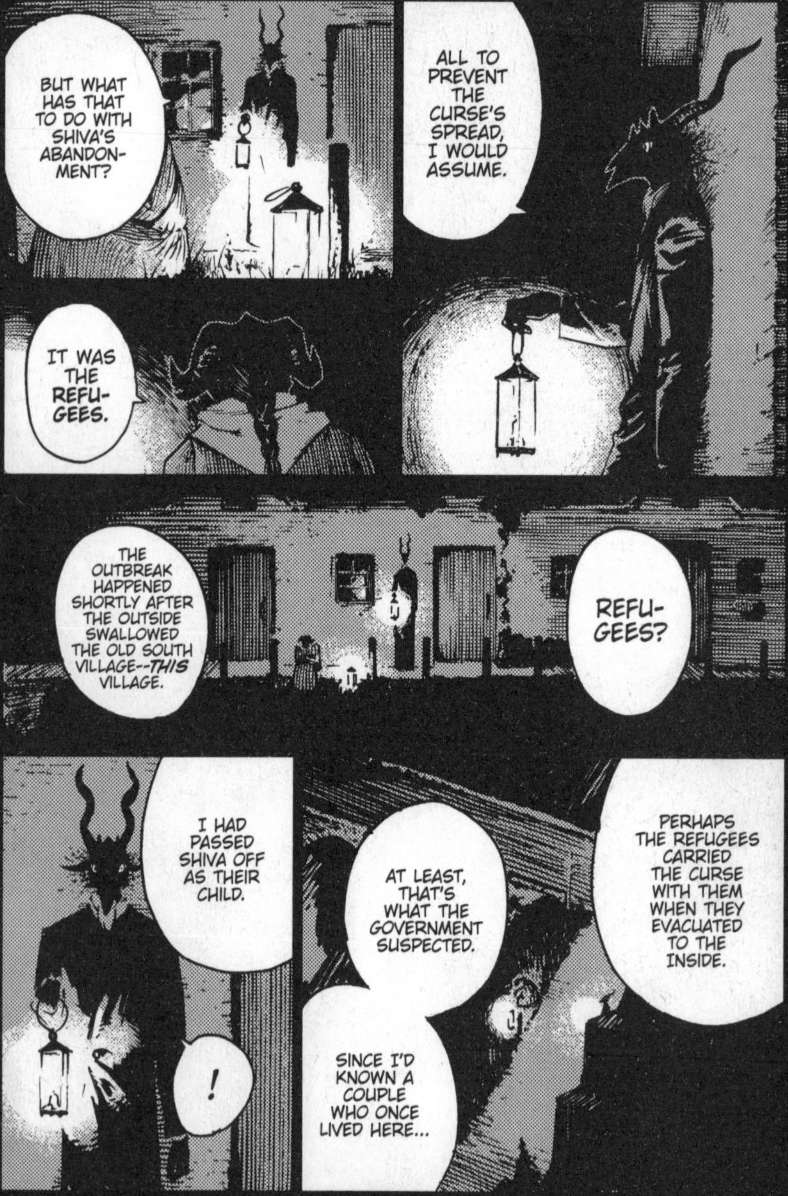
ALL TO PREVENT THE CURSE'S SPREAD, I WOULD ASSUME.
BUT WHAT HAS THAT TO DO WITH SHIVA'S ABANDONMENT?
IT WAS THE REFUGEES.
REFUGEES?
THE OUTBREAK HAPPENED SHORTLY AFTER THE OUTSIDE SWALLOWED THE OLD SOUTH VILLAGE--*THIS* VILLAGE.
PERHAPS THE REFUGEES CARRIED THE CURSE WITH THEM WHEN THEY EVACUATED TO THE INSIDE.
AT LEAST, THAT'S WHAT THE GOVERNMENT SUSPECTED.
SINCE I'D KNOWN A COUPLE WHO ONCE LIVED HERE...
I HAD PASSED SHIVA OFF AS THEIR CHILD.
!

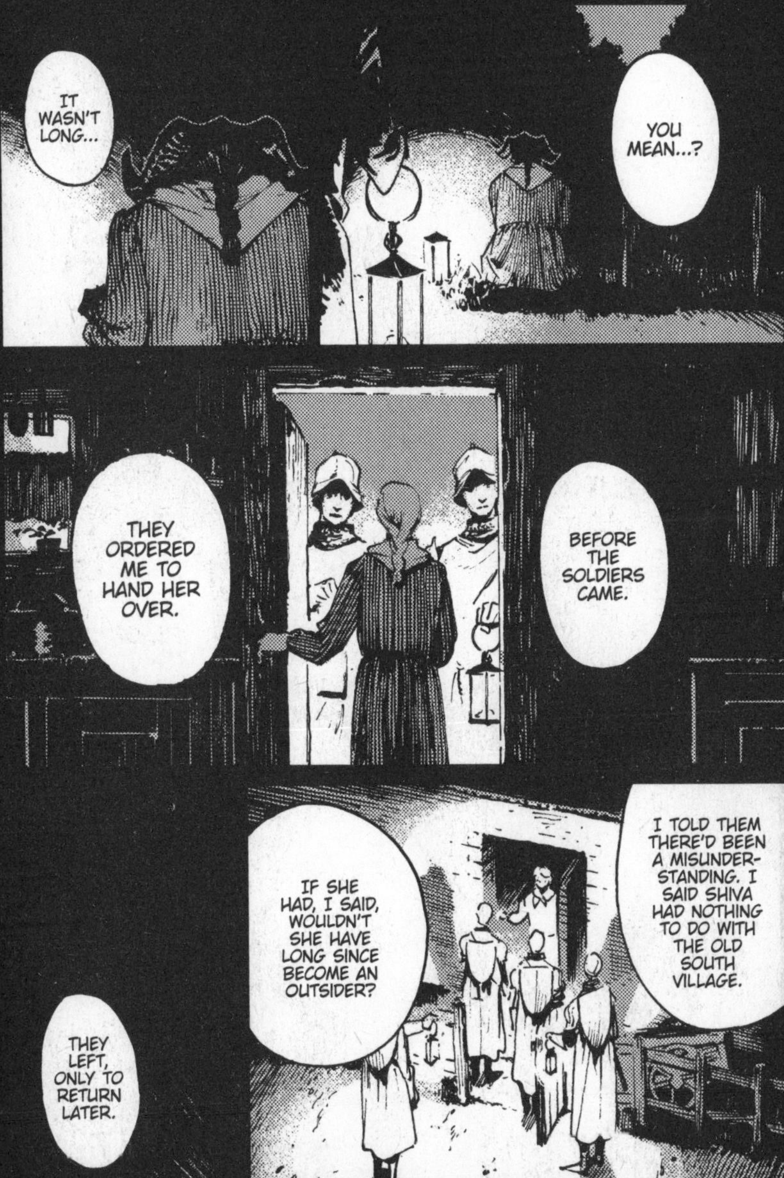
YOU MEAN...?
IT WASN'T LONG...
BEFORE THE SOLDIERS CAME.
THEY ORDERED ME TO HAND HER OVER.
I TOLD THEM THERE'D BEEN A MISUNDER-STANDING. I SAID SHIVA HAD NOTHING TO DO WITH THE OLD SOUTH VILLAGE.
IF SHE HAD, I SAID, WOULDN'T SHE HAVE LONG SINCE BECOME AN OUTSIDER?
THEY LEFT, ONLY TO RETURN LATER.

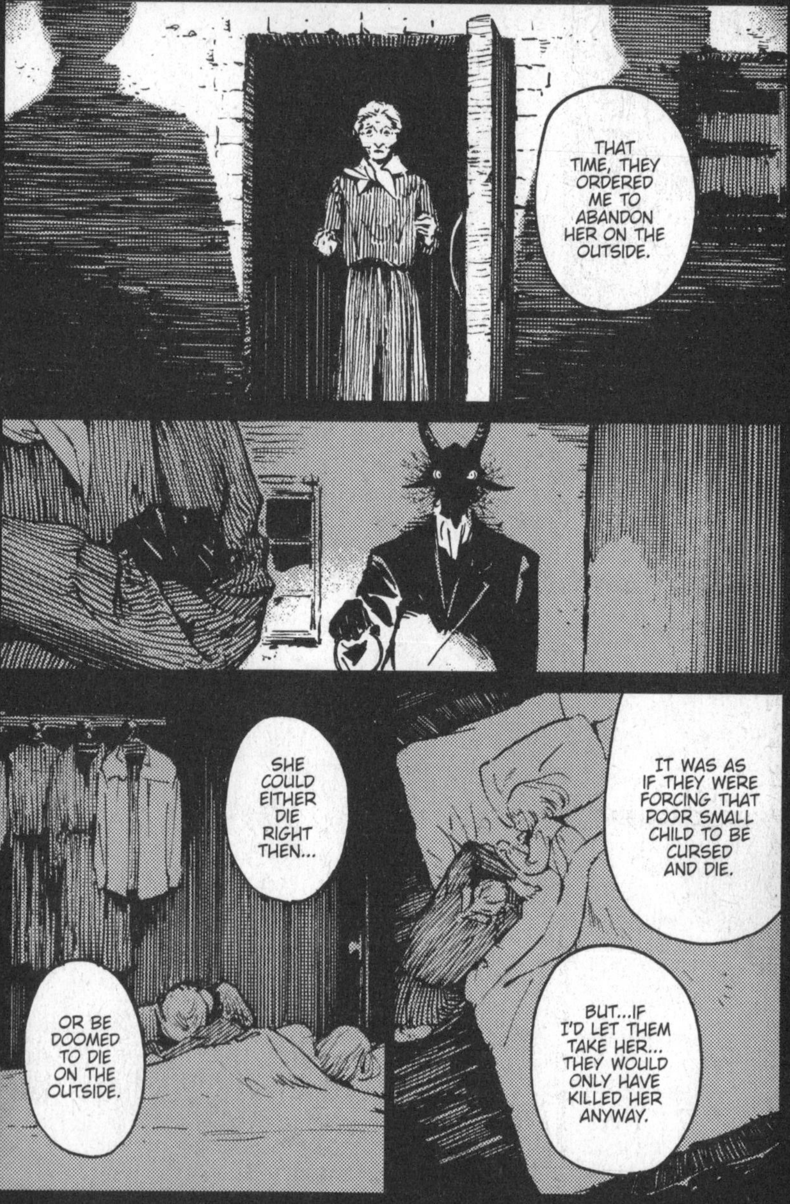
THAT TIME, THEY ORDERED ME TO ABANDON HER ON THE OUTSIDE.
IT WAS AS IF THEY WERE FORCING THAT POOR SMALL CHILD TO BE CURSED AND DIE.
BUT...IF I'D LET THEM TAKE HER... THEY WOULD ONLY HAVE KILLED HER ANYWAY.
SHE COULD EITHER DIE RIGHT THEN...
OR BE DOOMED TO DIE ON THE OUTSIDE.

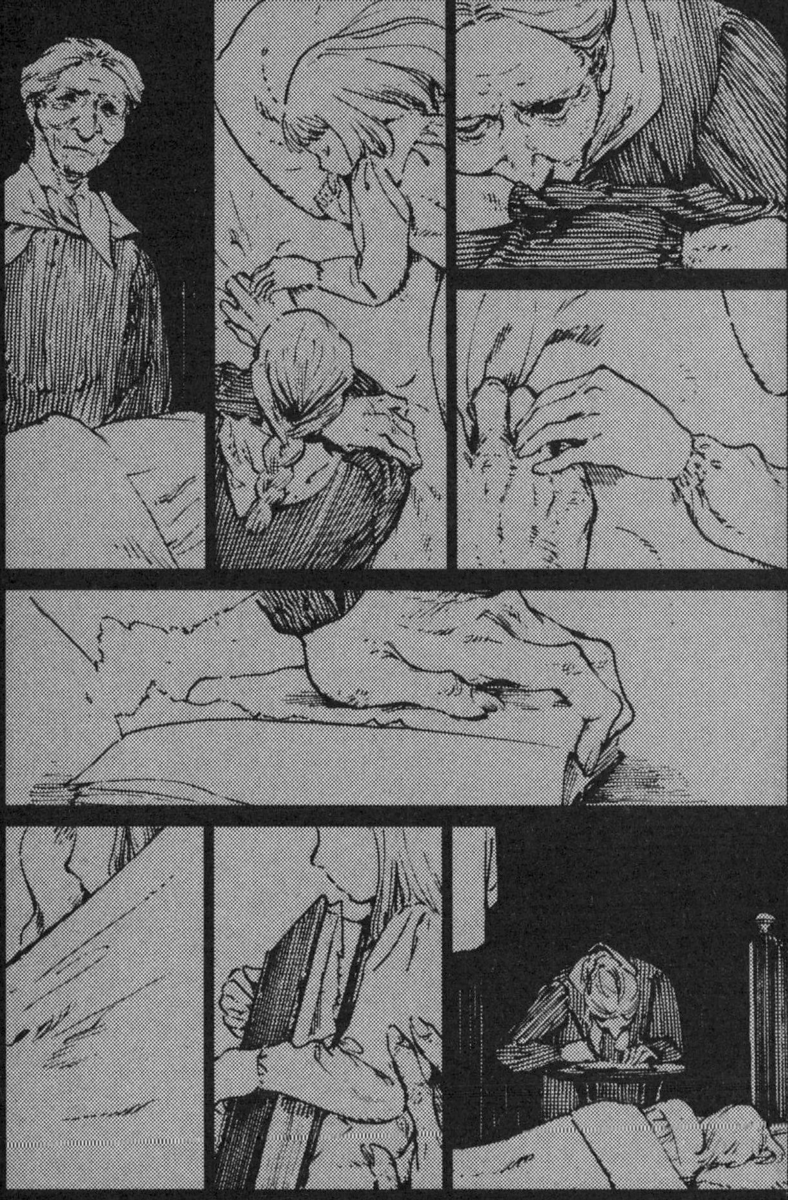

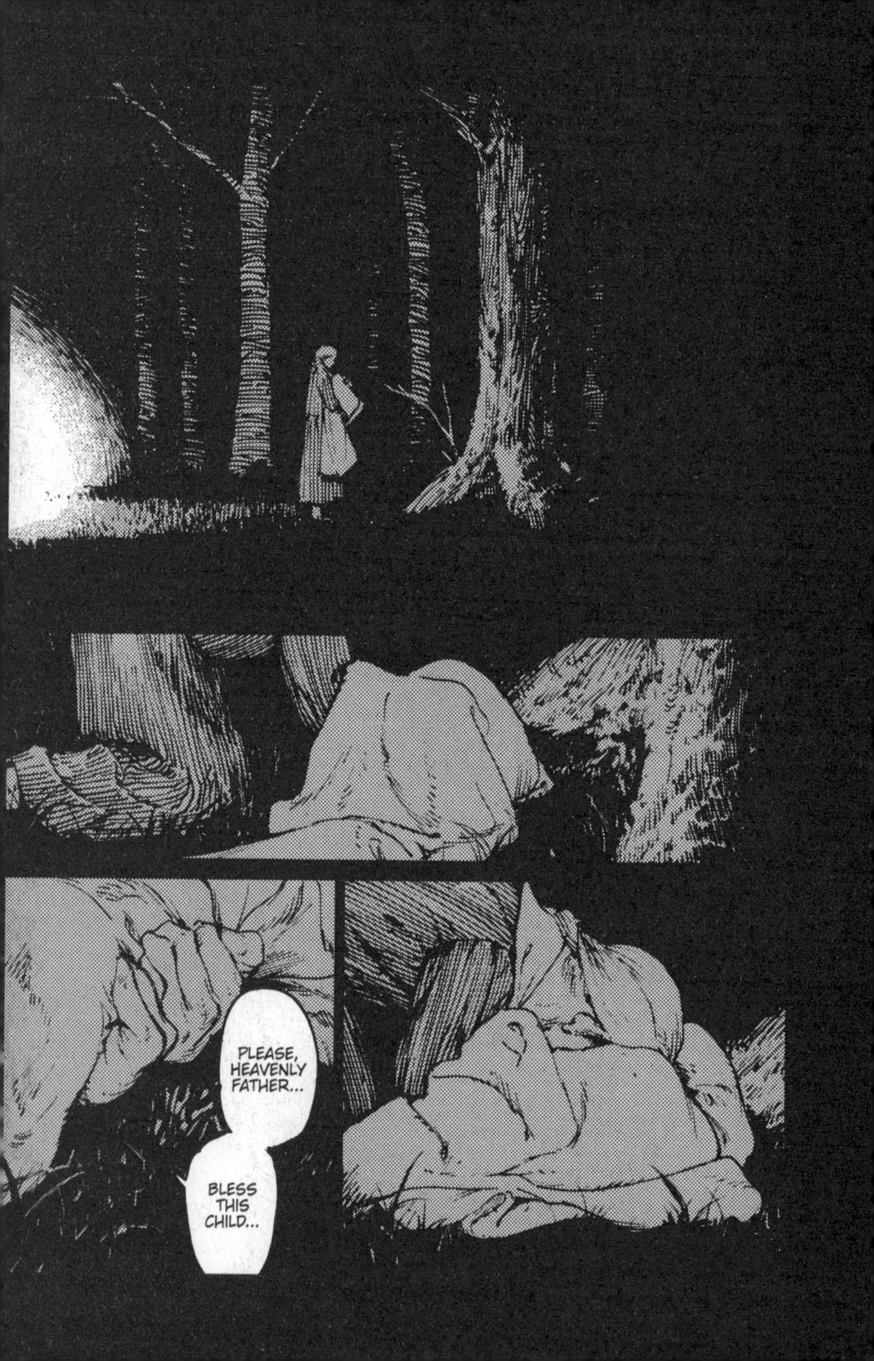
PLEASE, HEAVENLY FATHER...
BLESS THIS CHILD...

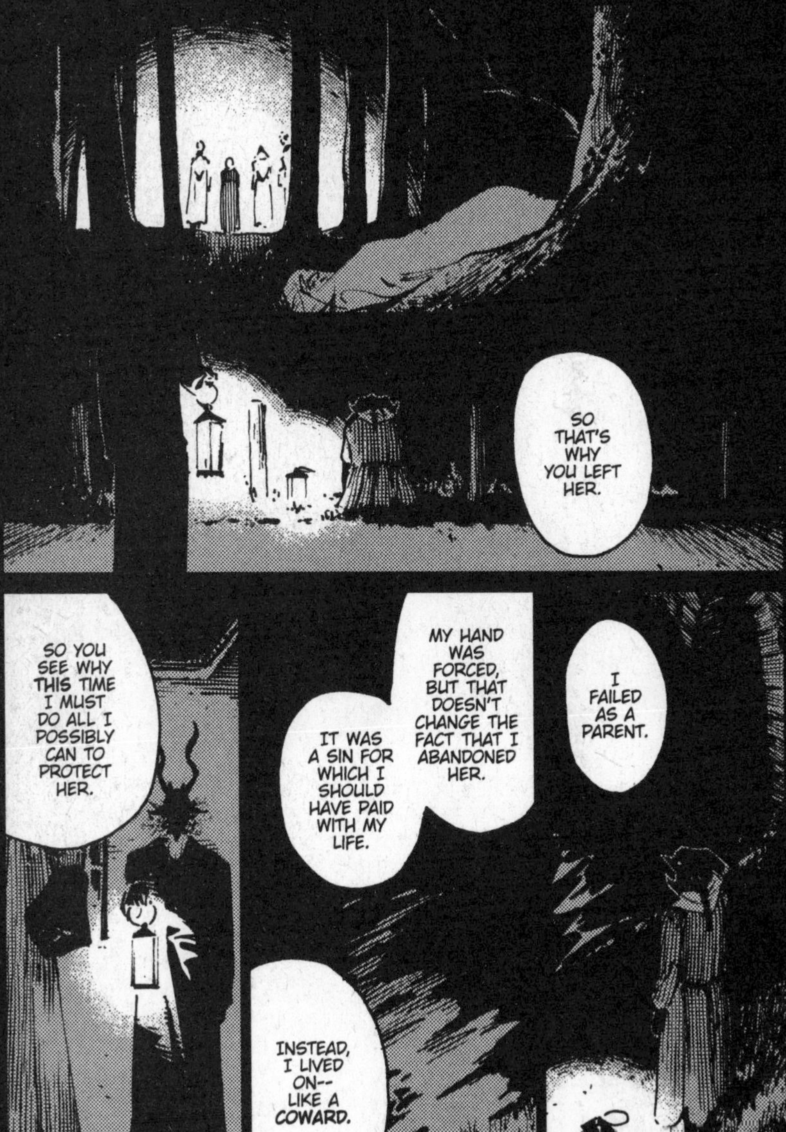
SO THAT'S WHY YOU LEFT HER.
I FAILED AS A PARENT.
MY HAND WAS FORCED, BUT THAT DOESN'T CHANGE THE FACT THAT I ABANDONED HER.
IT WAS A SIN FOR WHICH I SHOULD HAVE PAID WITH MY LIFE.
INSTEAD, I LIVED ON-- LIKE A COWARD.
SO YOU SEE WHY THIS TIME I MUST DO ALL I POSSIBLY CAN TO PROTECT HER.

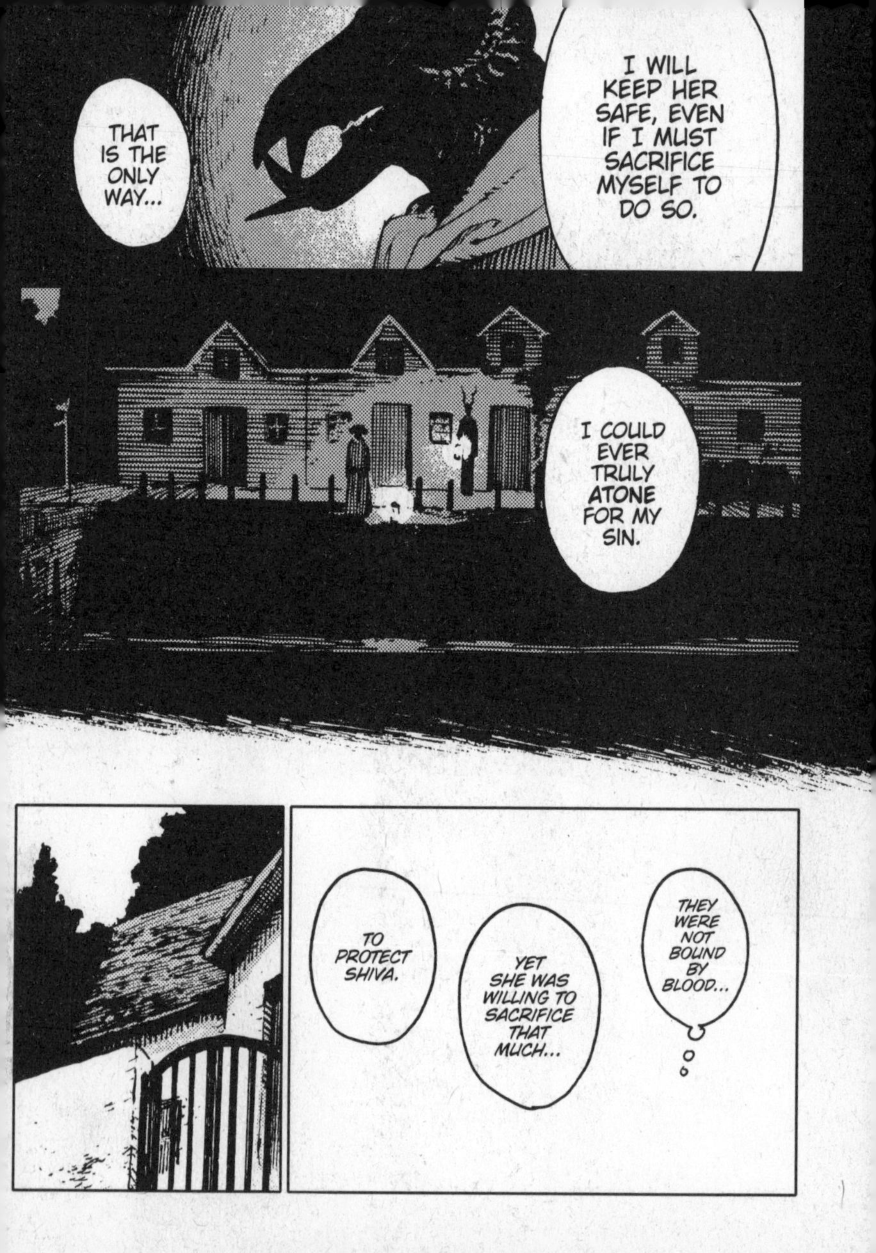
I WILL KEEP HER SAFE, EVEN IF I MUST SACRIFICE MYSELF TO DO SO.
THAT IS THE ONLY WAY...
I COULD EVER TRULY ATONE FOR MY SIN.
THEY WERE NOT BOUND BY BLOOD...
YET SHE WAS WILLING TO SACRIFICE THAT MUCH...
TO PROTECT SHIVA.

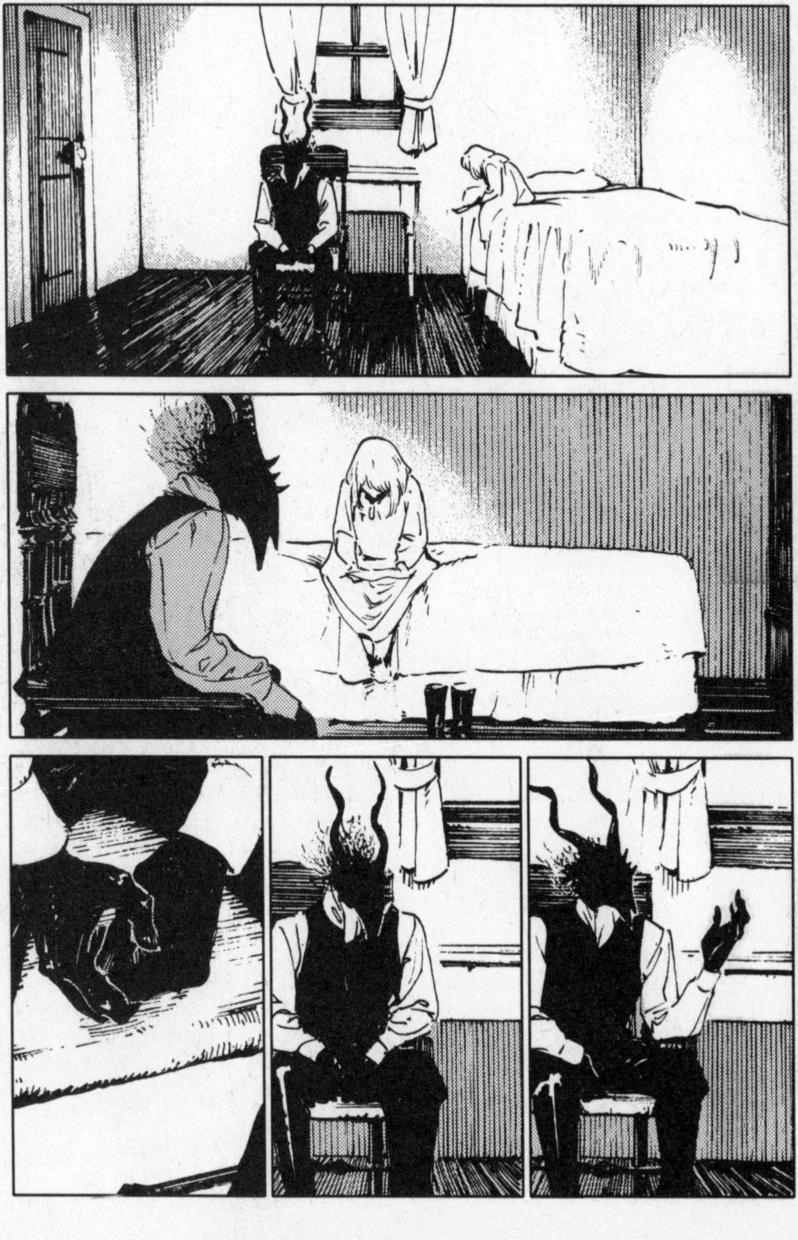

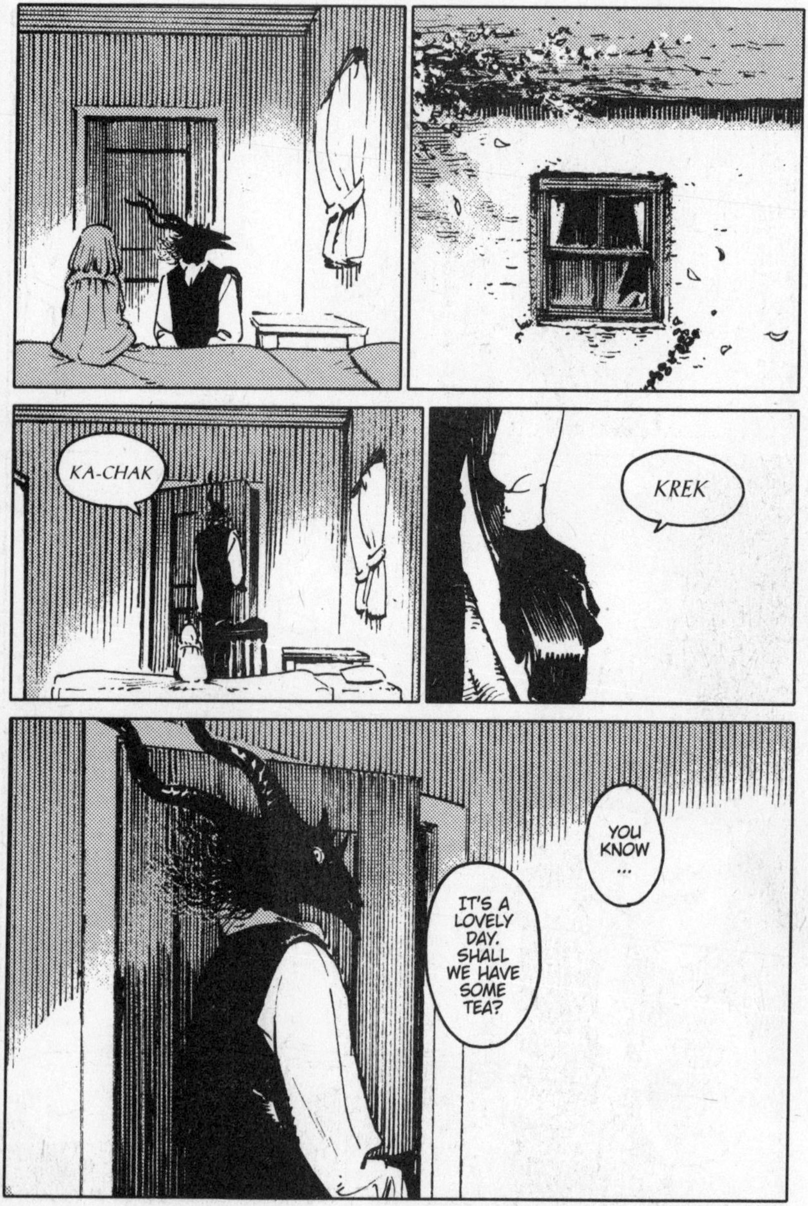
KREK
KA-CHAK
YOU KNOW ...
IT'S A LOVELY DAY. SHALL WE HAVE SOME TEA?

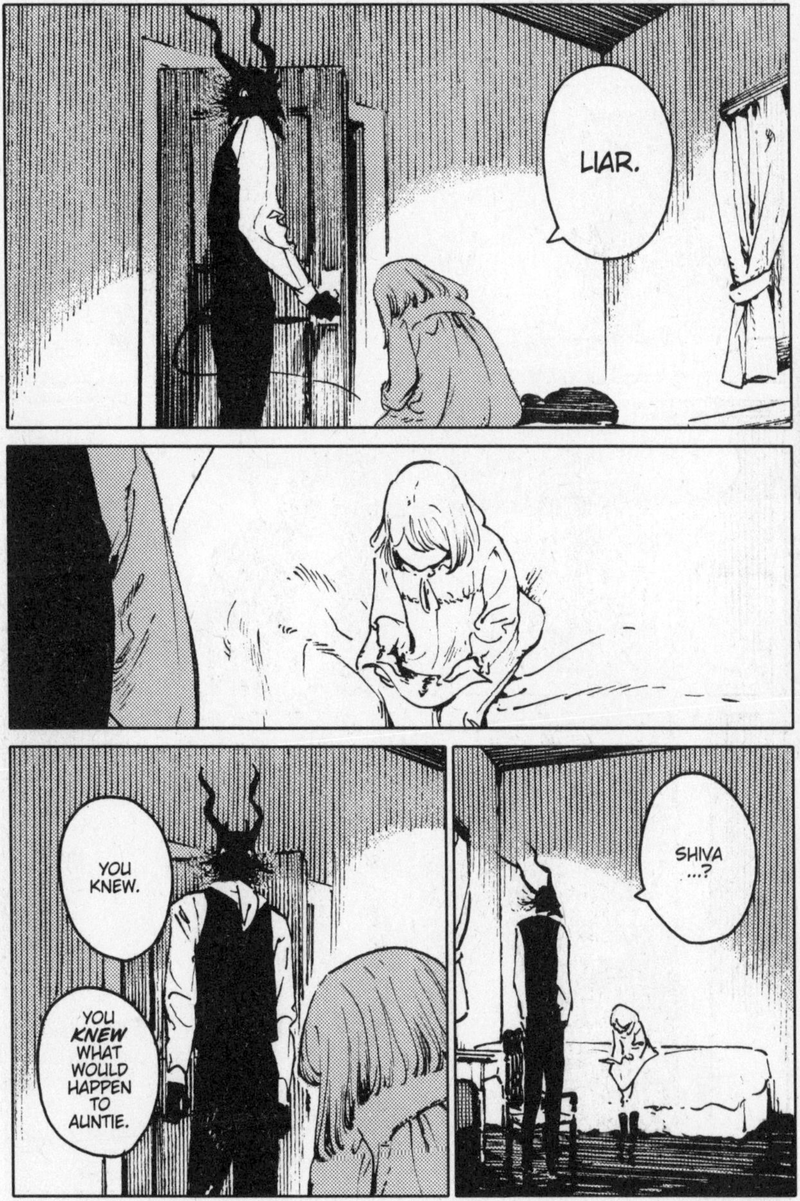
LIAR.
SHIVA ...?
YOU KNEW.
YOU *KNEW* WHAT WOULD HAPPEN TO AUNTIE.

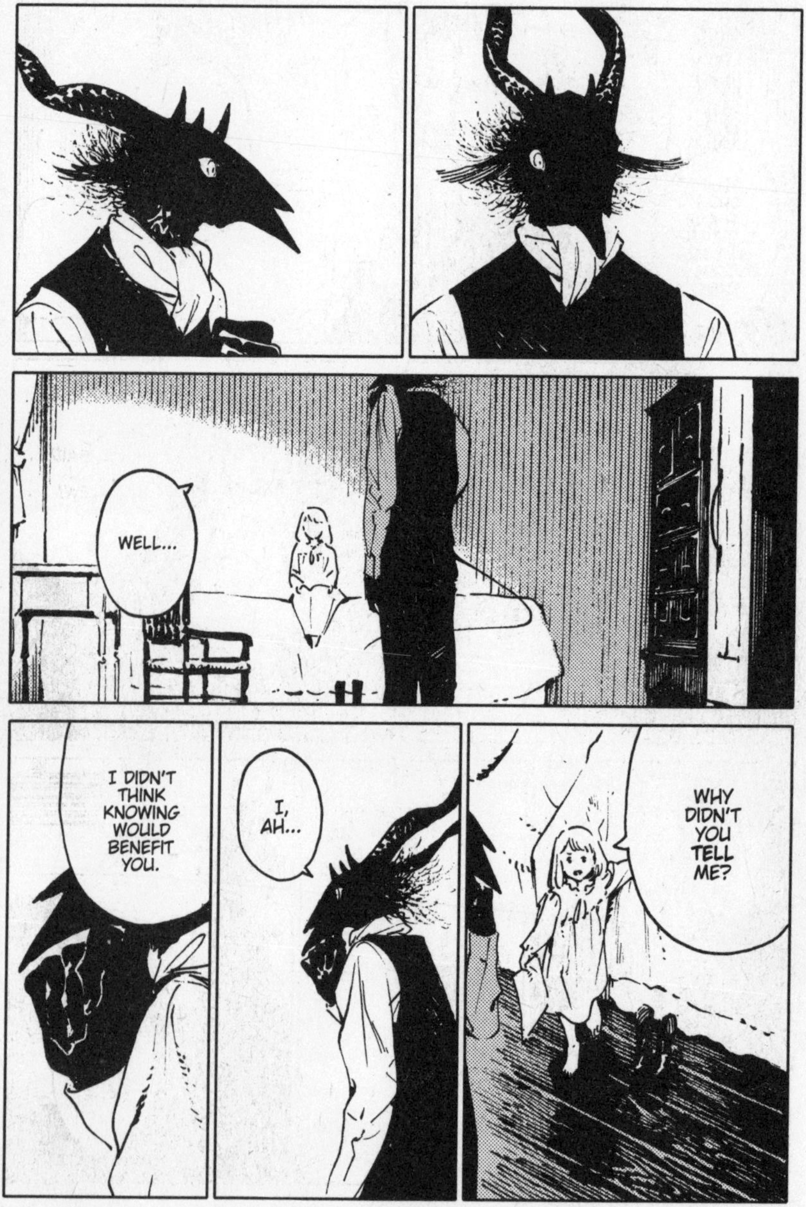
WELL...
WHY DIDN'T YOU TELL ME?
I, AH...
I DIDN'T THINK KNOWING WOULD BENEFIT YOU.

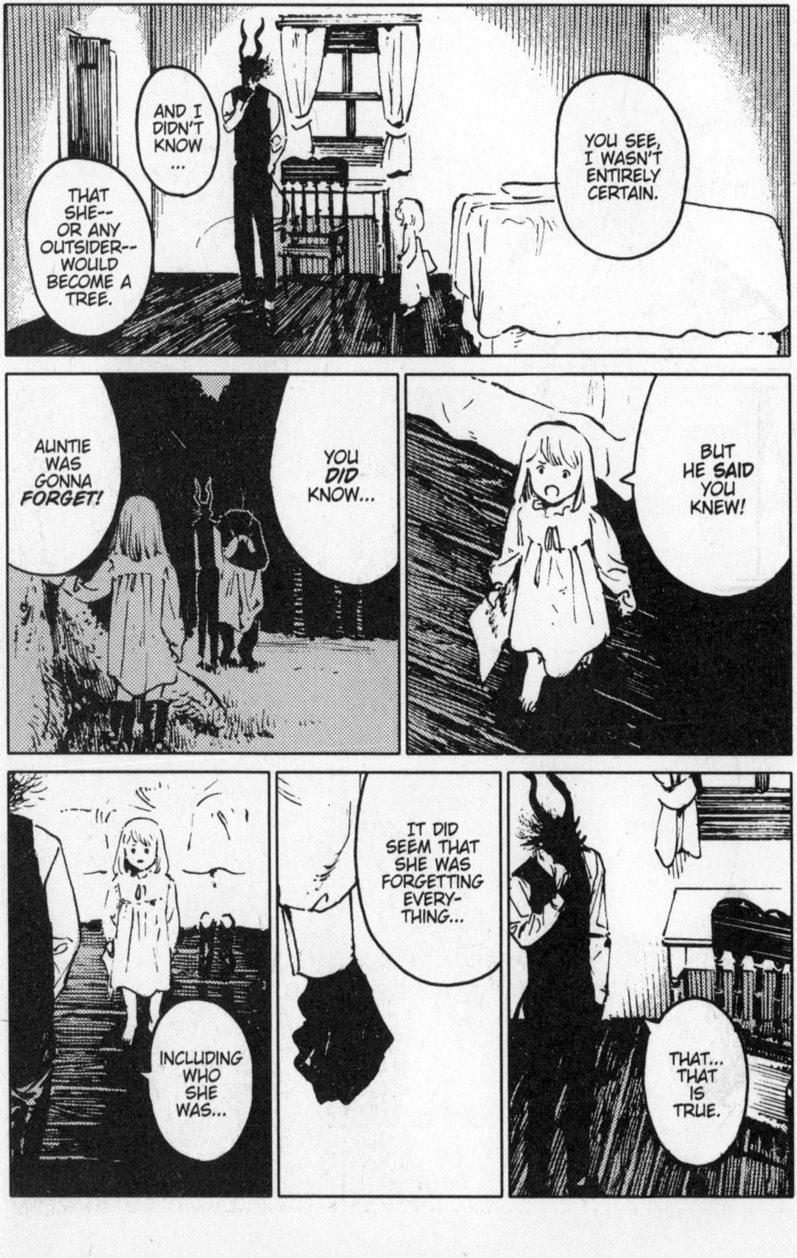
YOU SEE, I WASN'T ENTIRELY CERTAIN.
AND I DIDN'T KNOW ...
THAT SHE-- OR ANY OUTSIDER-- WOULD BECOME A TREE.
BUT HE SAID YOU KNEW!
YOU DID KNOW...
AUNTIE WAS GONNA FORGET!
THAT... THAT IS TRUE.
IT DID SEEM THAT SHE WAS FORGETTING EVERY-THING...
INCLUDING WHO SHE WAS...

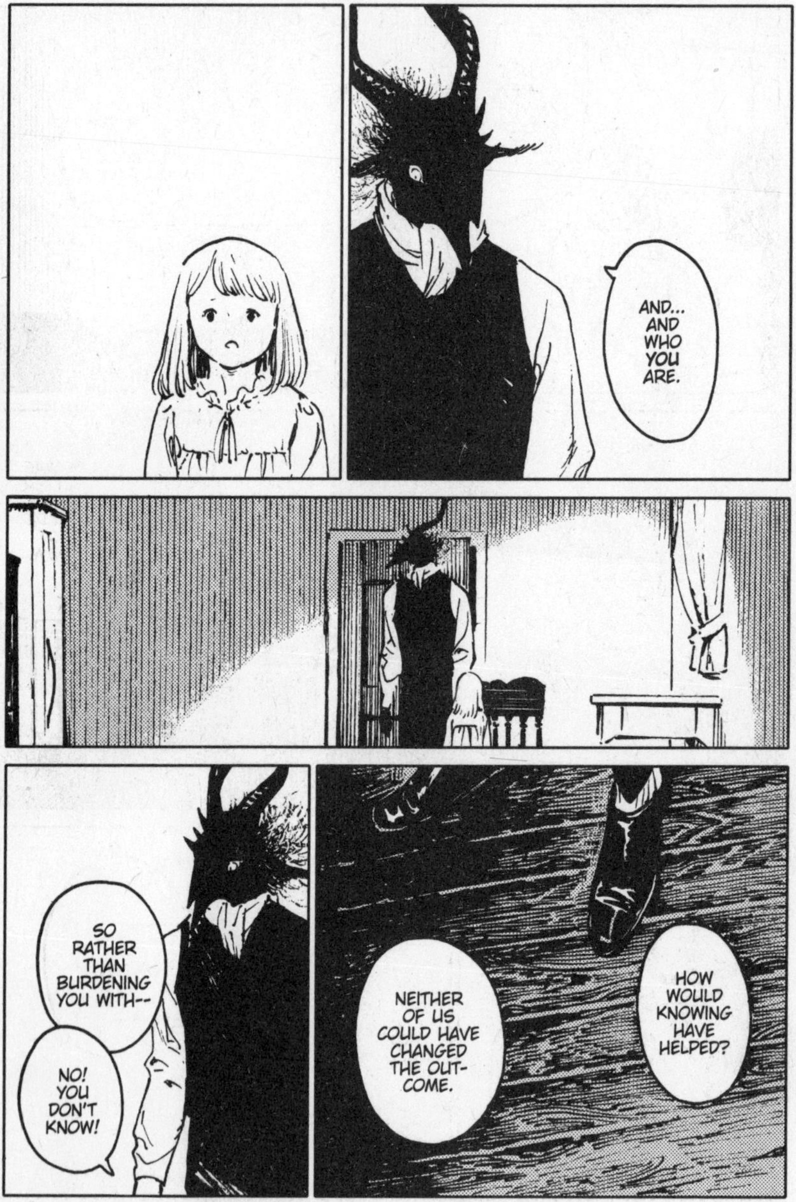
AND... AND WHO YOU ARE.
HOW WOULD KNOWING HAVE HELPED?
NEITHER OF US COULD HAVE CHANGED THE OUT-COME.
SO RATHER THAN BURDENING YOU WITH--
NO! YOU DON'T KNOW!

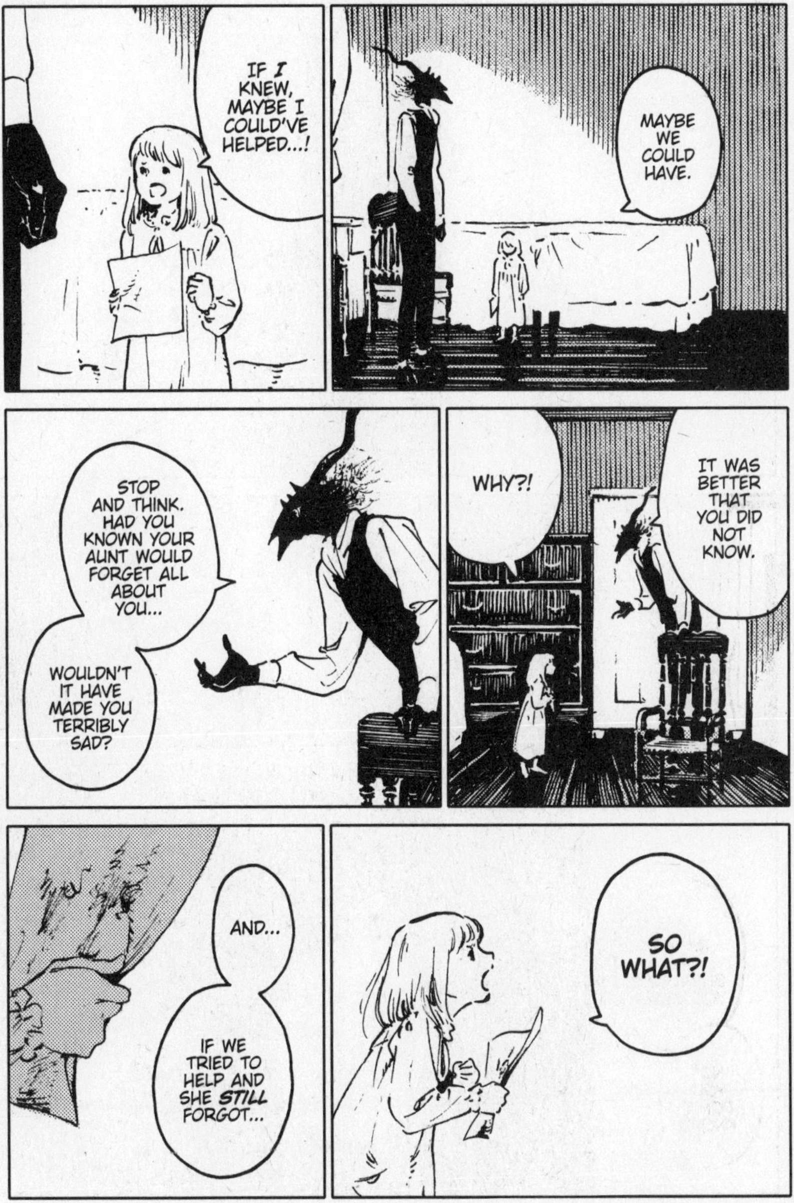
MAYBE WE COULD HAVE.
IF *I* KNEW, MAYBE I COULD'VE HELPED...!
IT WAS BETTER THAT YOU DID NOT KNOW.
WHY?!
STOP AND THINK. HAD YOU KNOWN YOUR AUNT WOULD FORGET ALL ABOUT YOU...
WOULDN'T IT HAVE MADE YOU TERRIBLY SAD?
SO WHAT?!
AND...
IF WE TRIED TO HELP AND SHE *STILL* FORGOT...

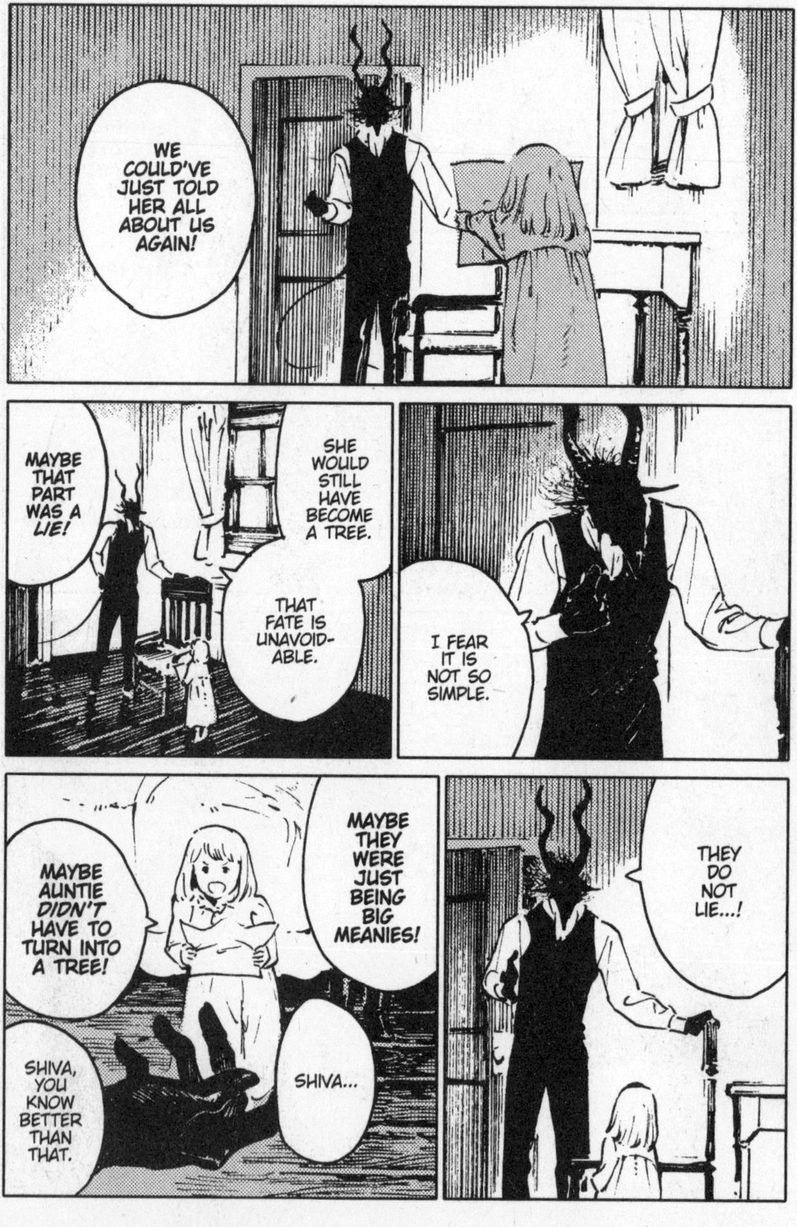
WE COULD'VE JUST TOLD HER ALL ABOUT US AGAIN!
I FEAR IT IS NOT SO SIMPLE.
SHE WOULD STILL HAVE BECOME A TREE.
THAT FATE IS UNAVOID-ABLE.
MAYBE THAT PART WAS A *LIE!*
THEY DO NOT LIE...!
MAYBE THEY WERE JUST BEING BIG MEANIES!
MAYBE AUNTIE *DIDN'T* HAVE TO TURN INTO A TREE!
SHIVA...
SHIVA, YOU KNOW BETTER THAN THAT.

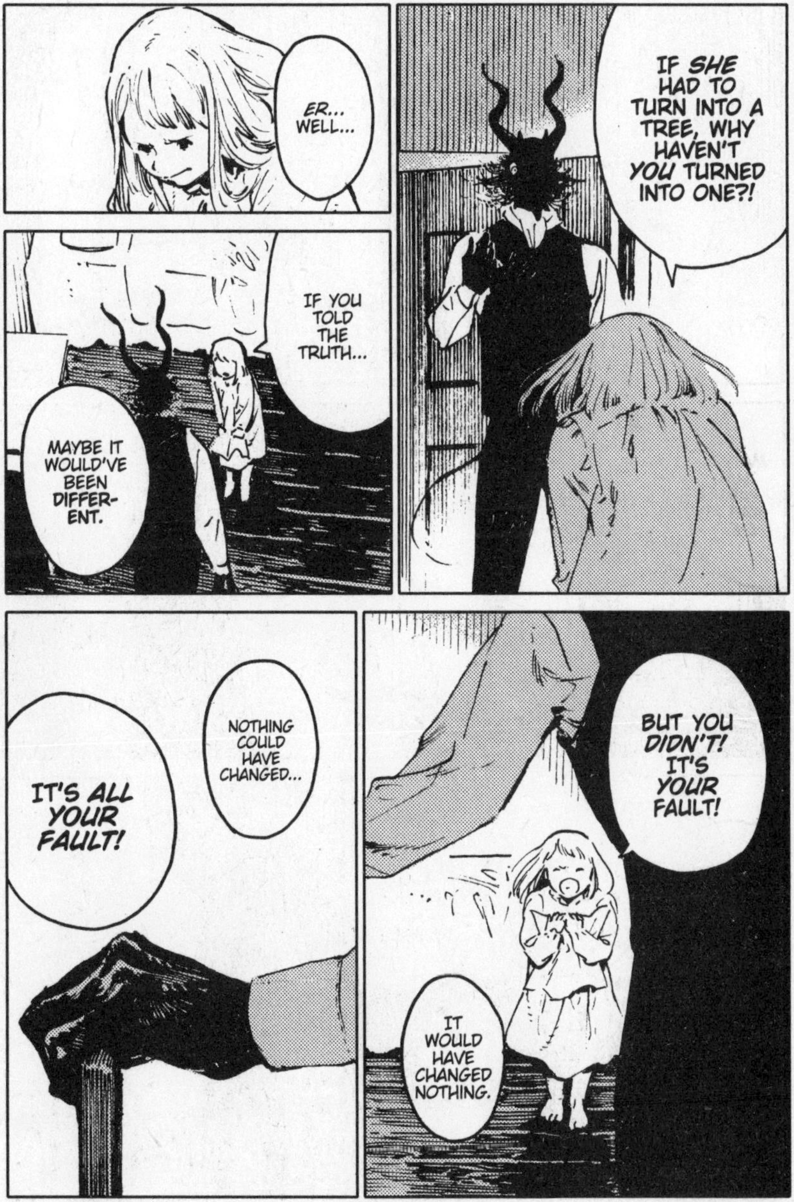
IF *SHE* HAD TO TURN INTO A TREE, WHY HAVEN'T *YOU* TURNED INTO ONE?!
ER... WELL...
IF YOU TOLD THE TRUTH...
MAYBE IT WOULD'VE BEEN DIFFER-ENT.
BUT YOU *DIDN'T!* IT'S *YOUR* FAULT!
IT WOULD HAVE CHANGED NOTHING.
NOTHING COULD HAVE CHANGED...
IT'S *ALL YOUR FAULT!*

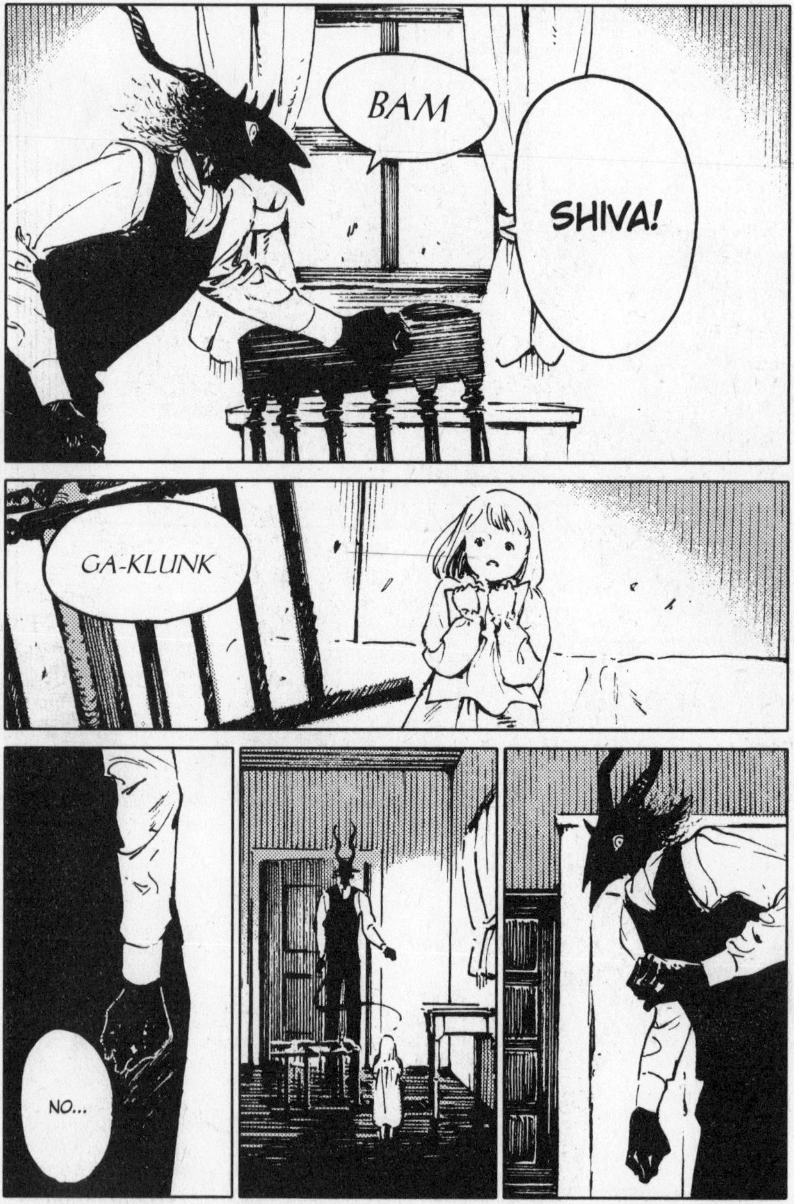
SHIVA!
BAM
GA-KLUNK
NO...

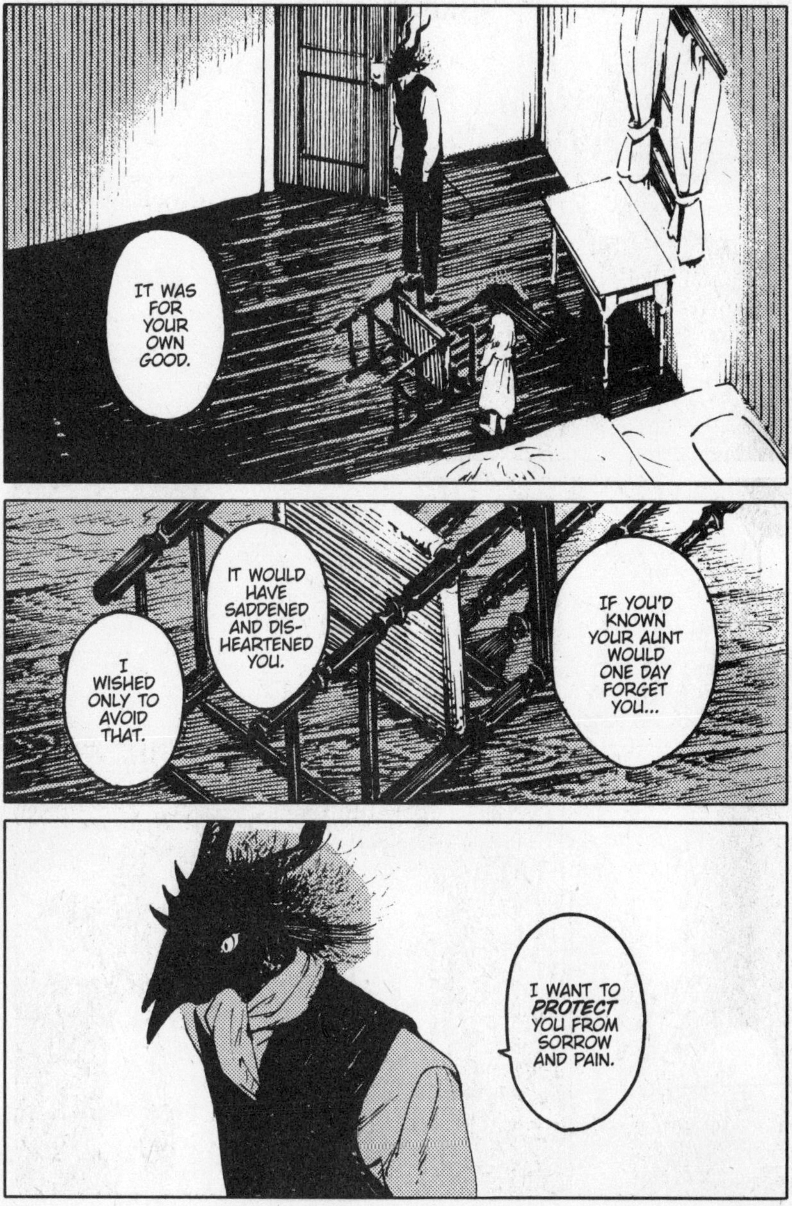
IT WAS FOR YOUR OWN GOOD.
IF YOU'D KNOWN YOUR AUNT WOULD ONE DAY FORGET YOU...
IT WOULD HAVE SADDENED AND DIS-HEARTENED YOU.
I WISHED ONLY TO AVOID THAT.
I WANT TO *PROTECT* YOU FROM SORROW AND PAIN.

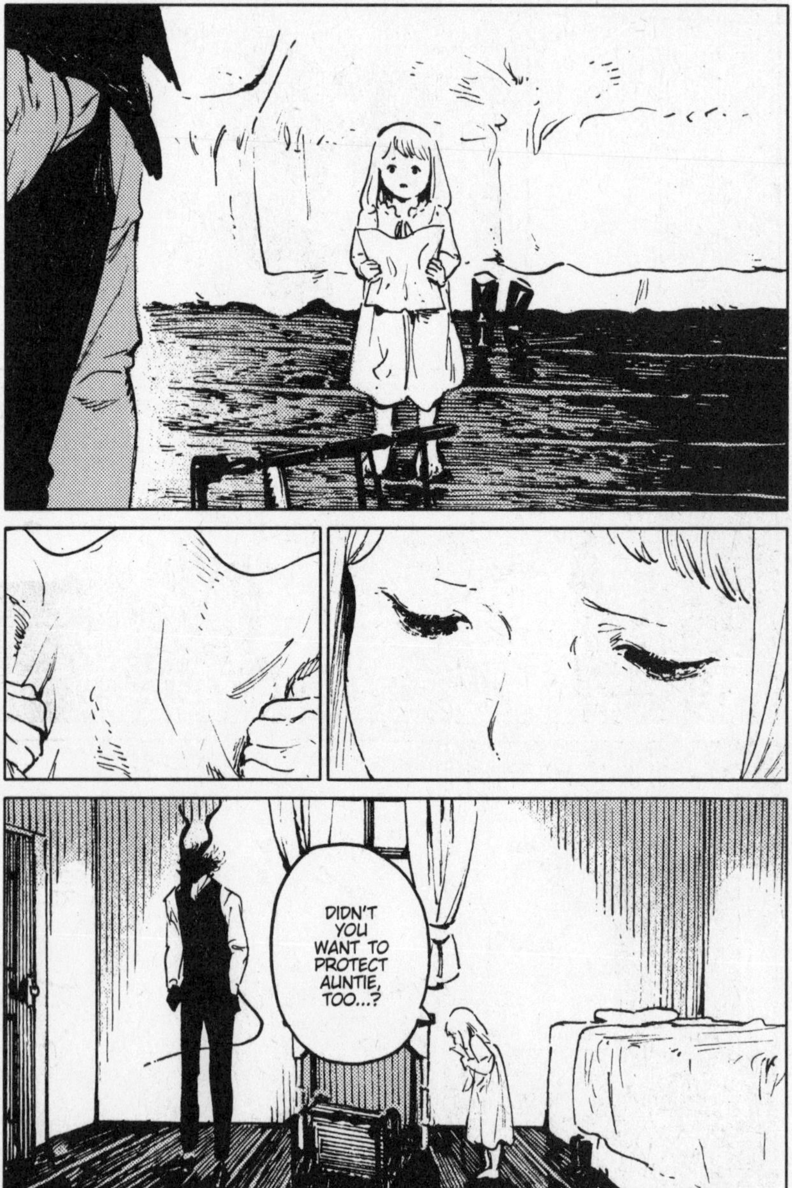
DIDN'T YOU WANT TO PROTECT AUNTIE, TOO...?

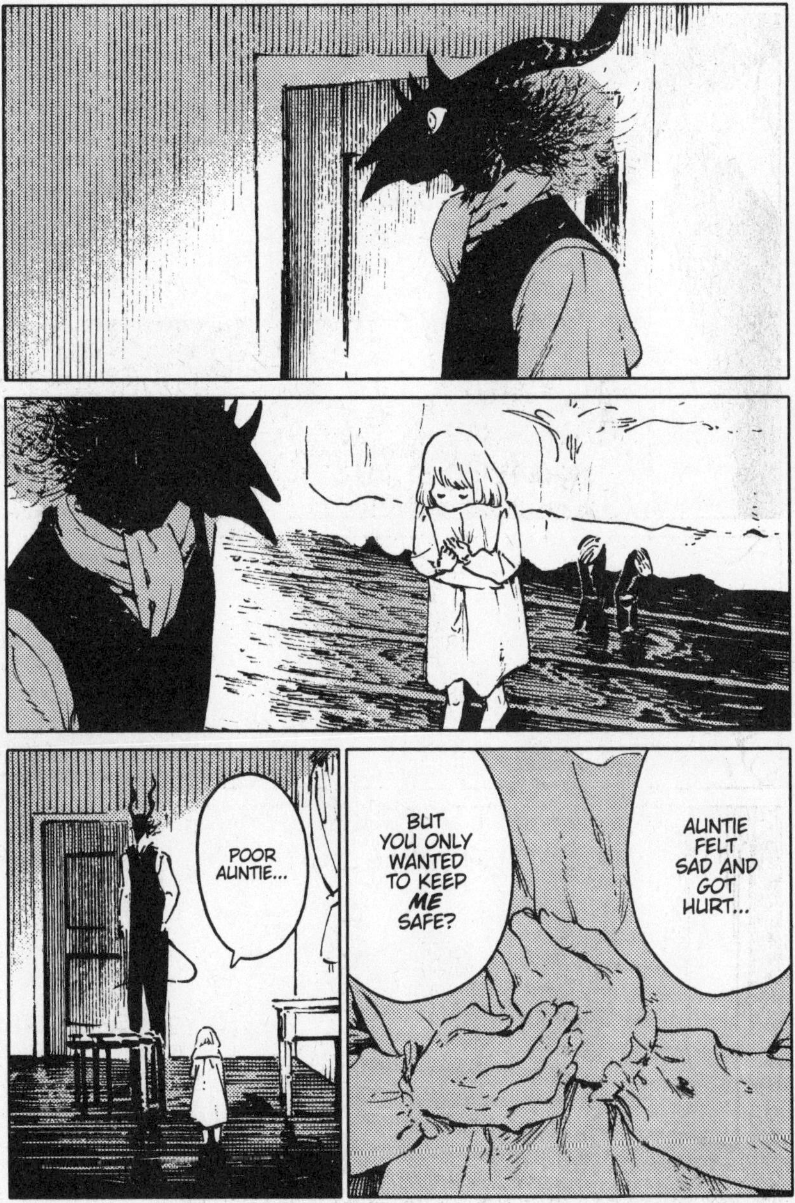
AUNTIE FELT SAD AND GOT HURT...
BUT YOU ONLY WANTED TO KEEP *ME* SAFE?
POOR AUNTIE...

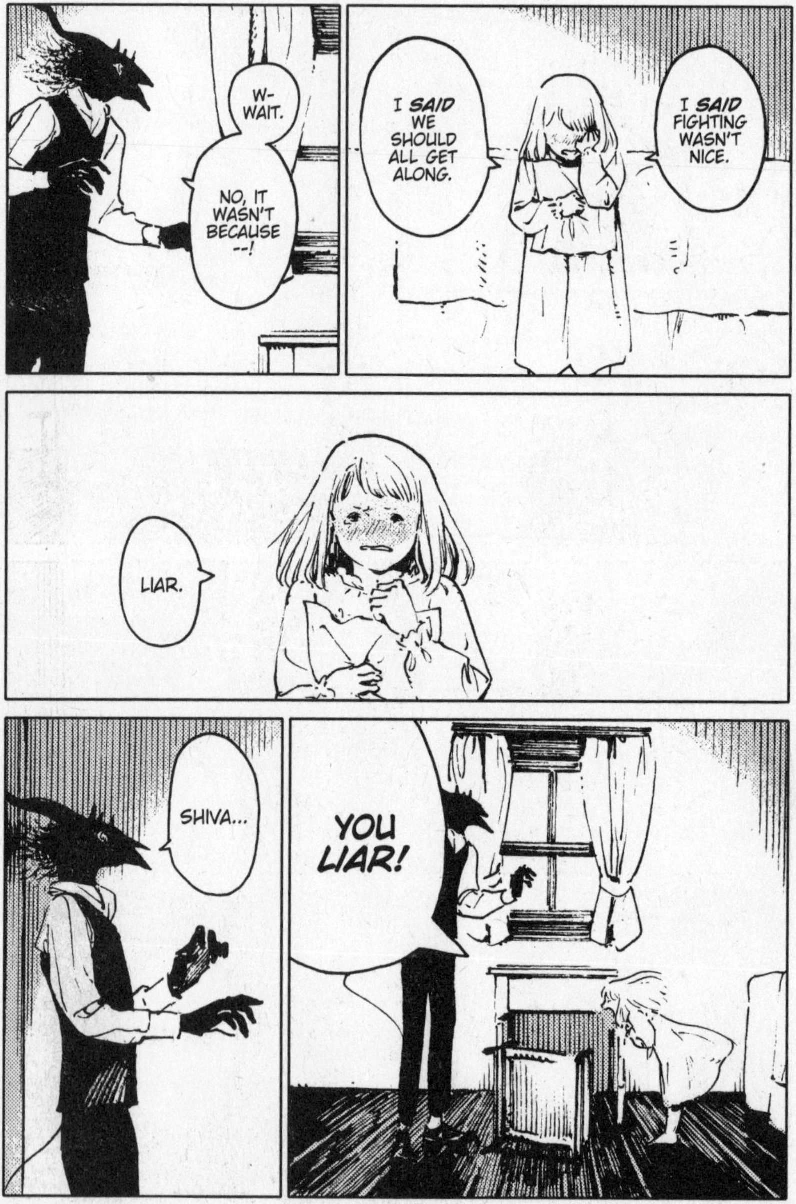
I SAID FIGHTING WASN'T NICE.
I SAID WE SHOULD ALL GET ALONG.
W-WAIT.
NO, IT WASN'T BECAUSE --!
LIAR.
YOU LIAR!
SHIVA...

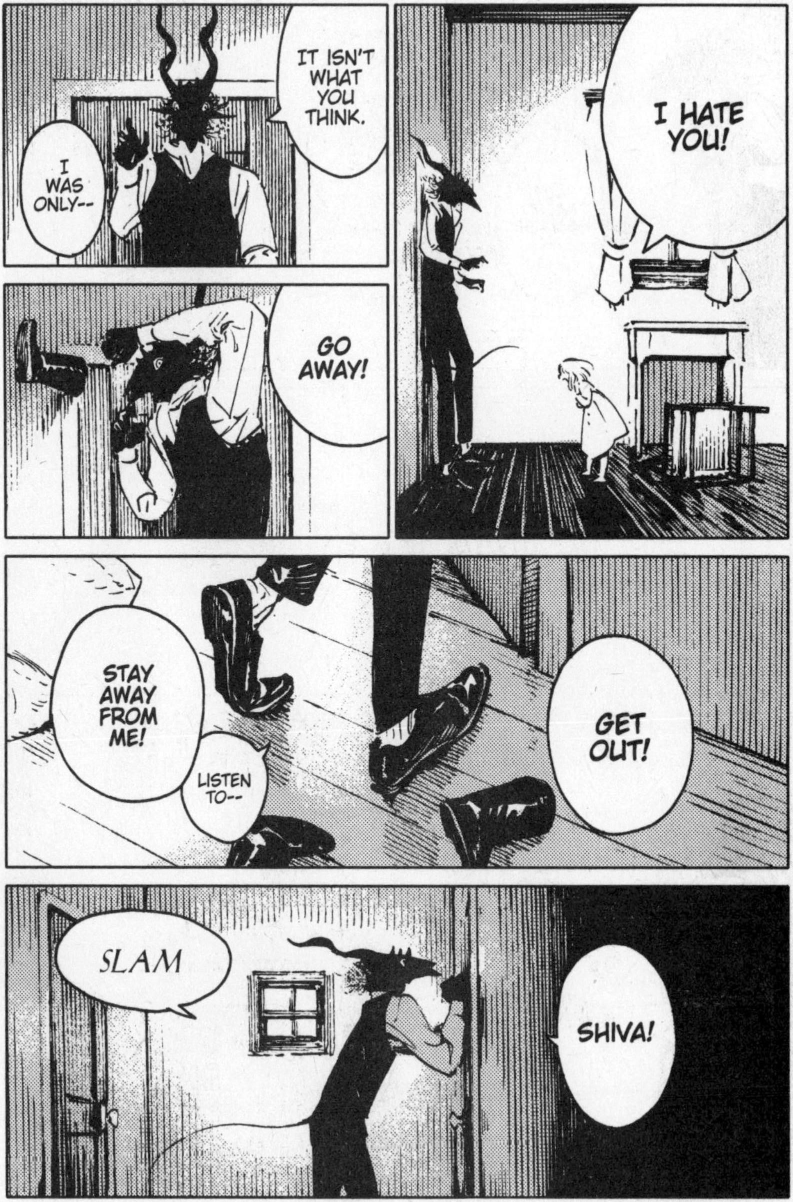
I HATE YOU!
IT ISN'T WHAT YOU THINK.
I WAS ONLY--
GO AWAY!
GET OUT!
STAY AWAY FROM ME!
LISTEN TO--
SHIVA!
SLAM

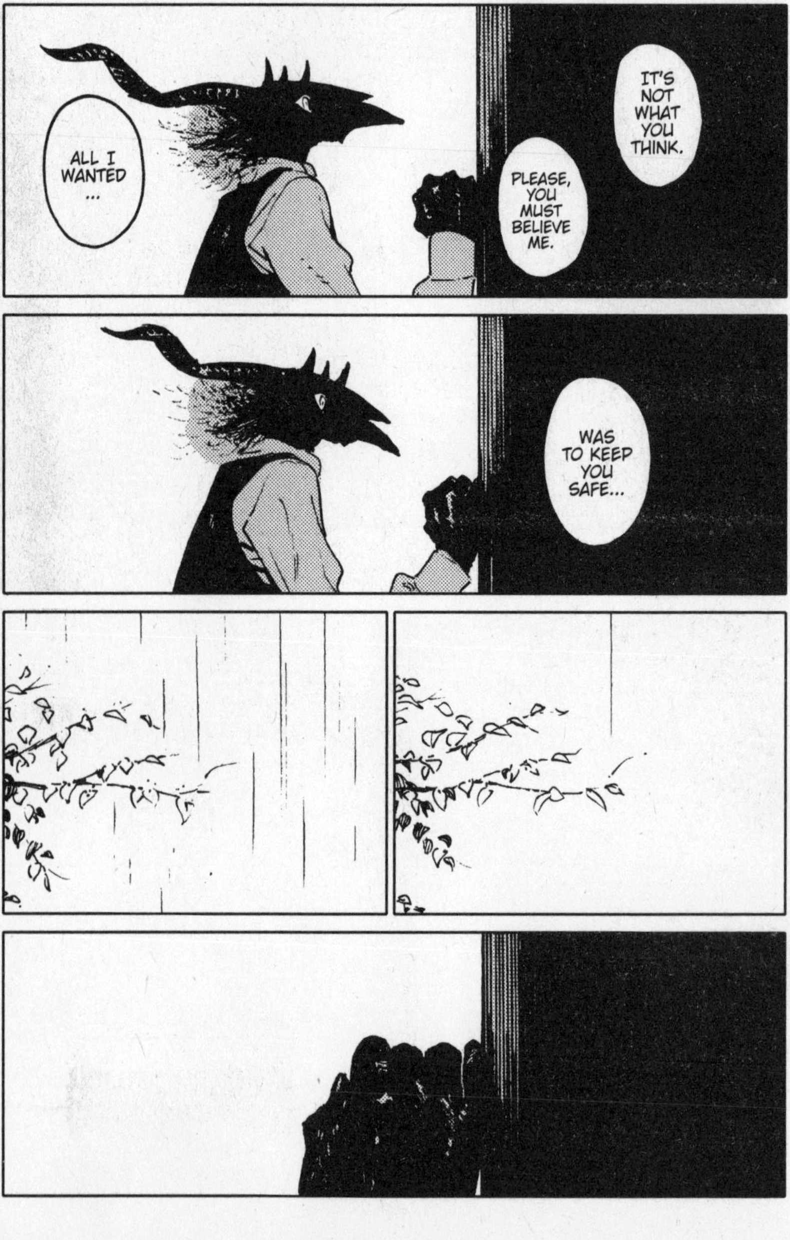
IT'S NOT WHAT YOU THINK.
PLEASE, YOU MUST BELIEVE ME.
ALL I WANTED ...
WAS TO KEEP YOU SAFE...

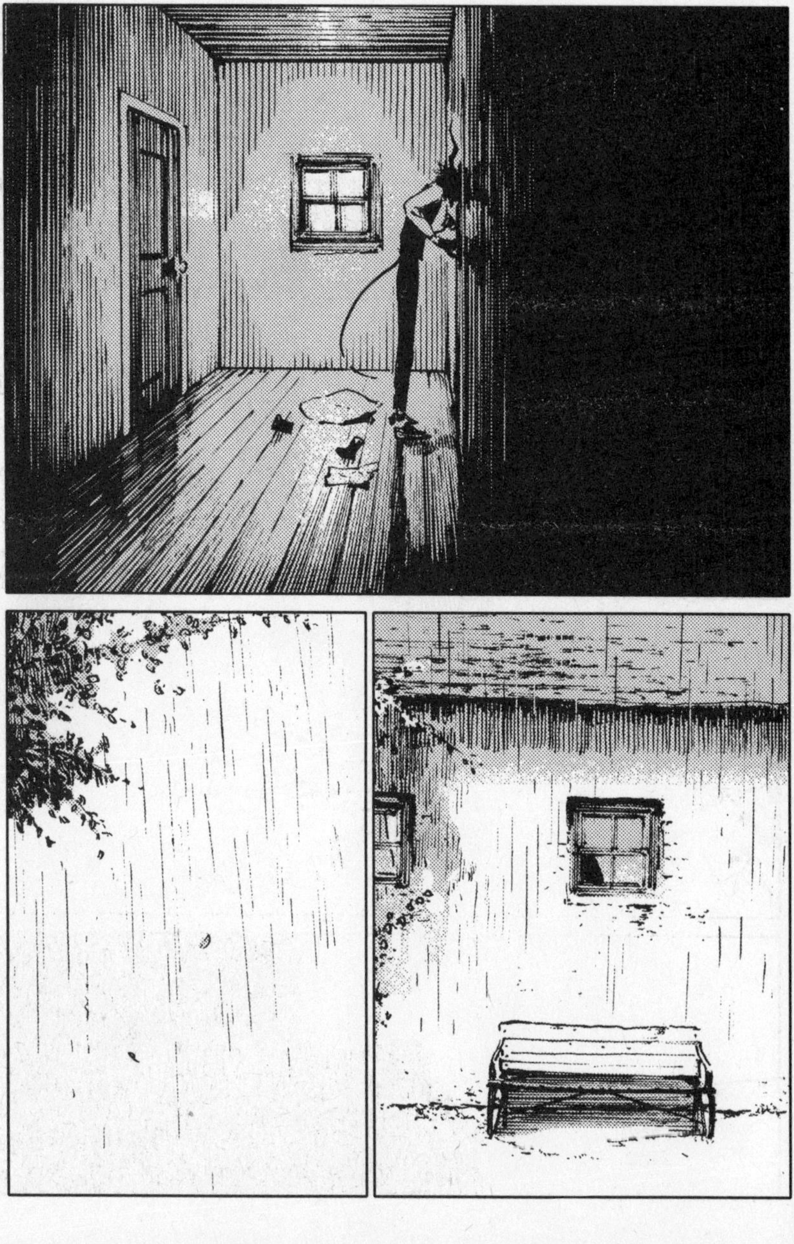

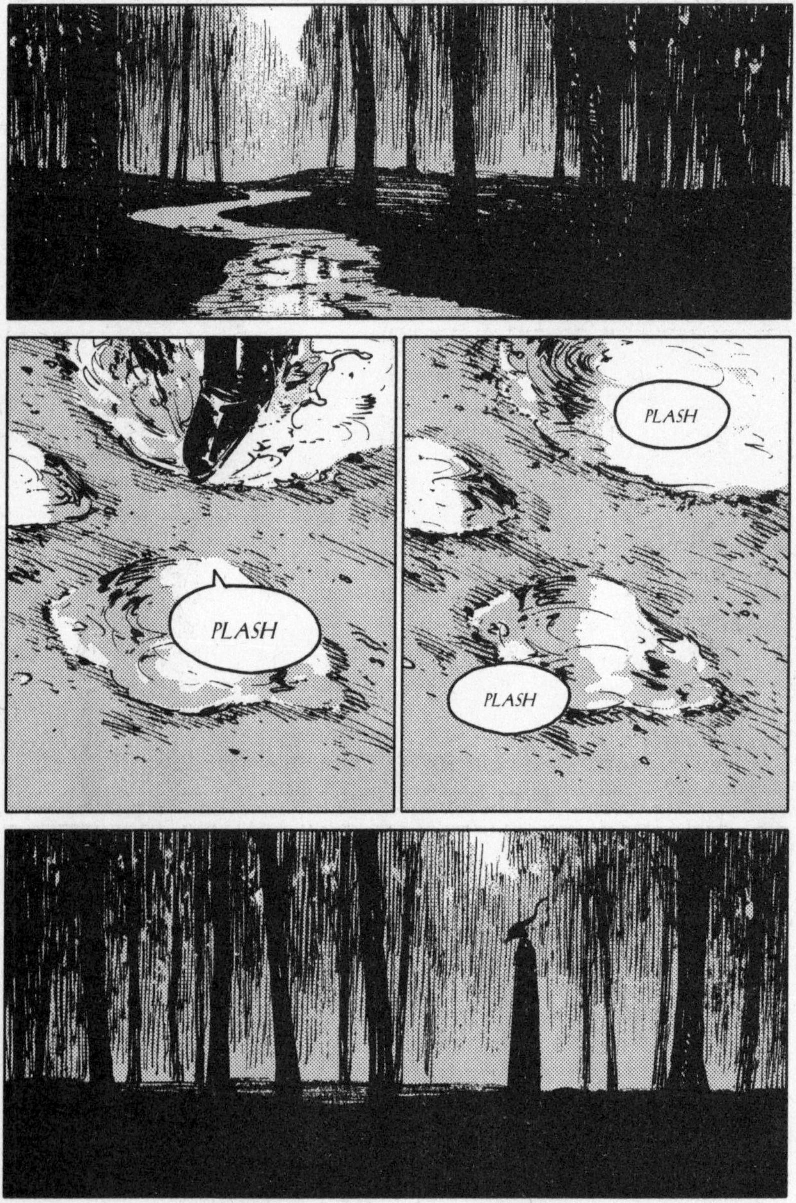
PLASH
PLASH
PLASH

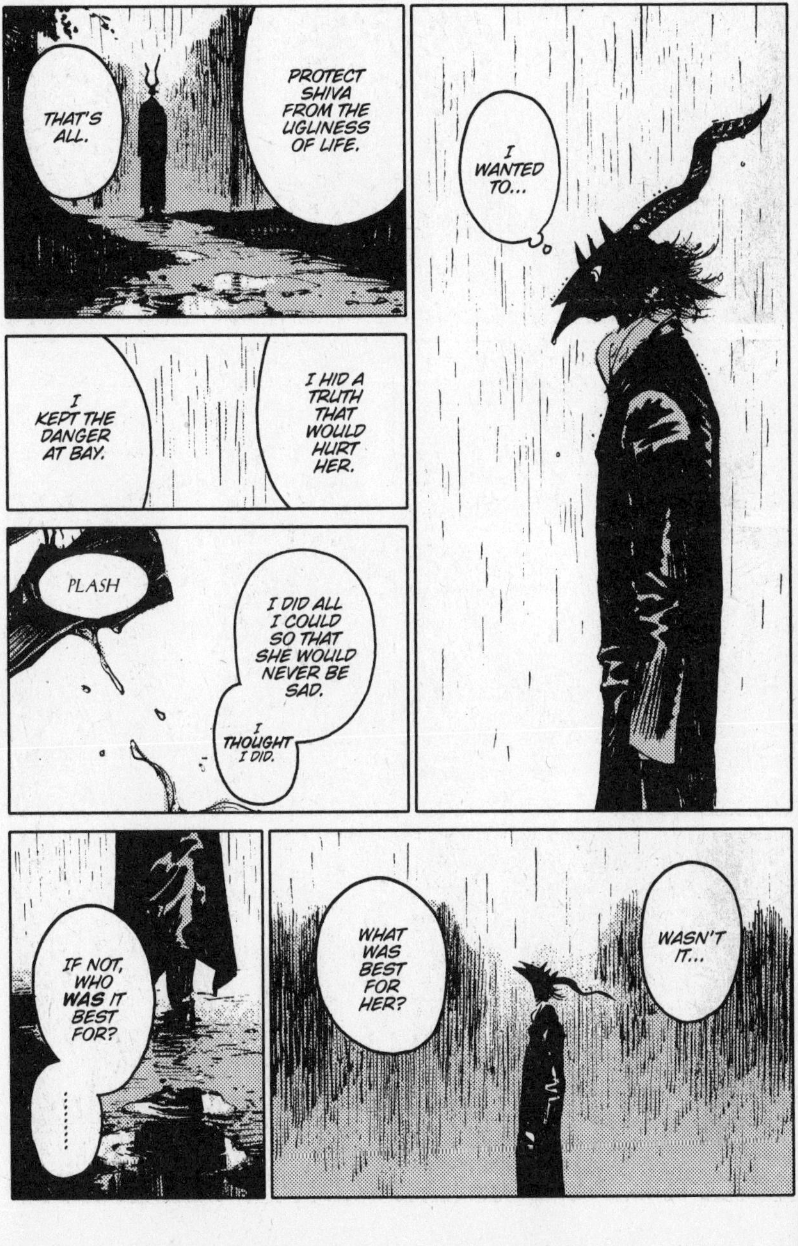
I WANTED TO...
PROTECT SHIVA FROM THE UGLINESS OF LIFE.
THAT'S ALL.
I HID A TRUTH THAT WOULD HURT HER.
I KEPT THE DANGER AT BAY.
I DID ALL I COULD SO THAT SHE WOULD NEVER BE SAD.
I THOUGHT I DID.
PLASH
WASN'T IT...
WHAT WAS BEST FOR HER?
IF NOT, WHO **WAS** IT BEST FOR?
......

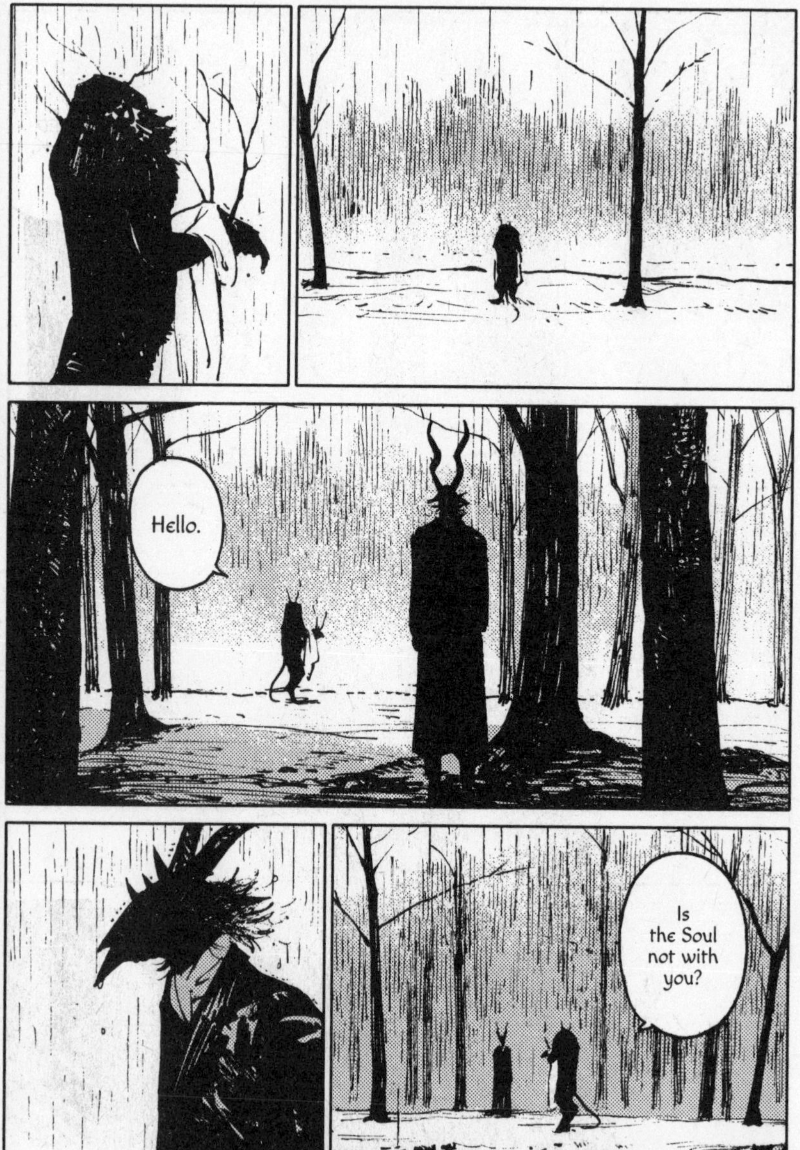
Hello.
Is the Soul not with you?

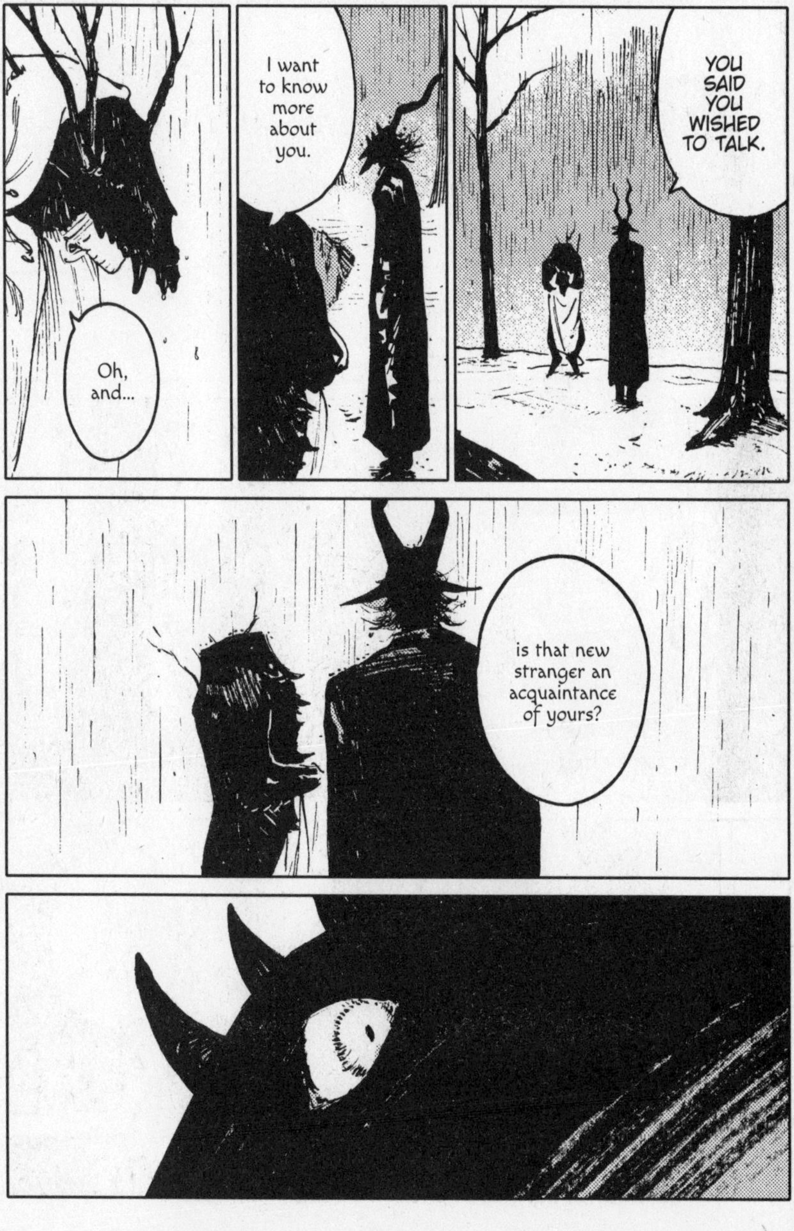
YOU SAID YOU WISHED TO TALK.
I want to know more about you.
Oh, and...
is that new stranger an acquaintance of yours?

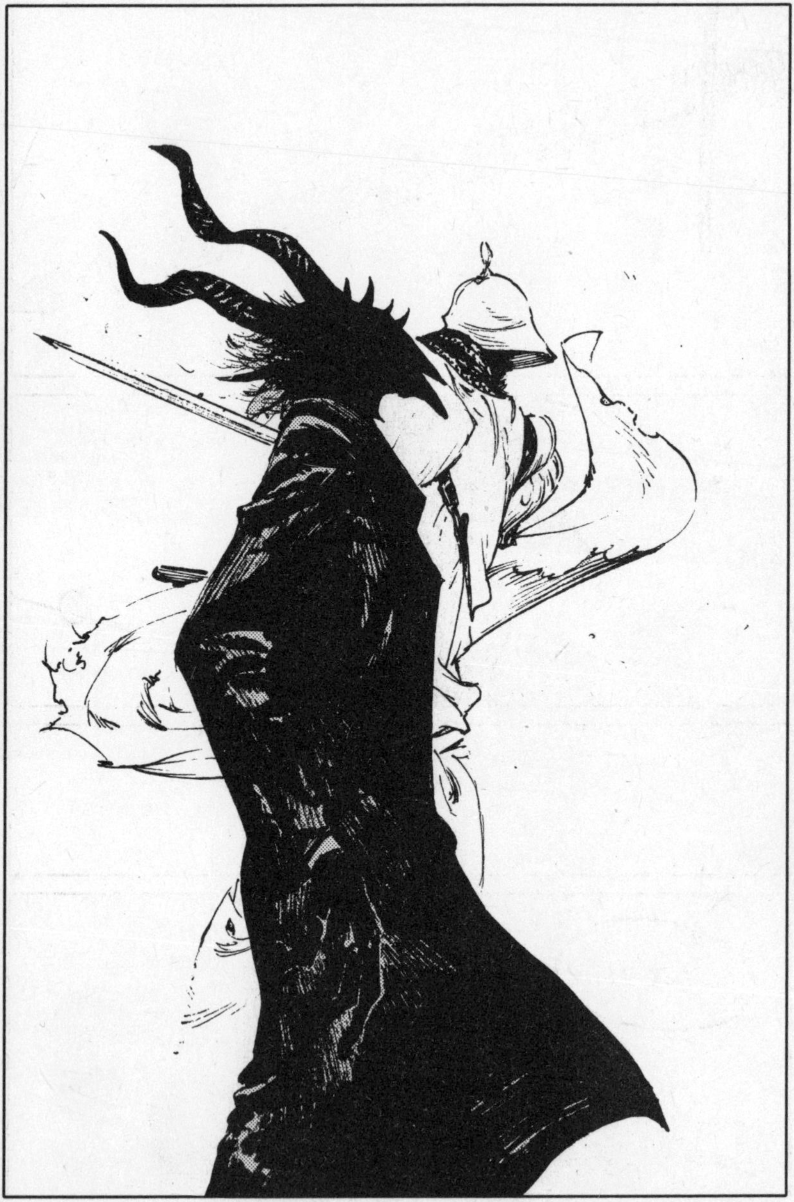

Chapter 23

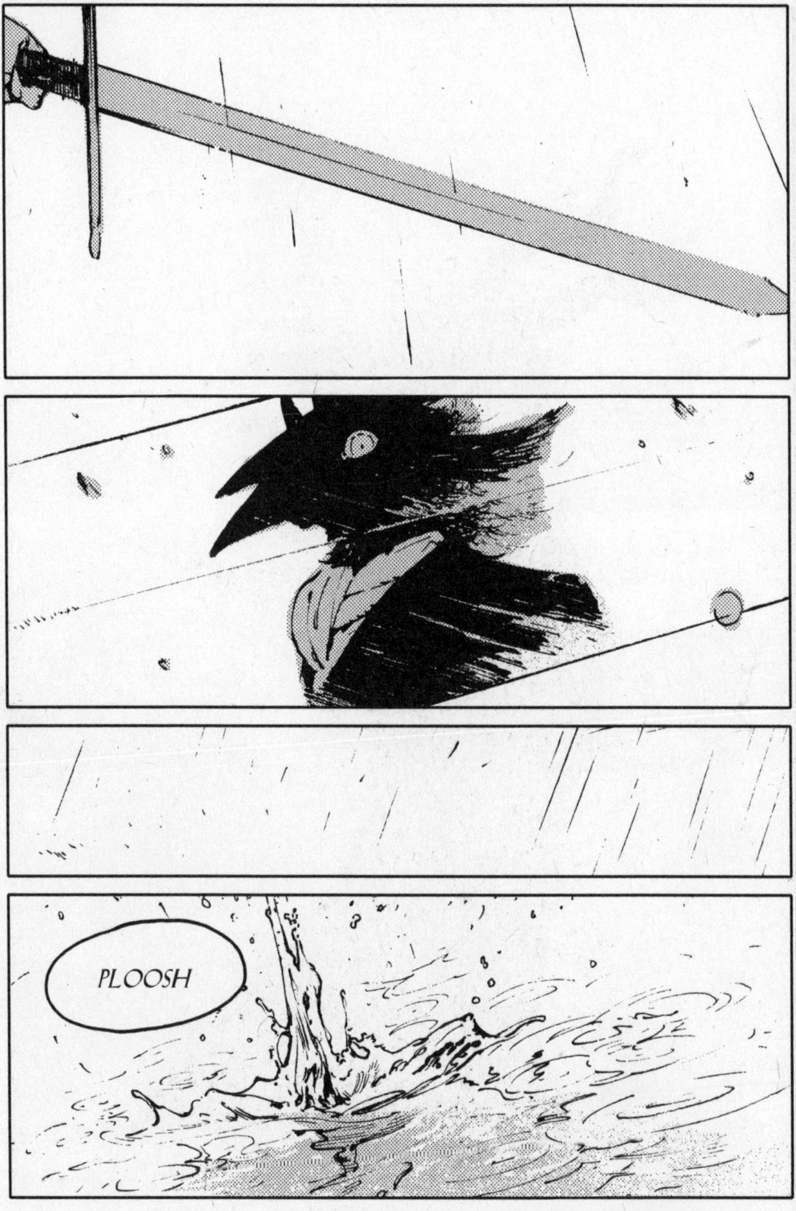
PLOOSH

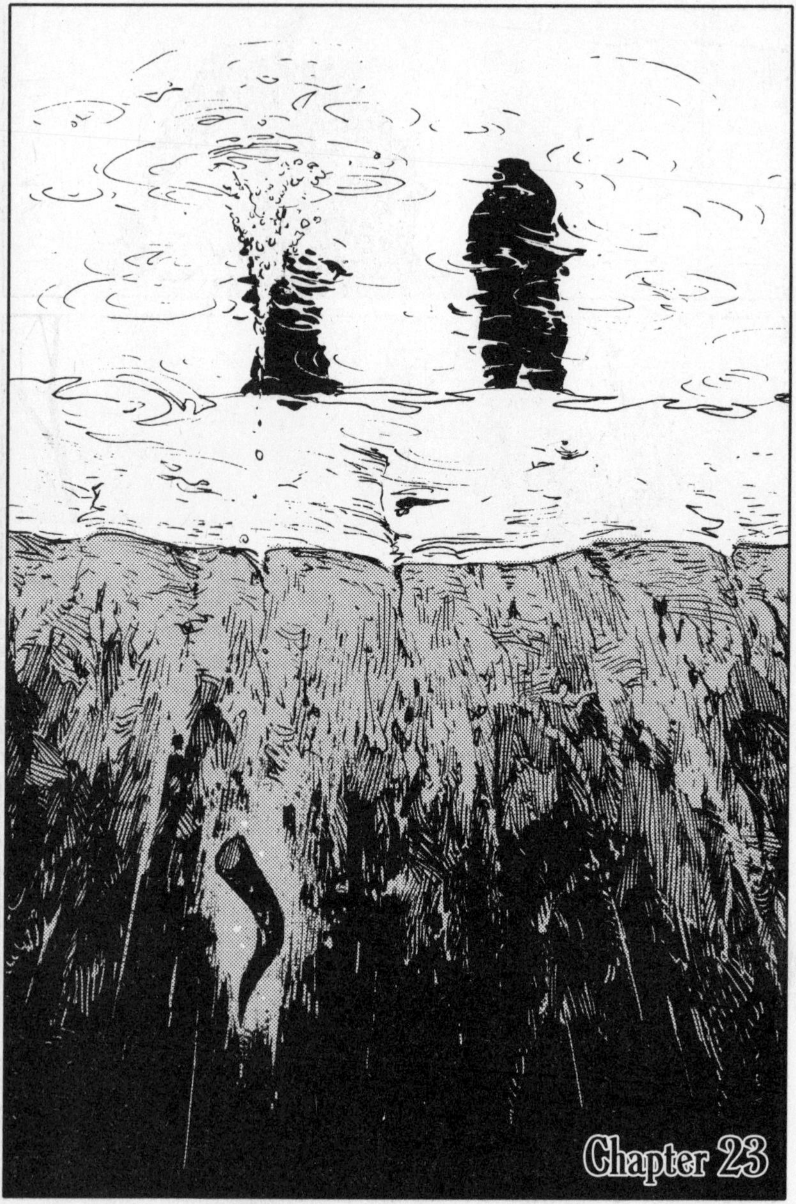
Chapter 23

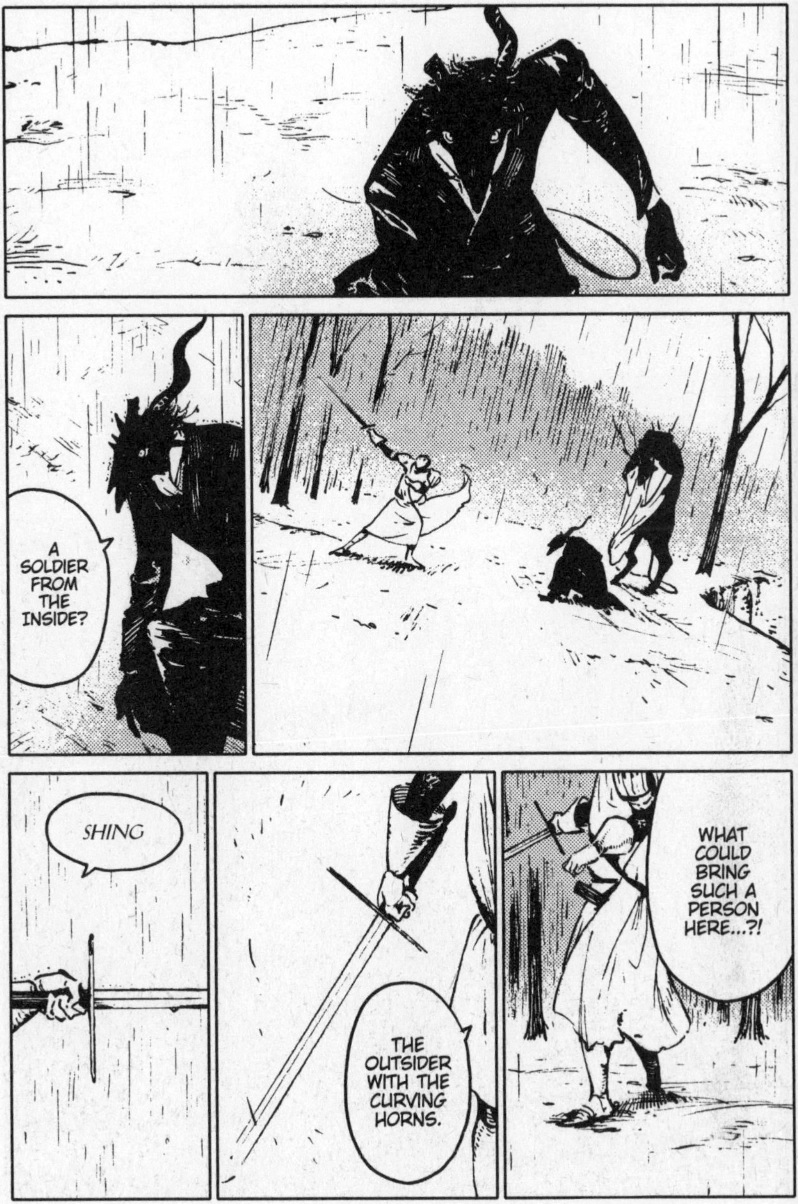
A SOLDIER FROM THE INSIDE?
WHAT COULD BRING SUCH A PERSON HERE...?!
THE OUTSIDER WITH THE CURVING HORNS.
SHING

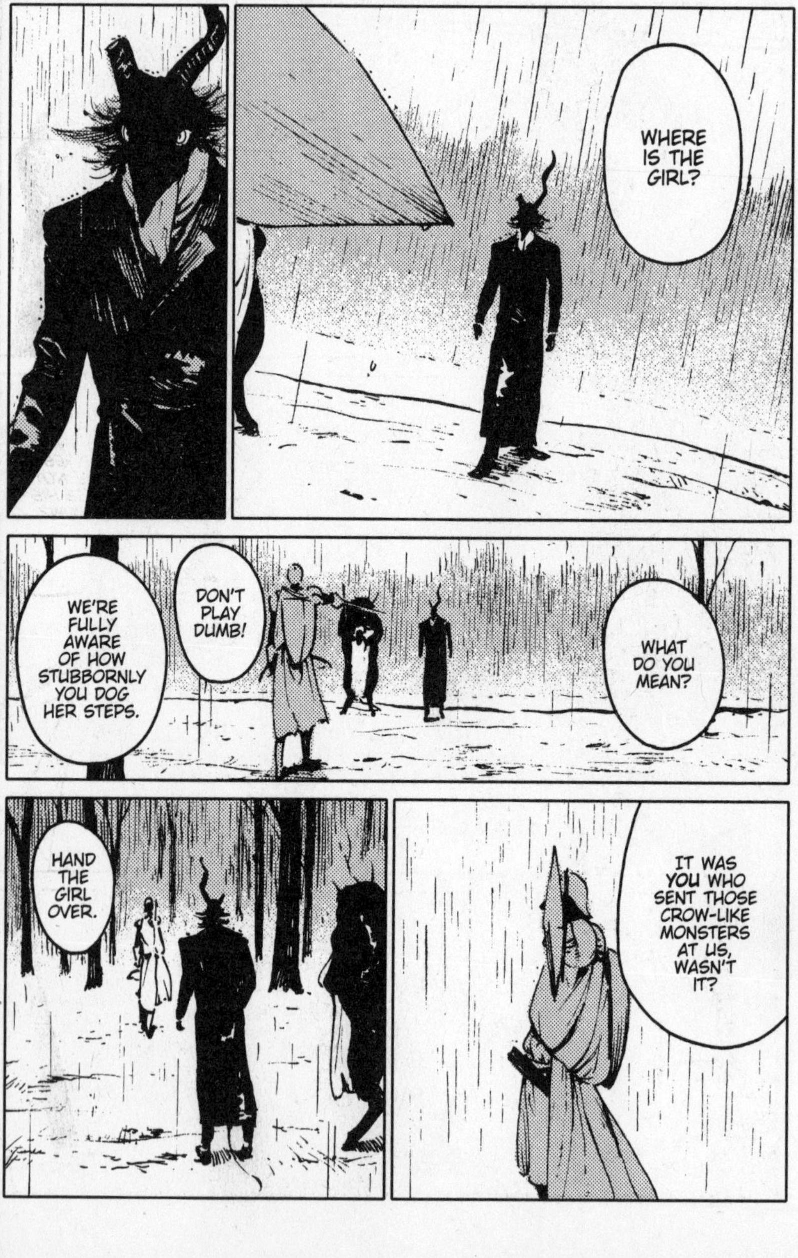
WHERE IS THE GIRL?
WHAT DO YOU MEAN?
DON'T PLAY DUMB!
WE'RE FULLY AWARE OF HOW STUBBORNLY YOU DOG HER STEPS.
IT WAS YOU WHO SENT THOSE CROW-LIKE MONSTERS AT US, WASN'T IT?
HAND THE GIRL OVER.

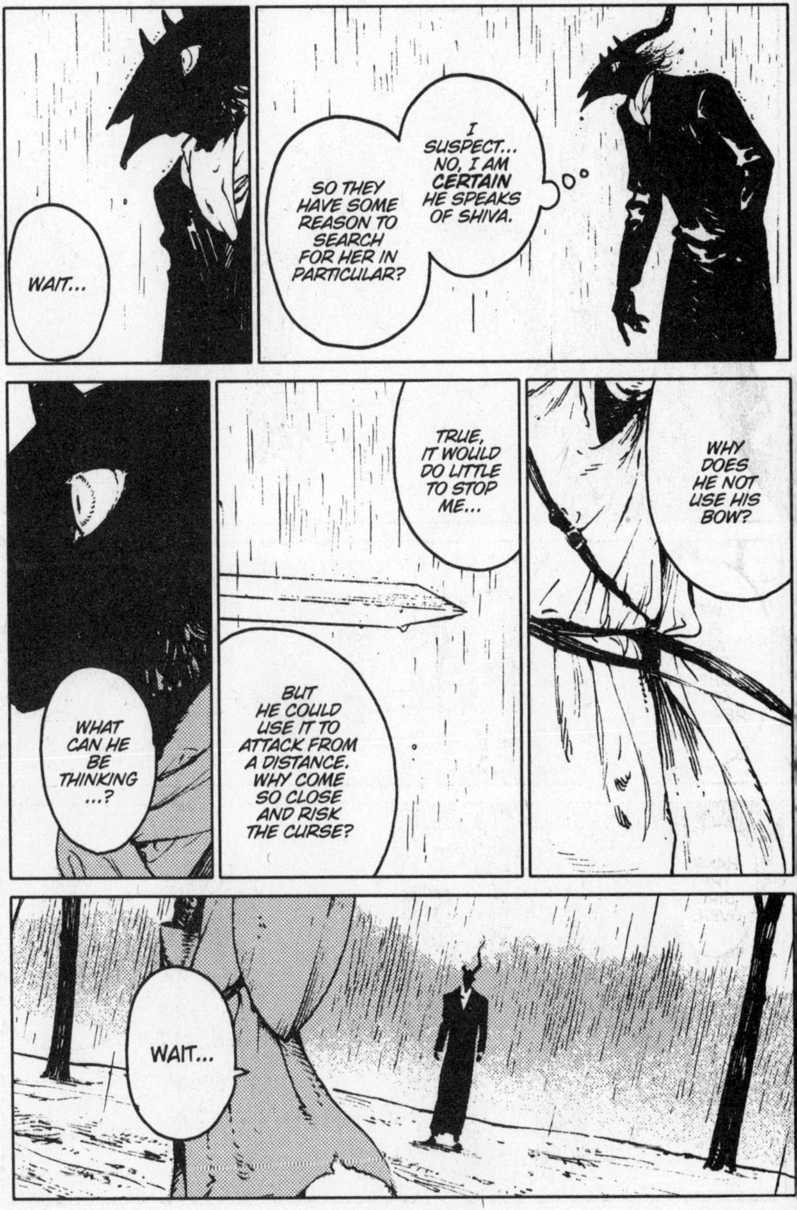
I SUSPECT... NO, I AM CERTAIN HE SPEAKS OF SHIVA.
SO THEY HAVE SOME REASON TO SEARCH FOR HER IN PARTICULAR?
WAIT...
WHY DOES HE NOT USE HIS BOW?
TRUE, IT WOULD DO LITTLE TO STOP ME...
BUT HE COULD USE IT TO ATTACK FROM A DISTANCE. WHY COME SO CLOSE AND RISK THE CURSE?
WHAT CAN HE BE THINKING ...?
WAIT...

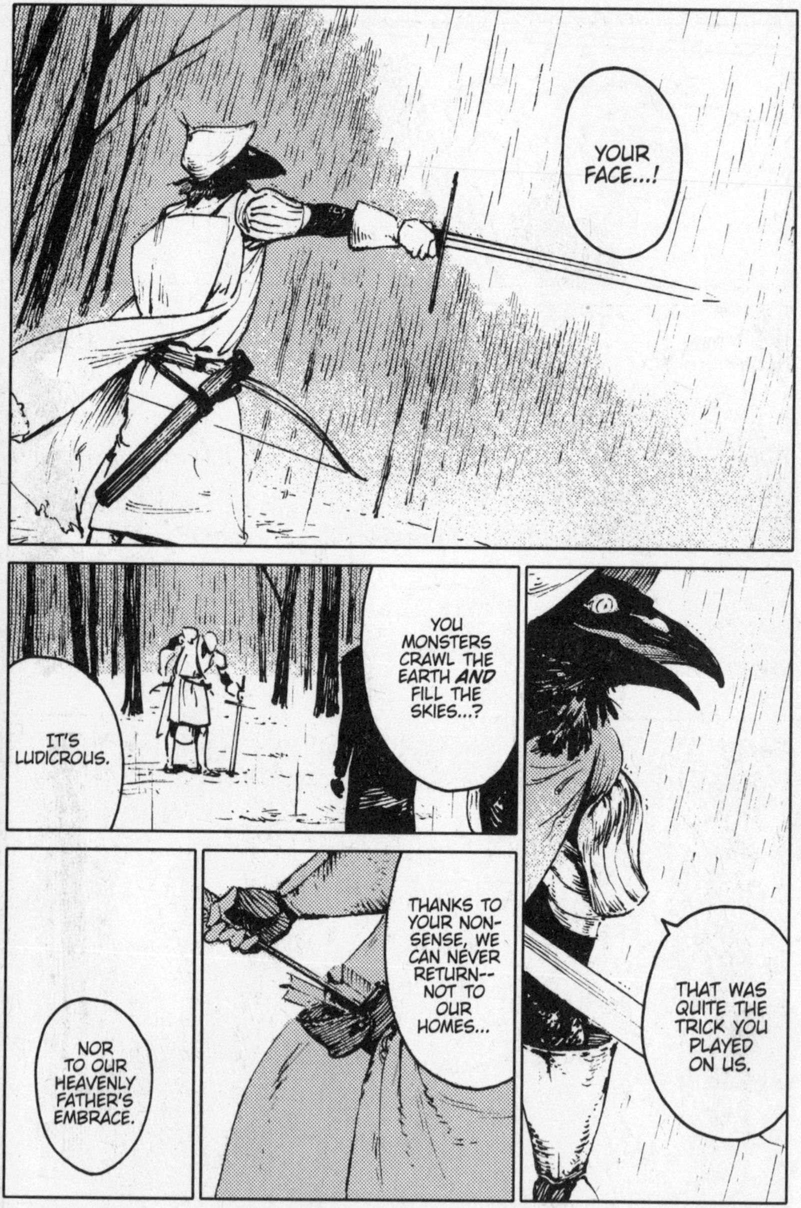
YOUR FACE...!
THAT WAS QUITE THE TRICK YOU PLAYED ON US.
YOU MONSTERS CRAWL THE EARTH *AND* FILL THE SKIES...?
IT'S LUDICROUS.
THANKS TO YOUR NON-SENSE, WE CAN NEVER RETURN-- NOT TO OUR HOMES...
NOR TO OUR HEAVENLY FATHER'S EMBRACE.

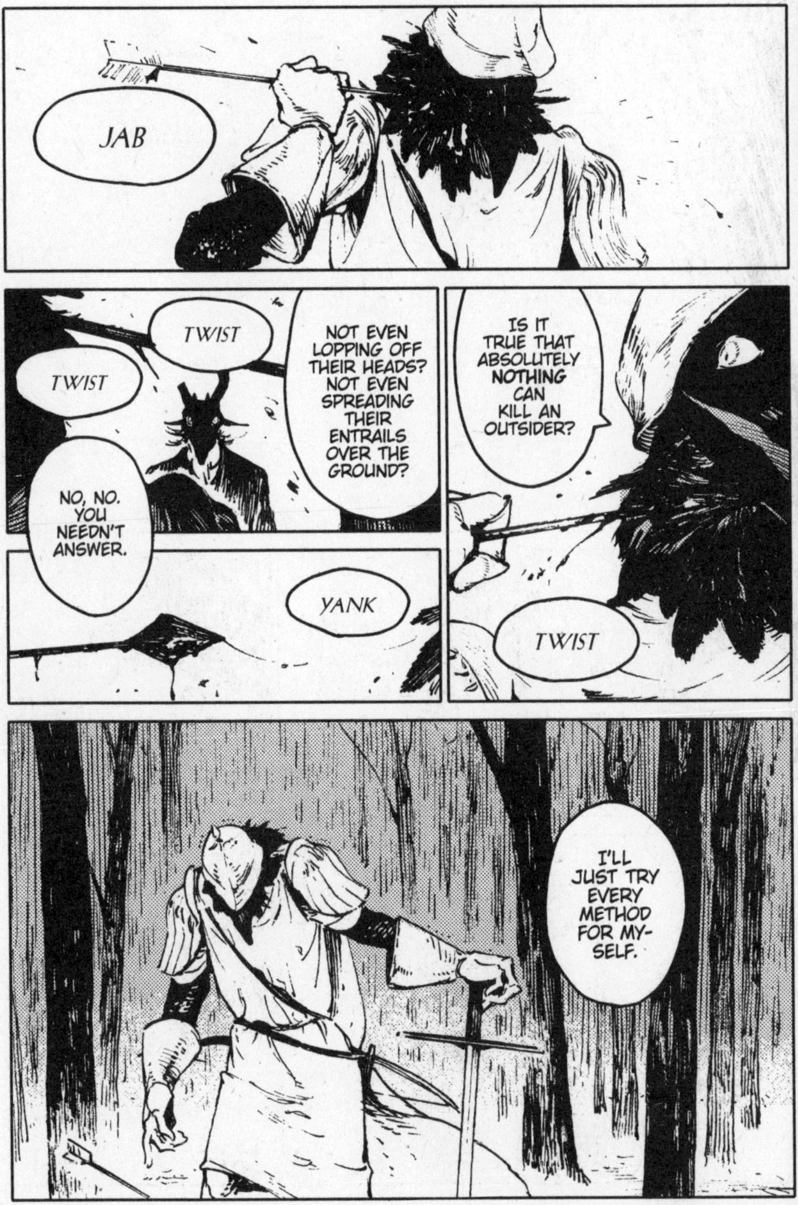
JAB
IS IT TRUE THAT ABSOLUTELY NOTHING CAN KILL AN OUTSIDER?
TWIST
NOT EVEN LOPPING OFF THEIR HEADS? NOT EVEN SPREADING THEIR ENTRAILS OVER THE GROUND?
TWIST
TWIST
NO, NO. YOU NEEDN'T ANSWER.
YANK
I'LL JUST TRY EVERY METHOD FOR MY-SELF.

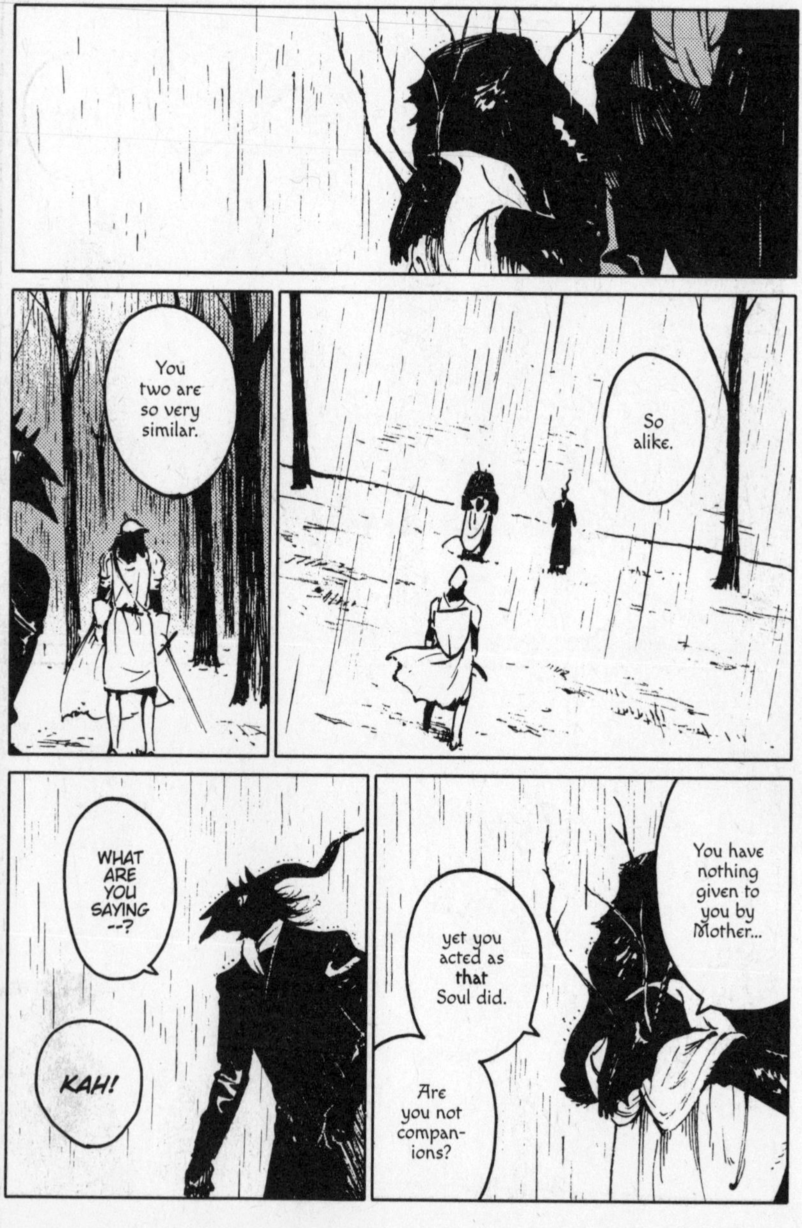
So alike.
You two are so very similar.
You have nothing given to you by Mother...
yet you acted as that Soul did.
Are you not companions?
WHAT ARE YOU SAYING --?
KAH!

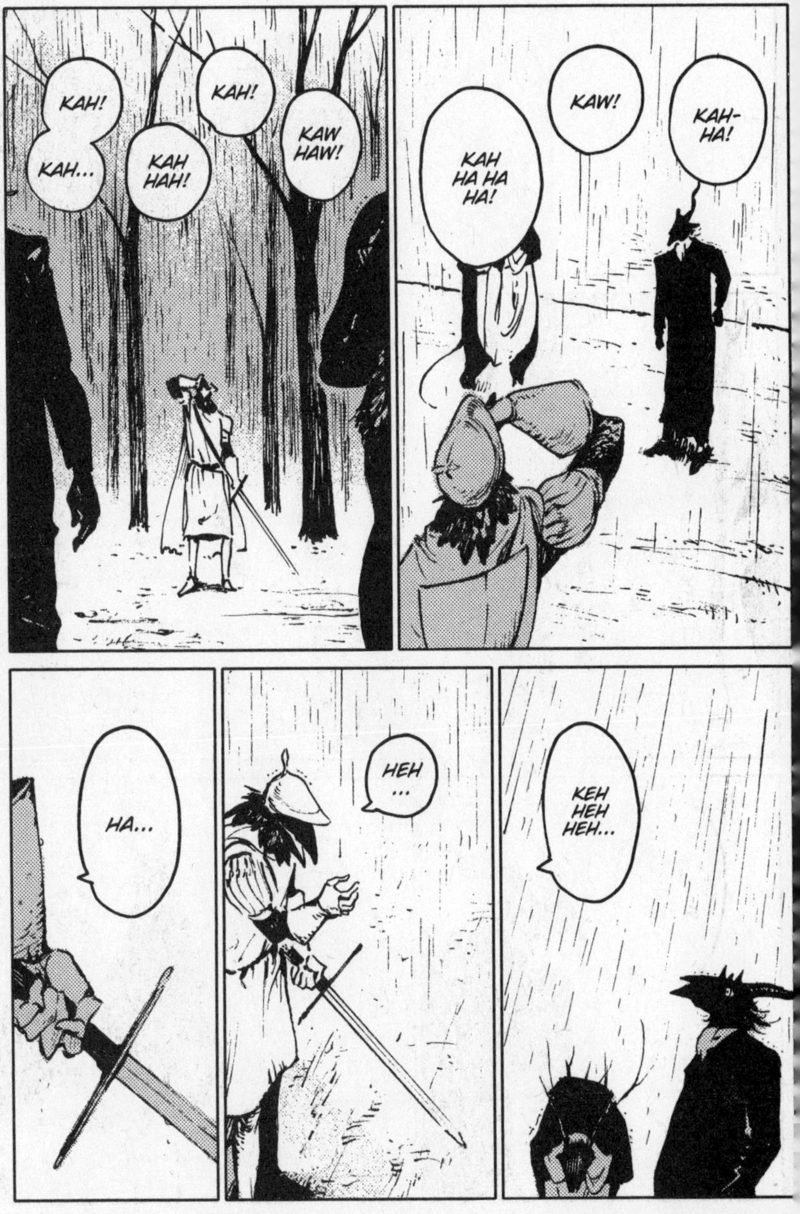
KAH-HA!
KAW!
KAH HA HA HA!
KAW HAW!
KAH!
KAH HAH!
KAH!
KAH...
KEH HEH HEH...
HEH ...
HA...

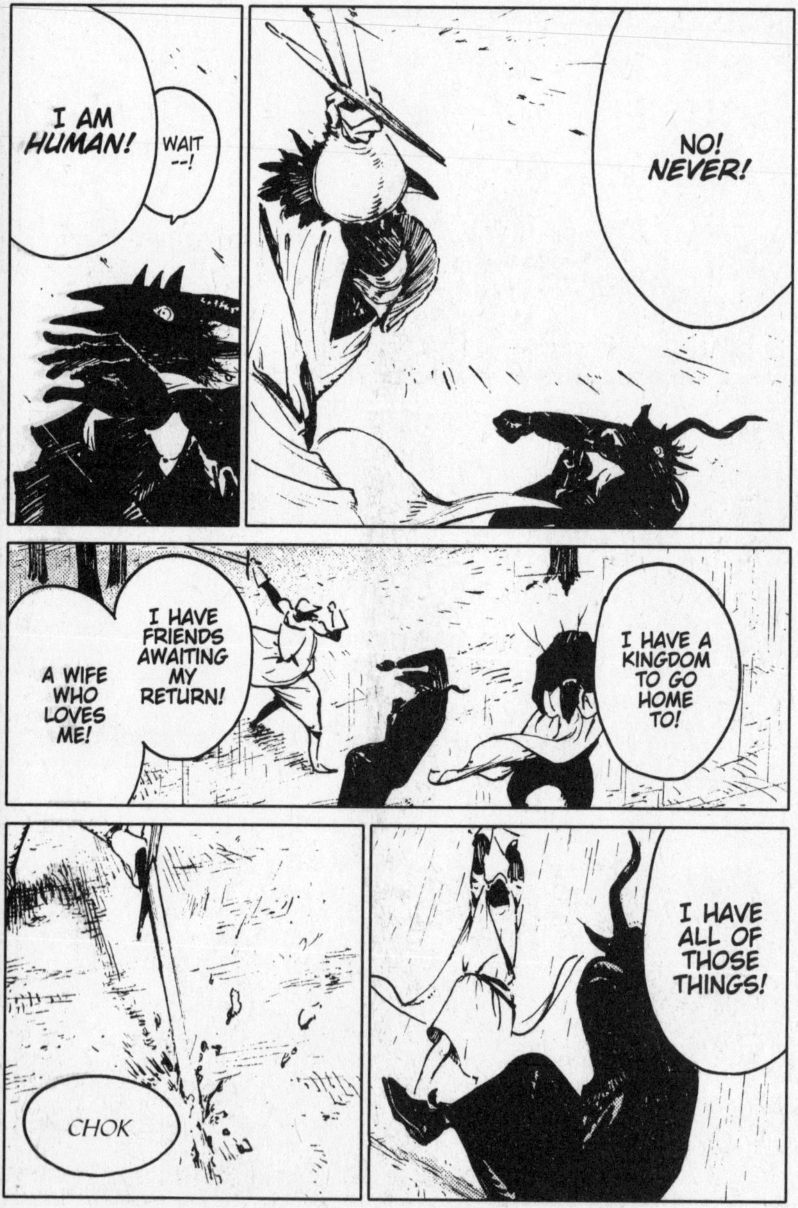
NO! NEVER!
WAIT --!
I AM HUMAN!
I HAVE A KINGDOM TO GO HOME TO!
I HAVE FRIENDS AWAITING MY RETURN!
A WIFE WHO LOVES ME!
I HAVE ALL OF THOSE THINGS!
CHOK

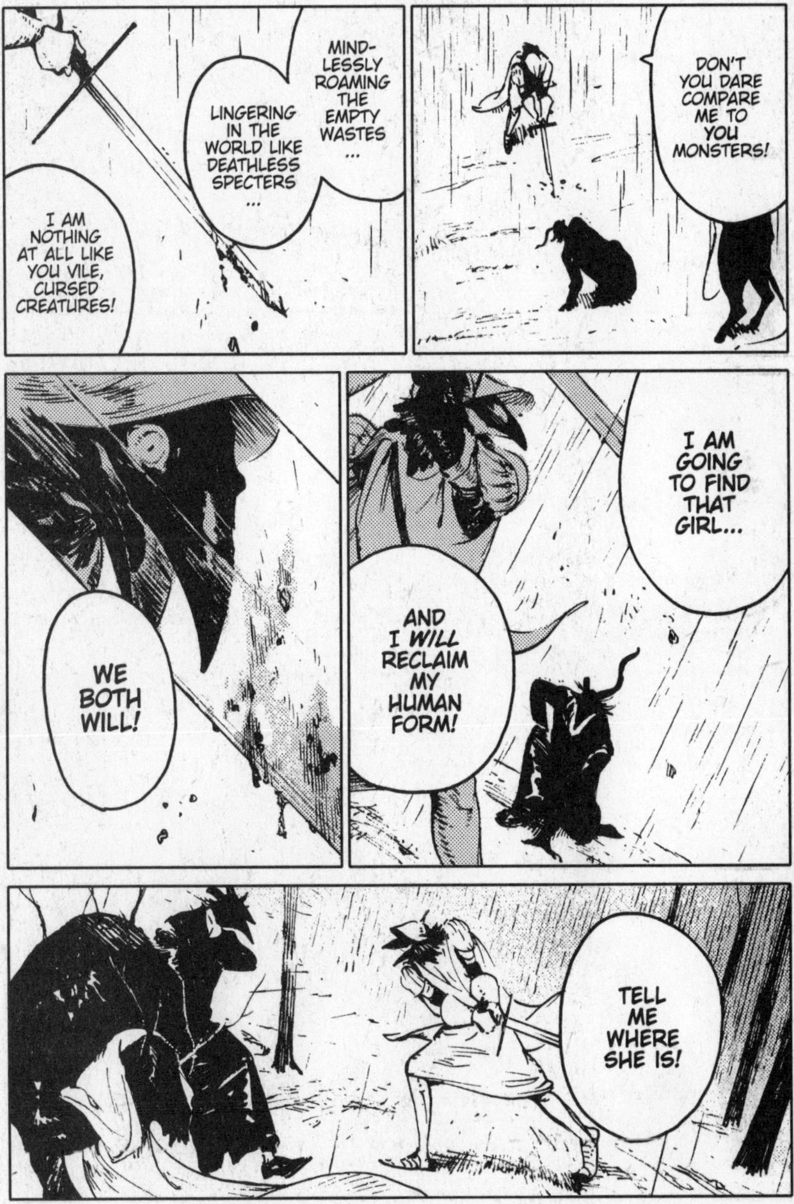
DON'T YOU DARE COMPARE ME TO YOU MONSTERS!
MIND-LESSLY ROAMING THE EMPTY WASTES ...
LINGERING IN THE WORLD LIKE DEATHLESS SPECTERS ...
I AM NOTHING AT ALL LIKE YOU VILE, CURSED CREATURES!
I AM GOING TO FIND THAT GIRL...
AND I *WILL* RECLAIM MY HUMAN FORM!
WE BOTH WILL!
TELL ME WHERE SHE IS!

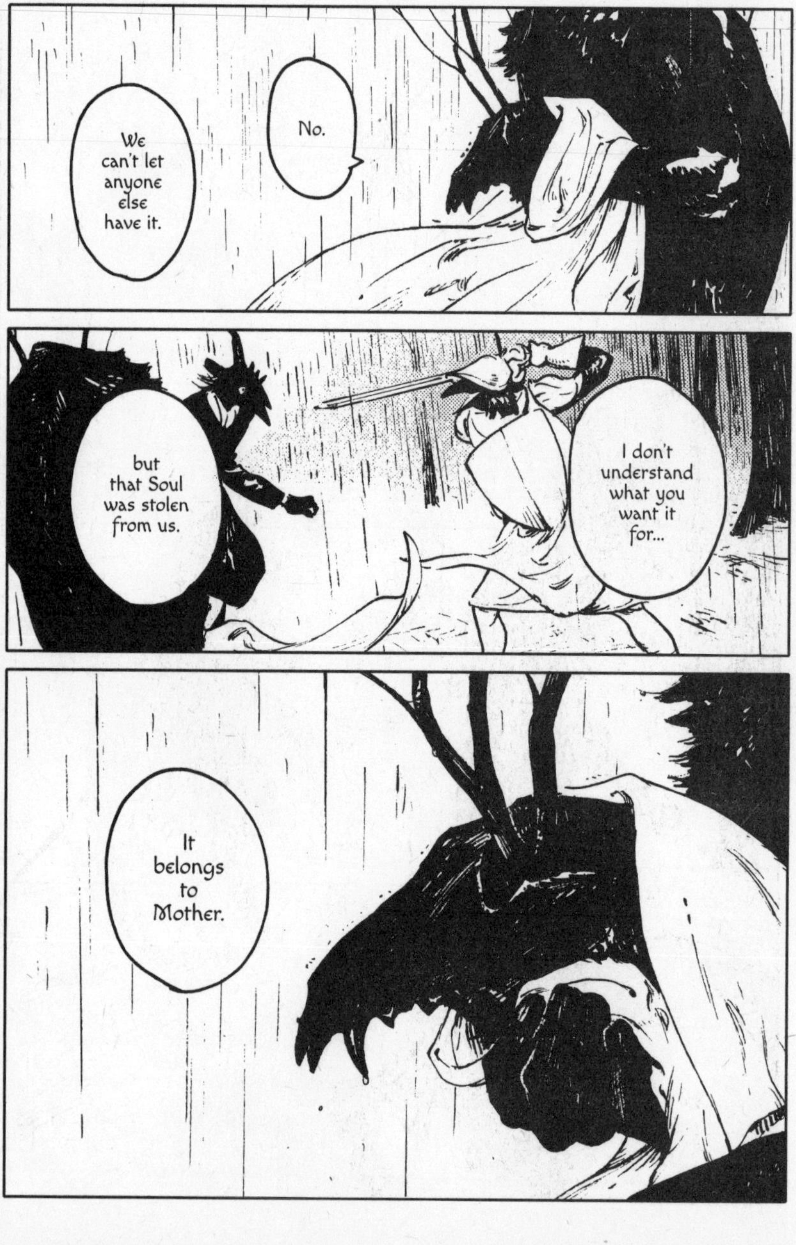
No.
We can't let anyone else have it.
I don't understand what you want it for...
but that Soul was stolen from us.
It belongs to Mother.

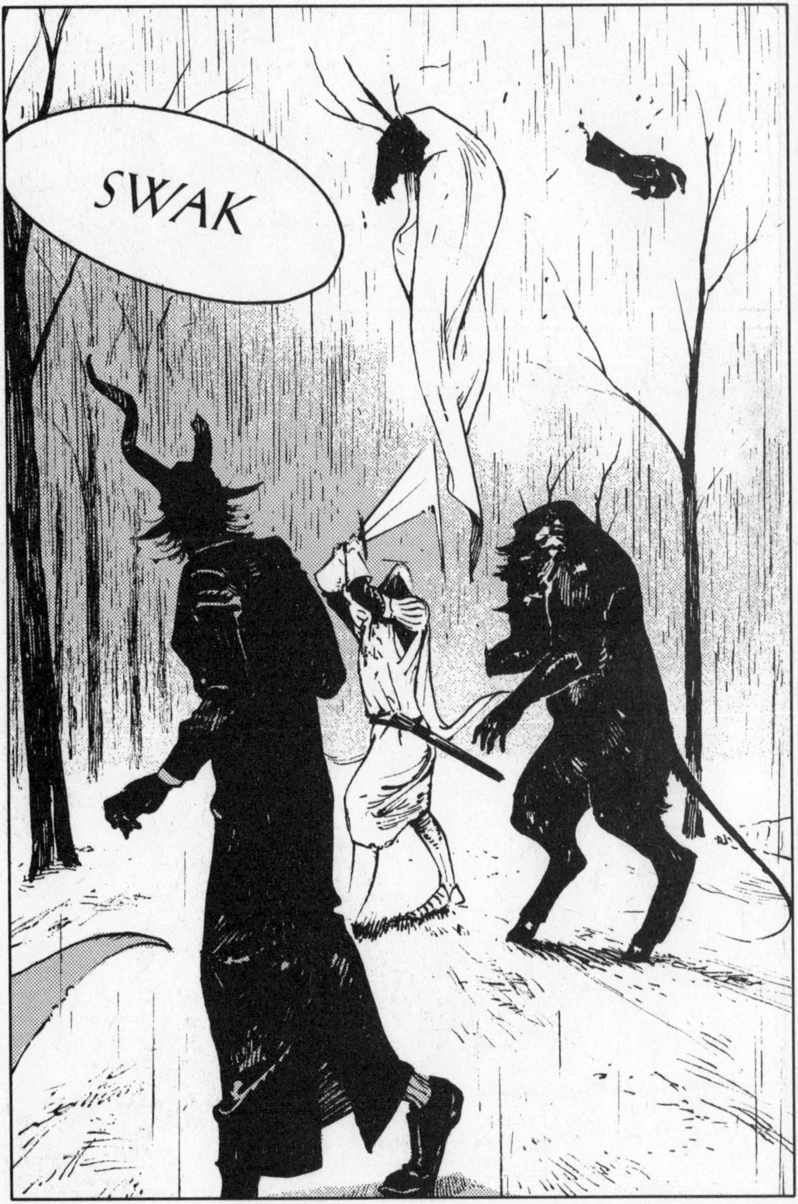
SWAK

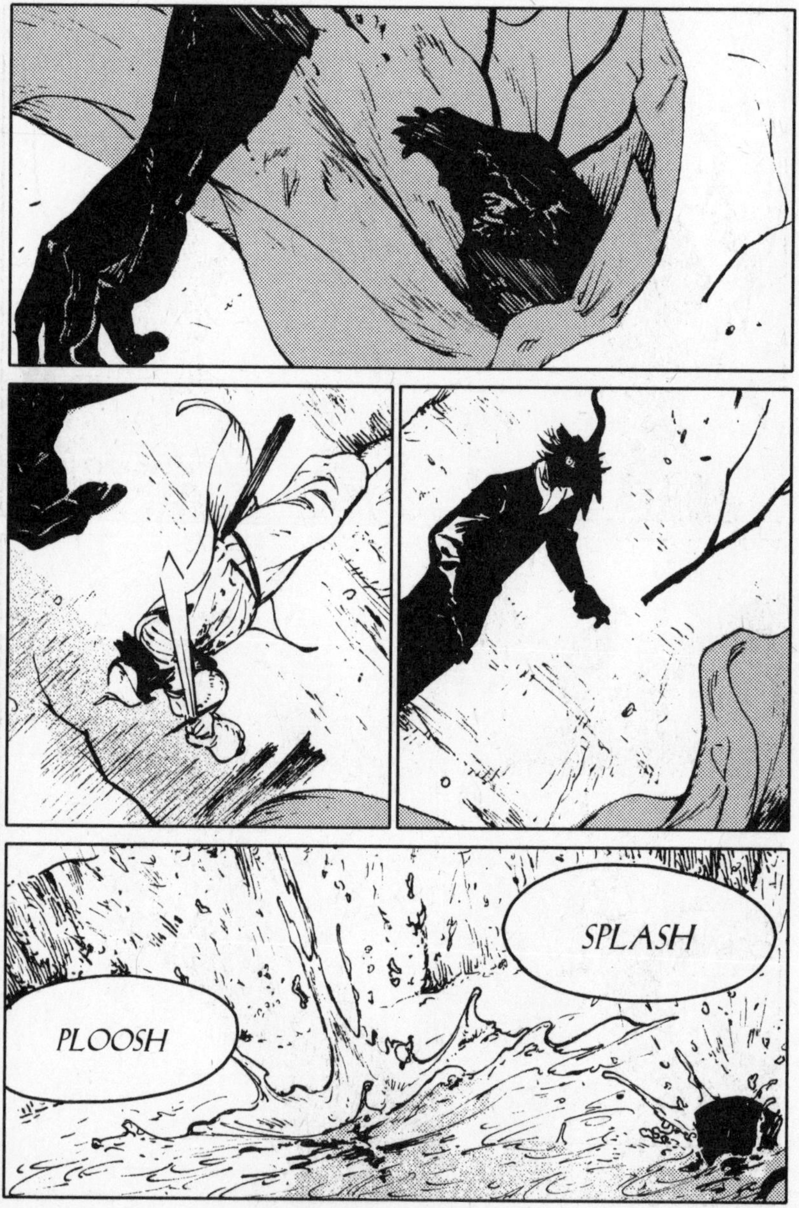
SPLASH
PLOOSH

ANOTHER ONE?!
SHOVE
!

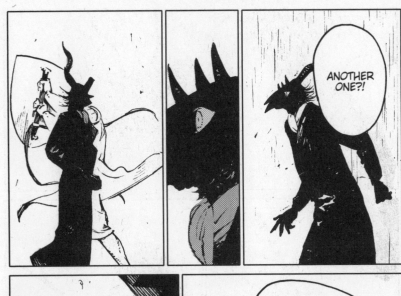

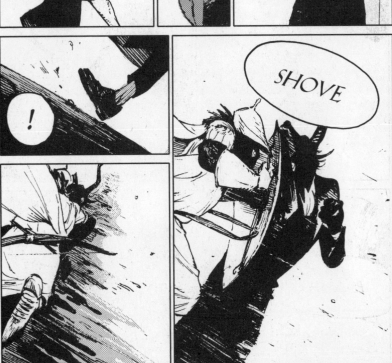

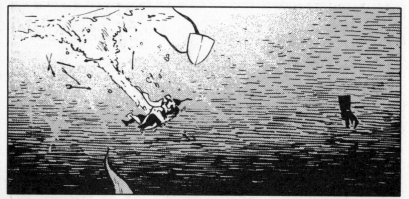

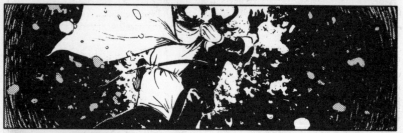

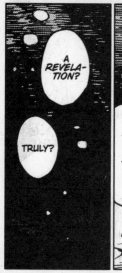

NGH ...!
WHY DO YOU WANT HER?
THERE'S NO PROOF SHE CAN AFFECT THE CURSE IN THE SLIGHTEST!
OH, BUT THERE IS!
THE REV-ELATION FROM THE HOLY FATHER!
A REVELA-TION?
TRULY?

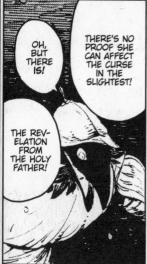

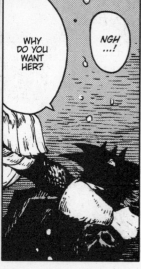

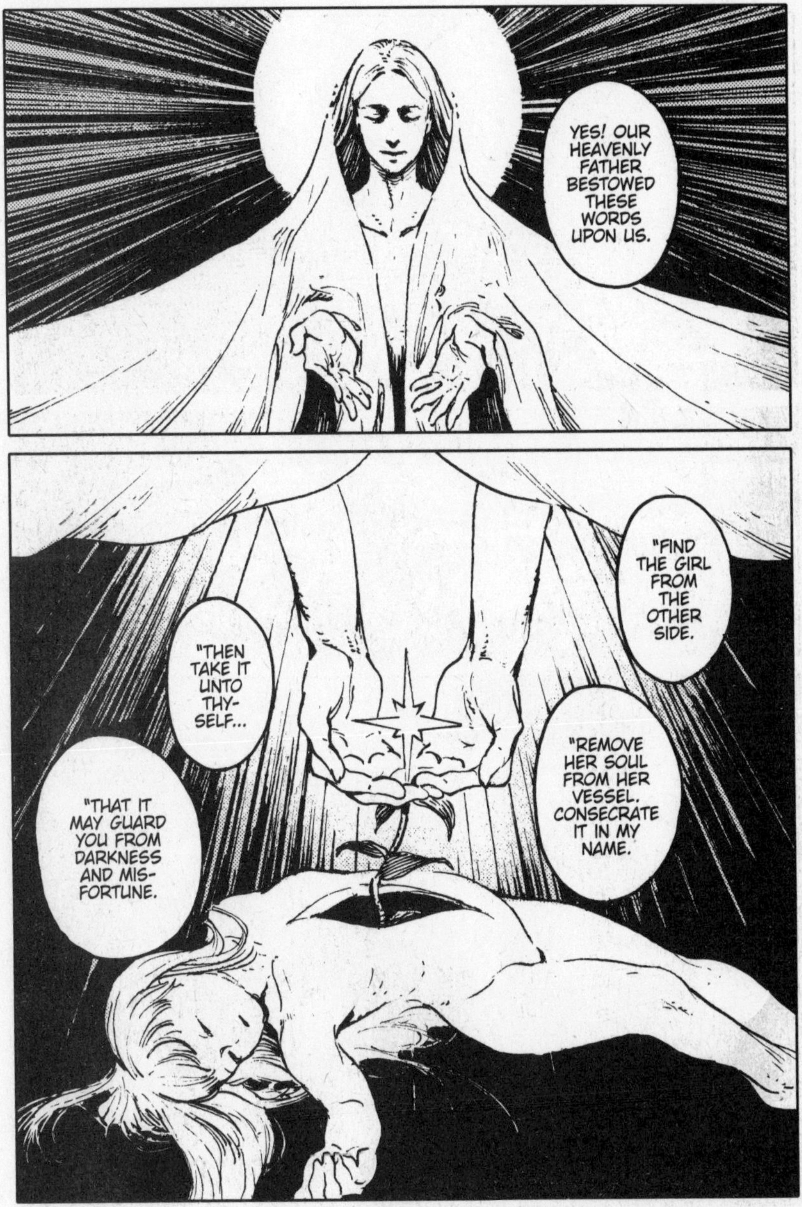
YES! OUR HEAVENLY FATHER BESTOWED THESE WORDS UPON US.
"FIND THE GIRL FROM THE OTHER SIDE.
"REMOVE HER SOUL FROM HER VESSEL. CONSECRATE IT IN MY NAME.
"THEN TAKE IT UNTO THY-SELF...
"THAT IT MAY GUARD YOU FROM DARKNESS AND MIS-FORTUNE.

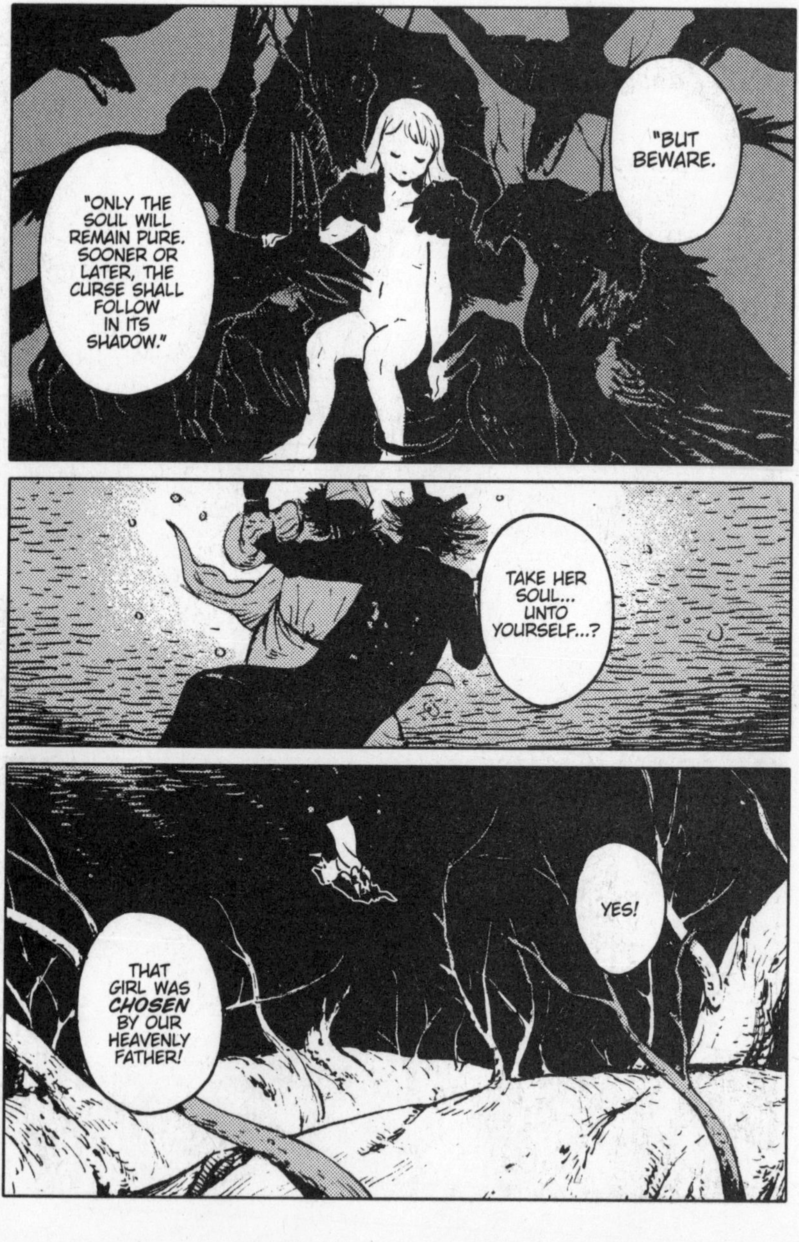
"BUT BEWARE.
"ONLY THE SOUL WILL REMAIN PURE. SOONER OR LATER, THE CURSE SHALL FOLLOW IN ITS SHADOW."
TAKE HER SOUL... UNTO YOURSELF...?
YES!
THAT GIRL WAS ***CHOSEN*** BY OUR HEAVENLY FATHER!

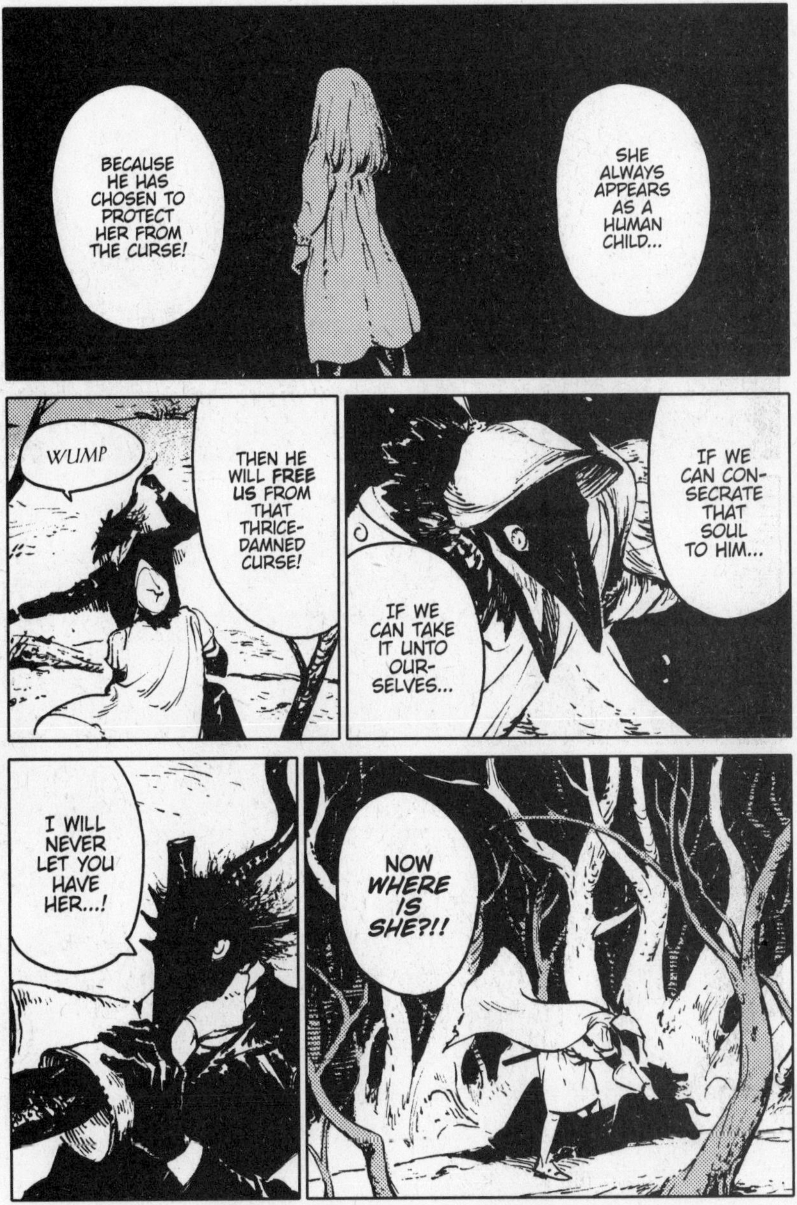
SHE ALWAYS APPEARS AS A HUMAN CHILD...
BECAUSE HE HAS CHOSEN TO PROTECT HER FROM THE CURSE!
IF WE CAN CON-SECRATE THAT SOUL TO HIM...
IF WE CAN TAKE IT UNTO OUR-SELVES...
THEN HE WILL FREE US FROM THAT THRICE-DAMNED CURSE!
WUMP
NOW WHERE IS SHE?!!
I WILL NEVER LET YOU HAVE HER...!

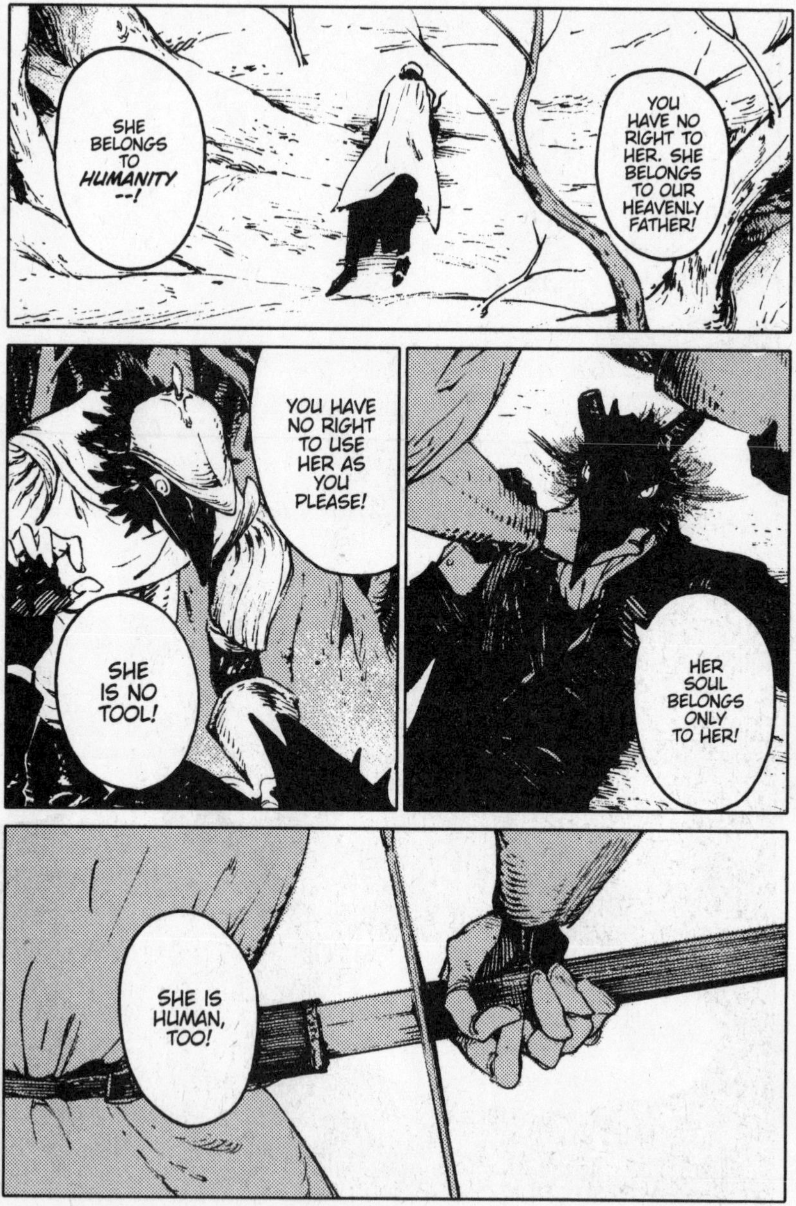
YOU HAVE NO RIGHT TO HER. SHE BELONGS TO OUR HEAVENLY FATHER!
SHE BELONGS TO *HUMANITY* --!
HER SOUL BELONGS ONLY TO HER!
YOU HAVE NO RIGHT TO USE HER AS YOU PLEASE!
SHE IS NO TOOL!
SHE IS HUMAN, TOO!

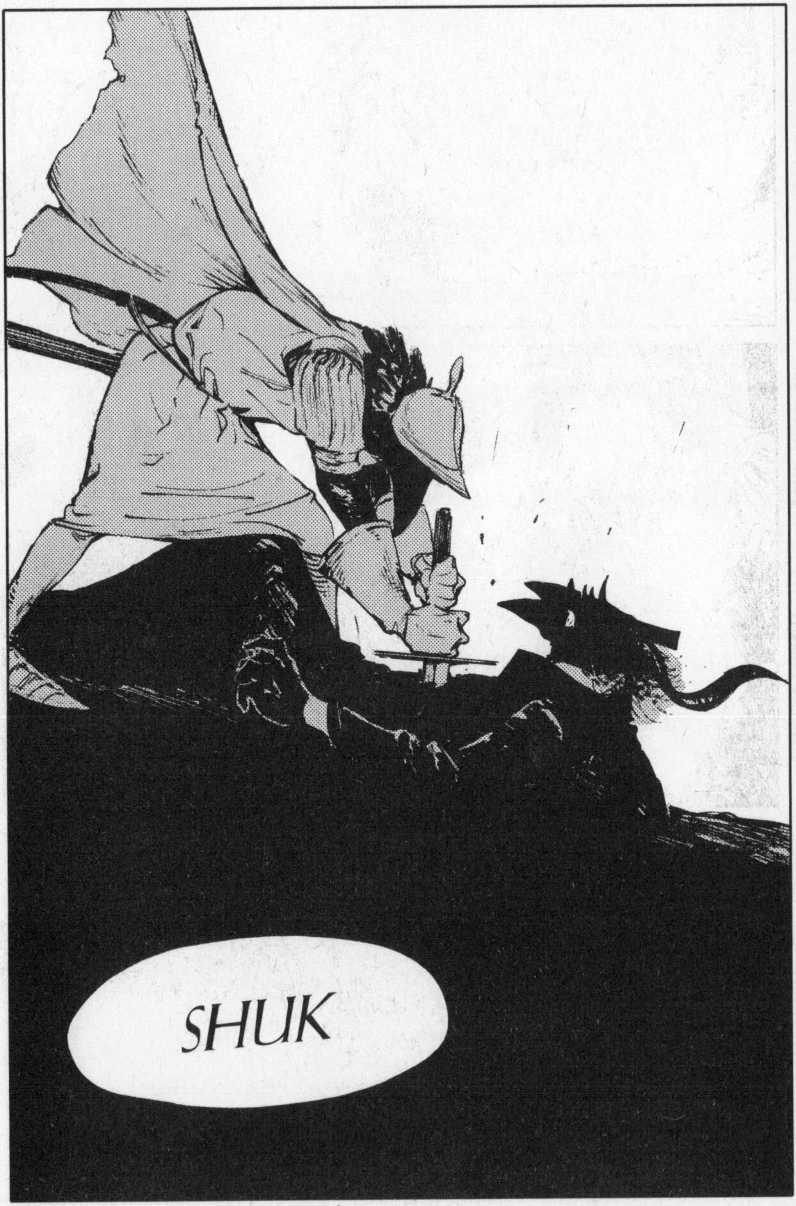
SHUK

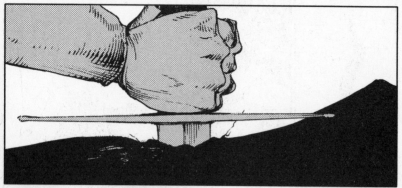

STOP PRETENDING YOU CAN COMPREHEND THIS.

YOU ARE NAUGHT BUT A FOUL *BEAST*...!

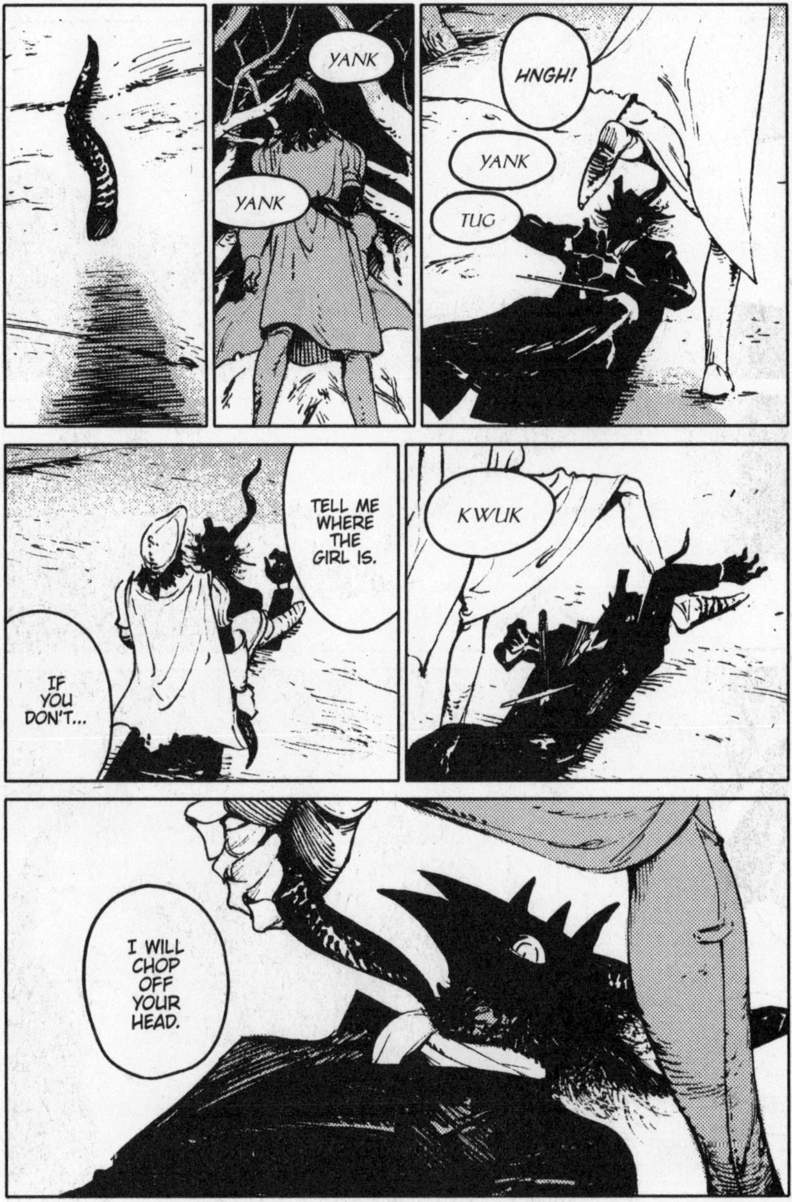
HNGH!
YANK
TUG
YANK
YANK
KWUK
TELL ME WHERE THE GIRL IS.
IF YOU DON'T...
I WILL CHOP OFF YOUR HEAD.

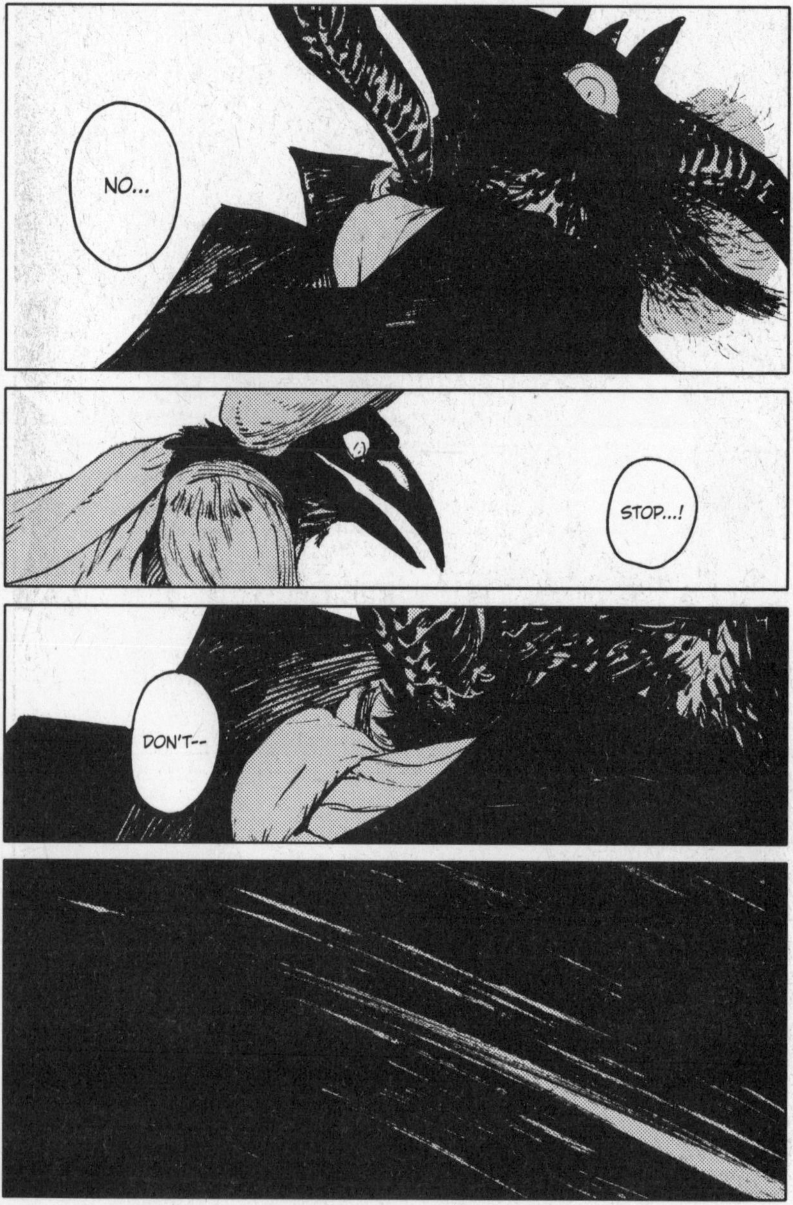
NO...
STOP...!
DON'T--

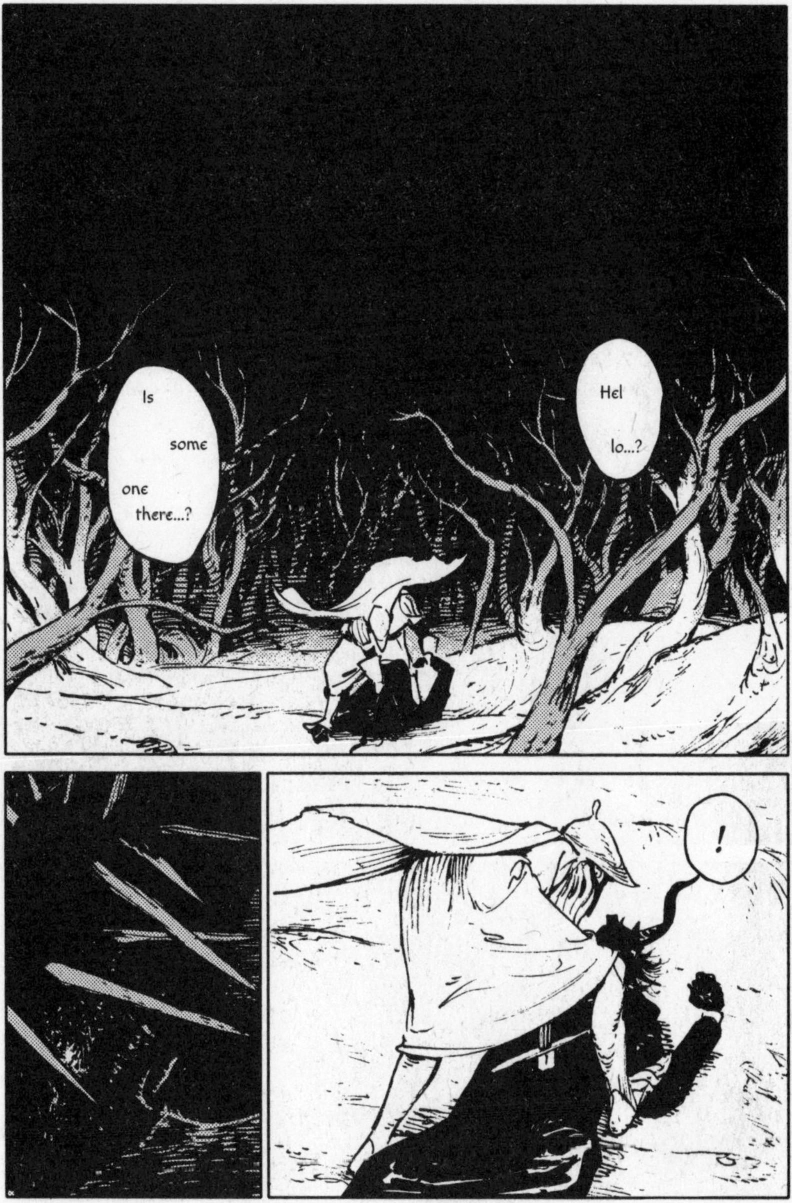
Hel lo...?
Is some one there...?
!

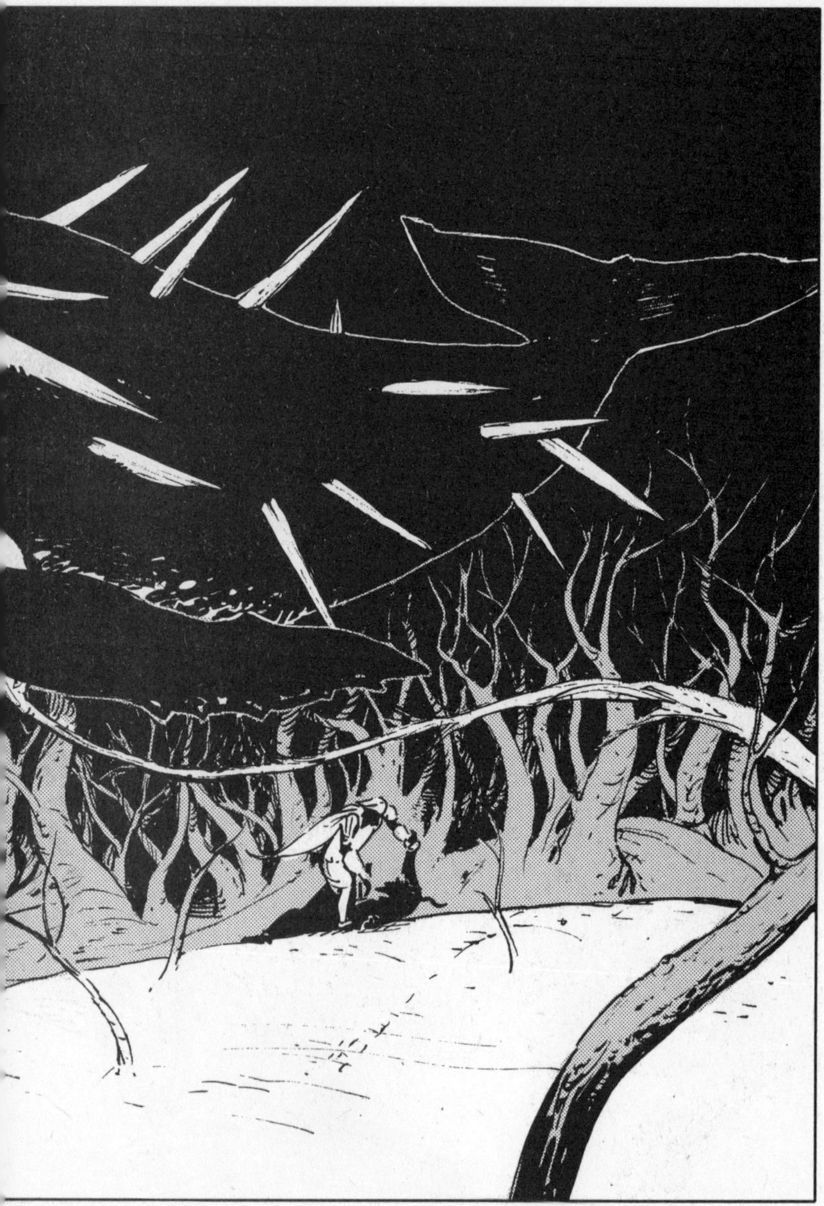

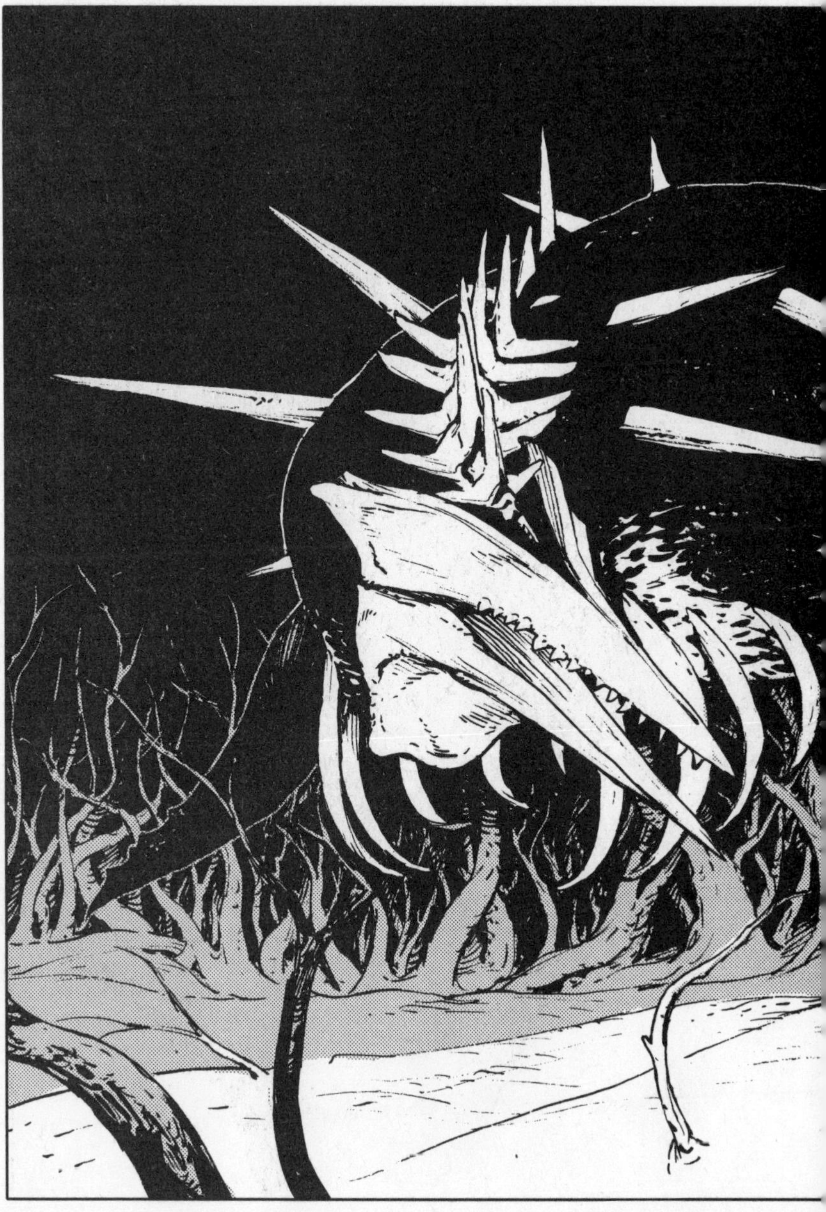

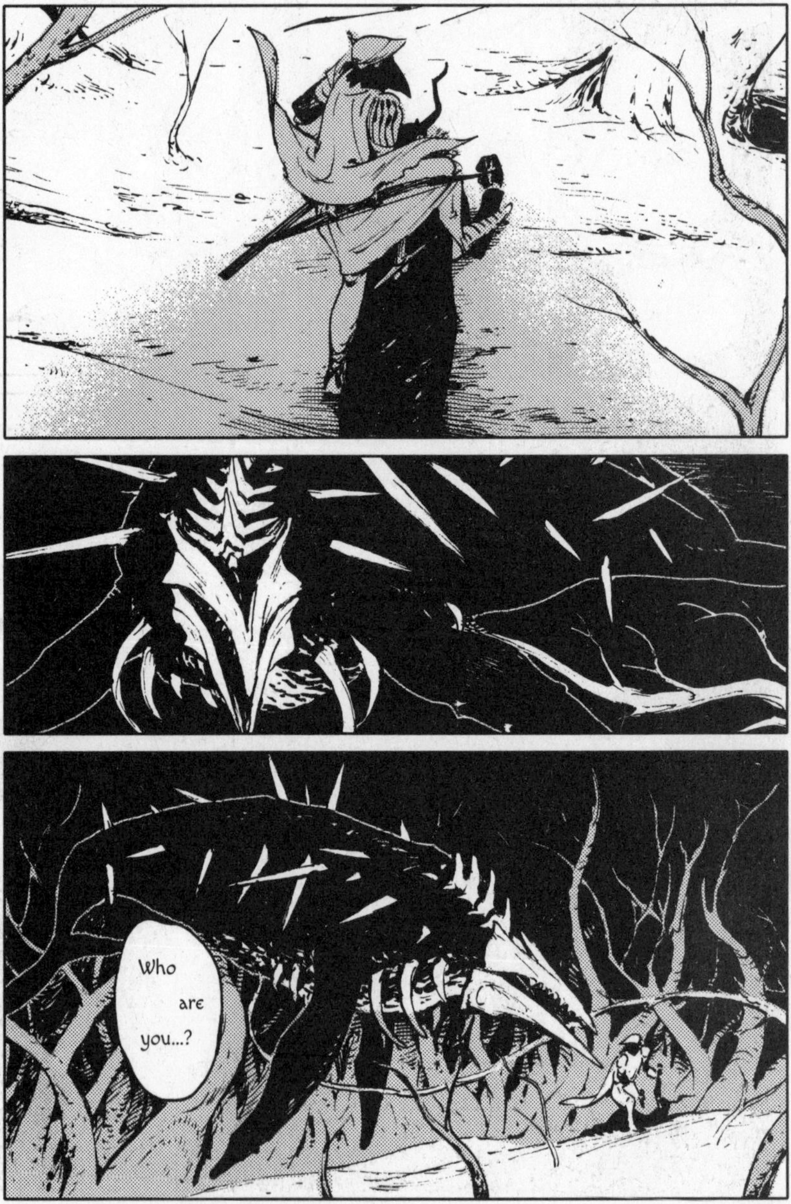
Who are you...?

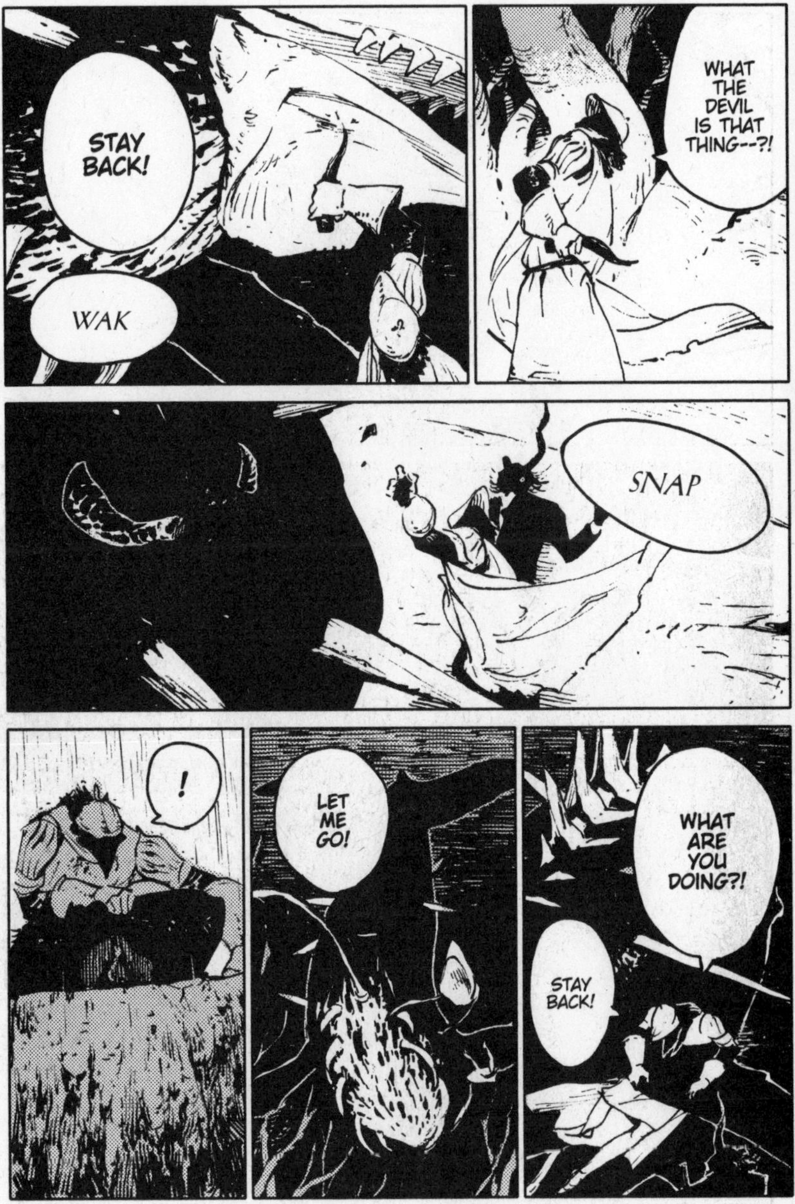
WHAT THE DEVIL IS THAT THING--?!
STAY BACK!
WAK
SNAP
WHAT ARE YOU DOING?!
STAY BACK!
LET ME GO!
!

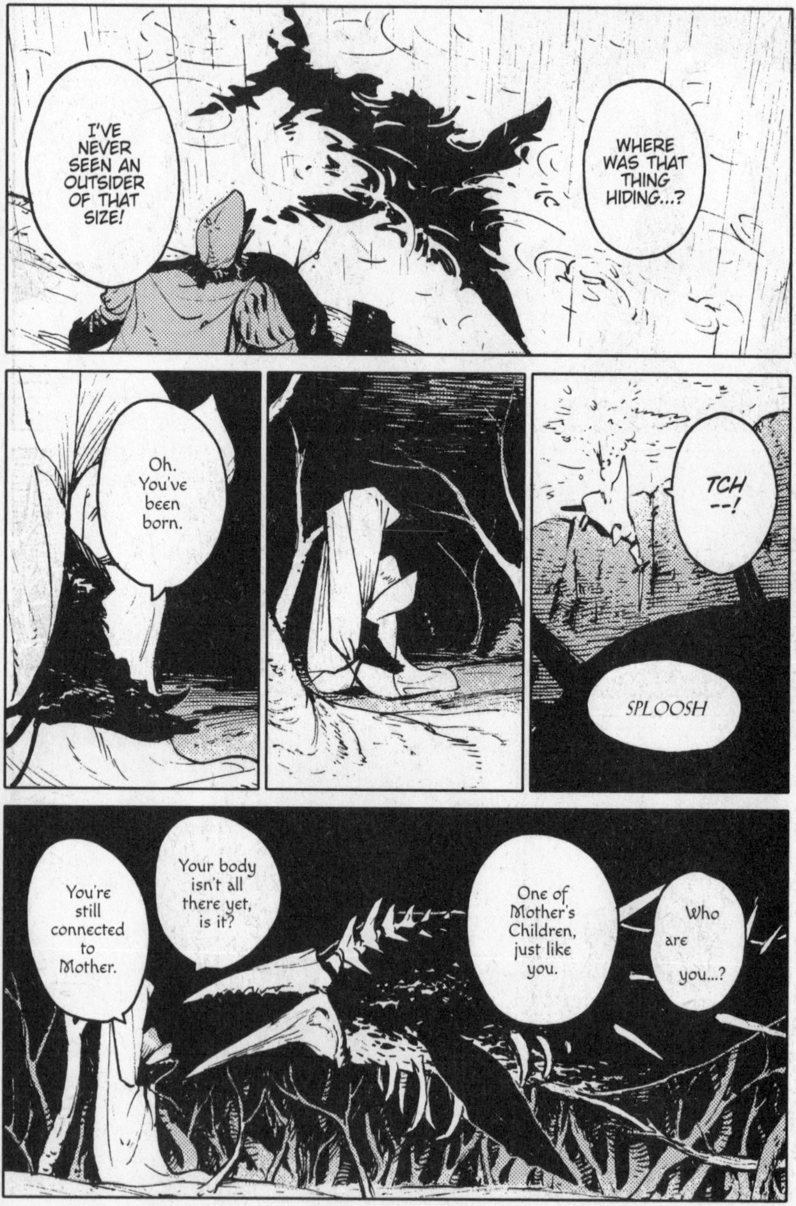
WHERE WAS THAT THING HIDING...?
I'VE NEVER SEEN AN OUTSIDER OF THAT SIZE!
TCH --!
SPLOOSH
Oh. You've been born.
Who are you...?
One of Mother's Children, just like you.
Your body isn't all there yet, is it?
You're still connected to Mother.

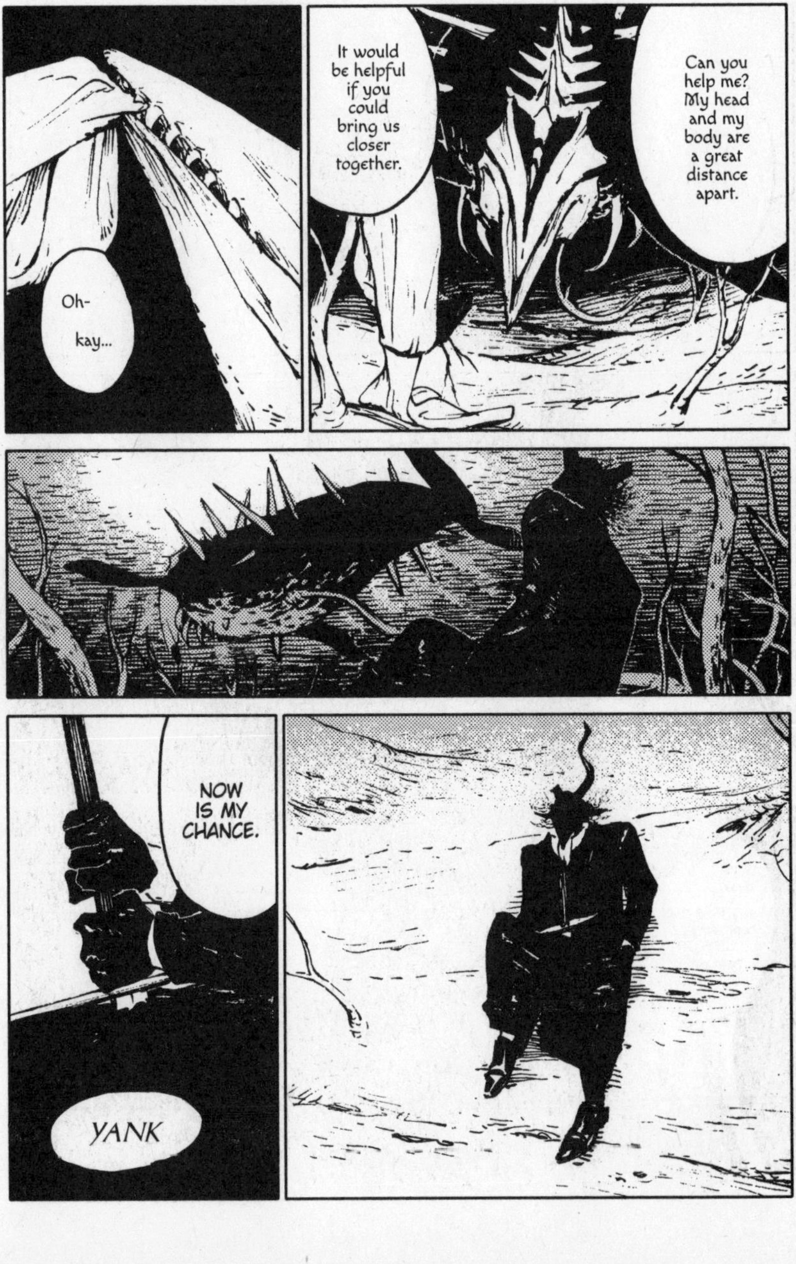
Can you help me? My head and my body are a great distance apart.
It would be helpful if you could bring us closer together.
Oh- kay...
NOW IS MY CHANCE.
YANK

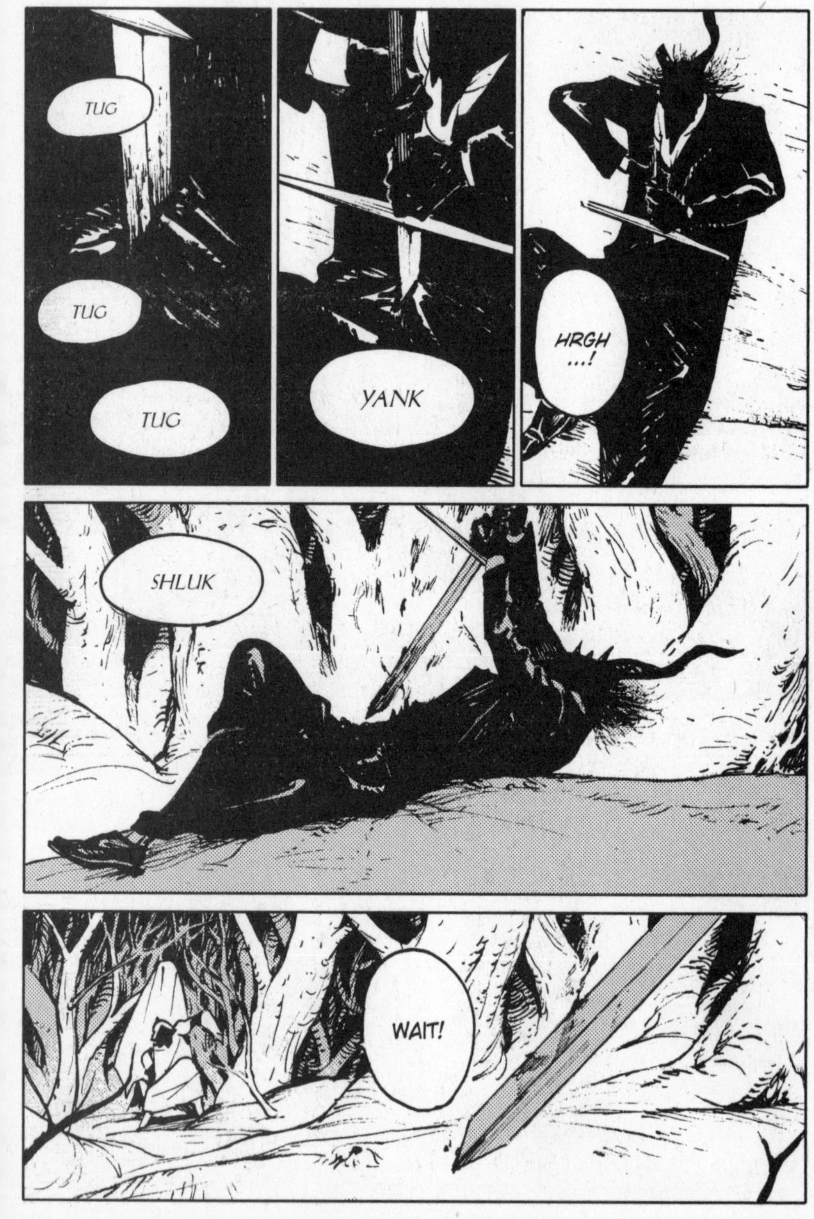
HRGH ...!
YANK
TUG
TUG
TUG
SHLUK
WAIT!

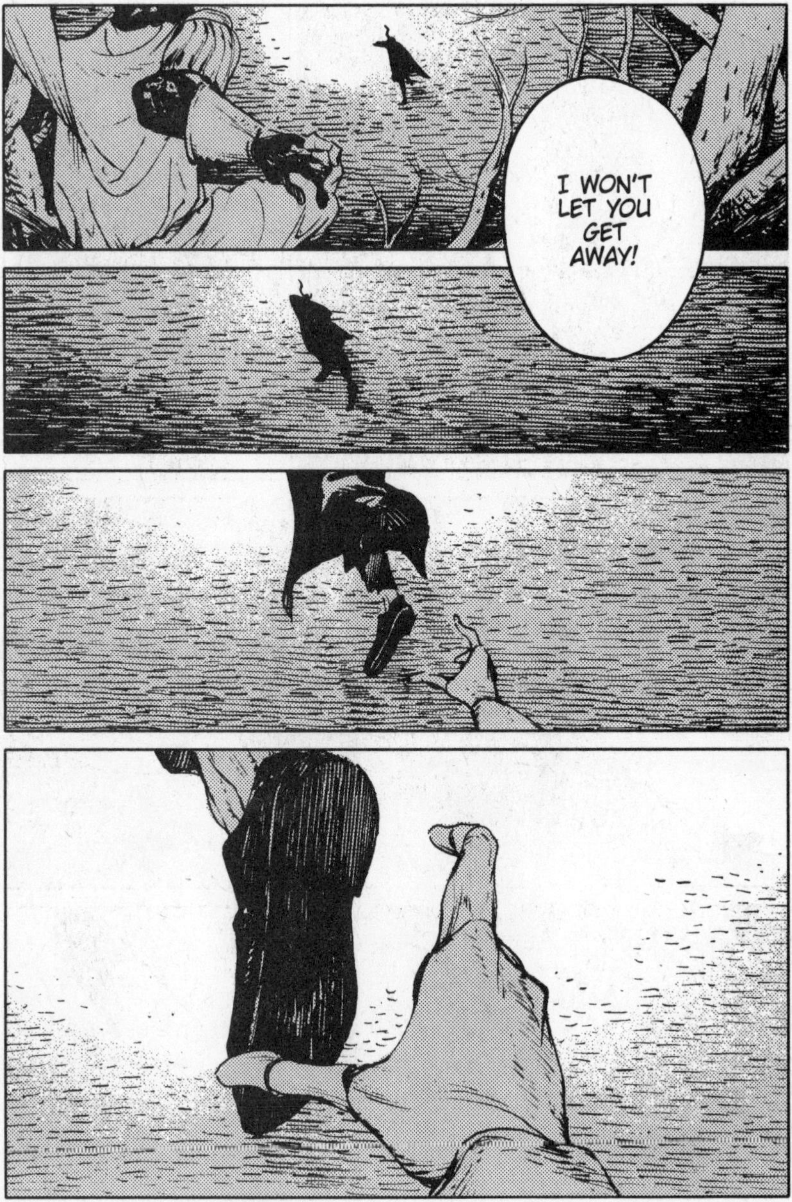
I WON'T LET YOU GET AWAY!

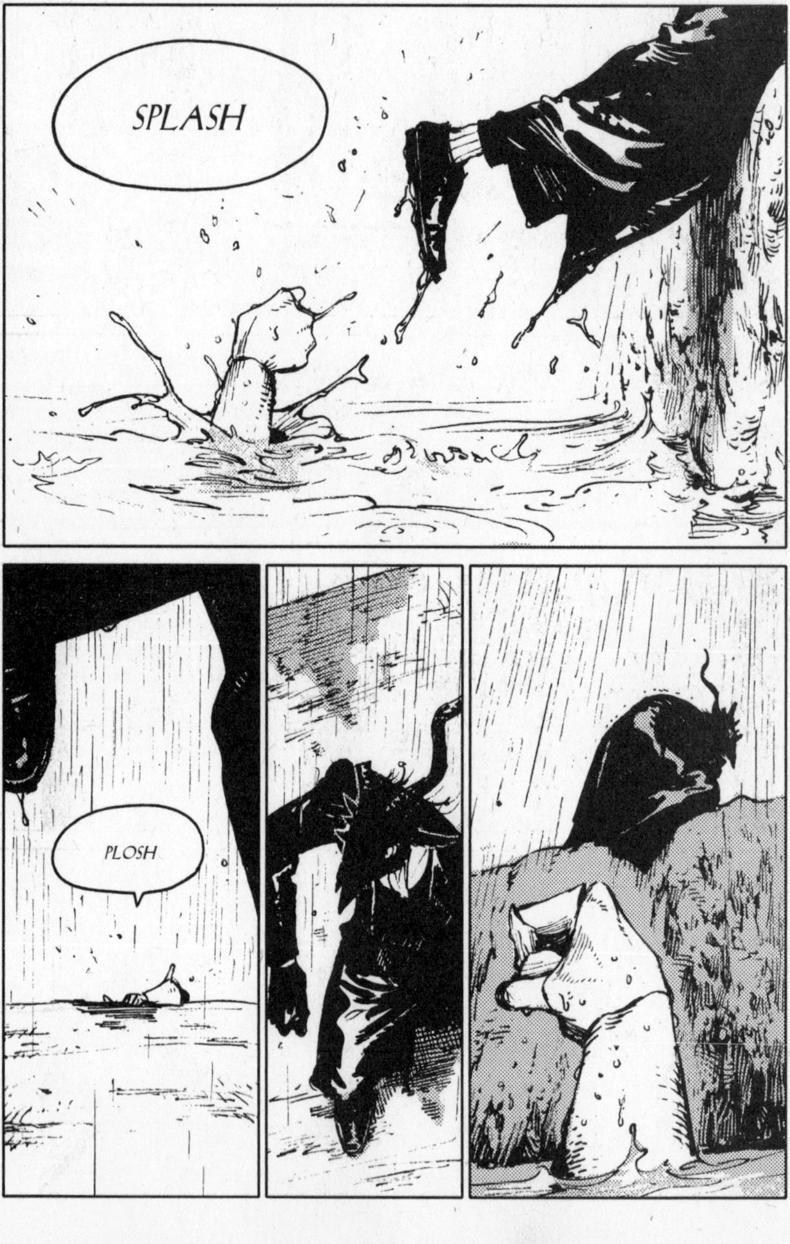
SPLASH
PLOSH

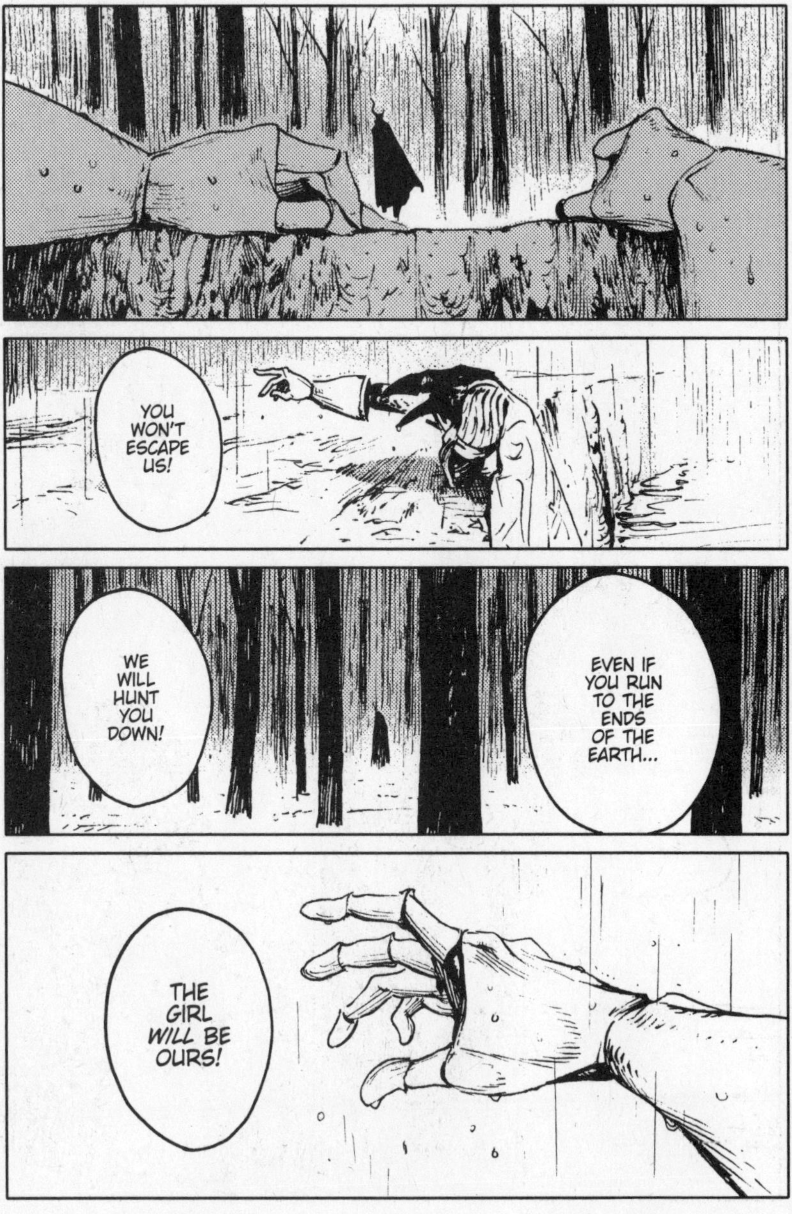
YOU WON'T ESCAPE US!
EVEN IF YOU RUN TO THE ENDS OF THE EARTH...
WE WILL HUNT YOU DOWN!
THE GIRL *WILL* BE OURS!

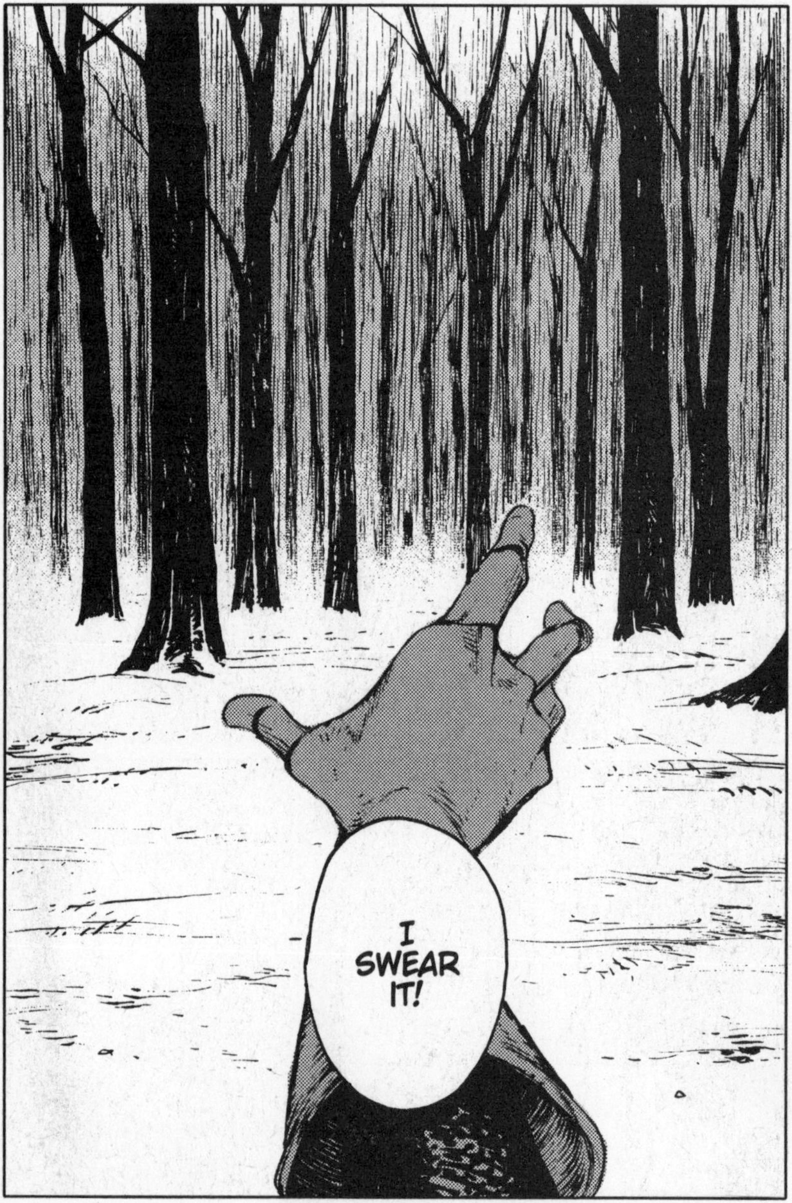
I SWEAR IT!

Chapter 24

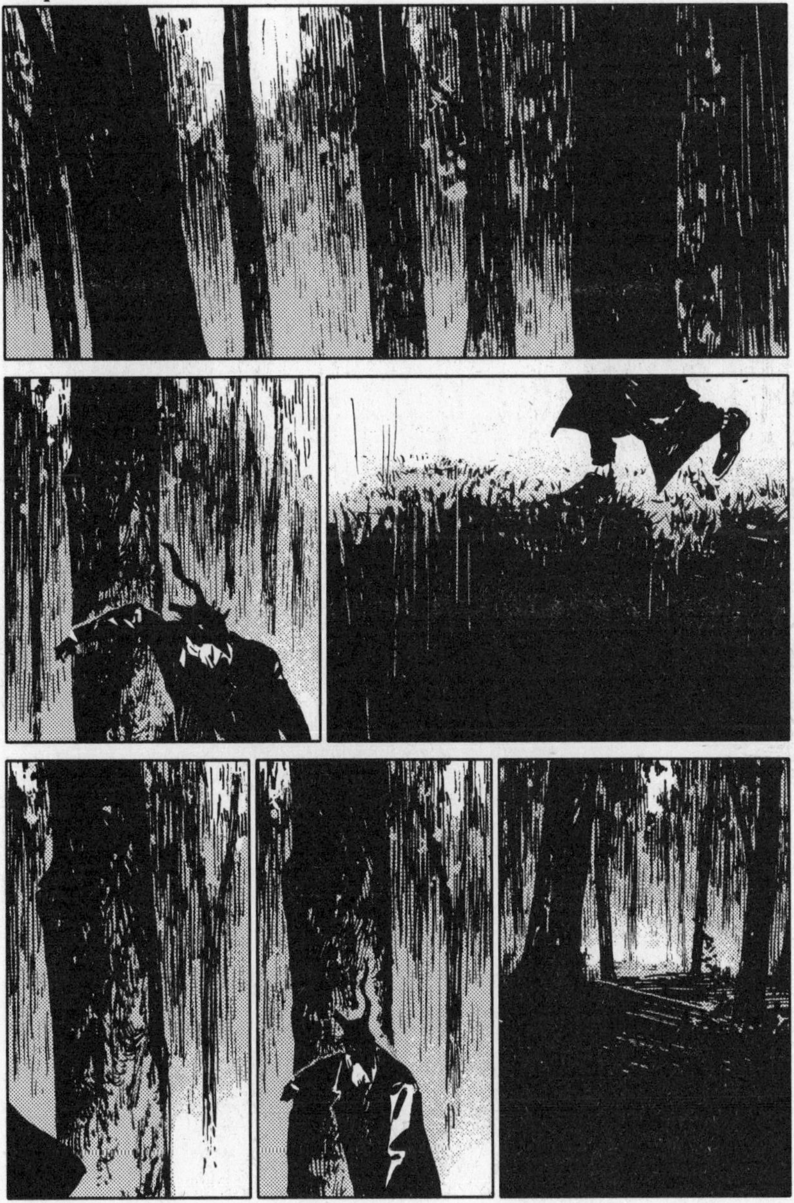

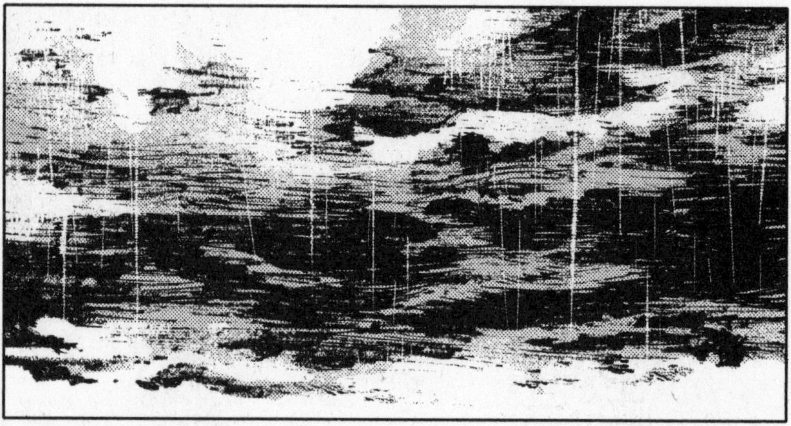

Chapter 24

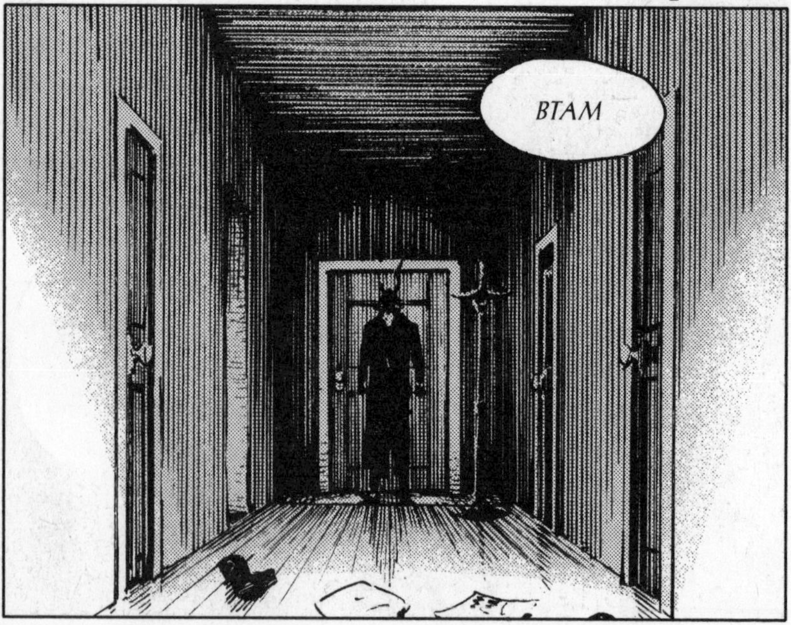
BTAM

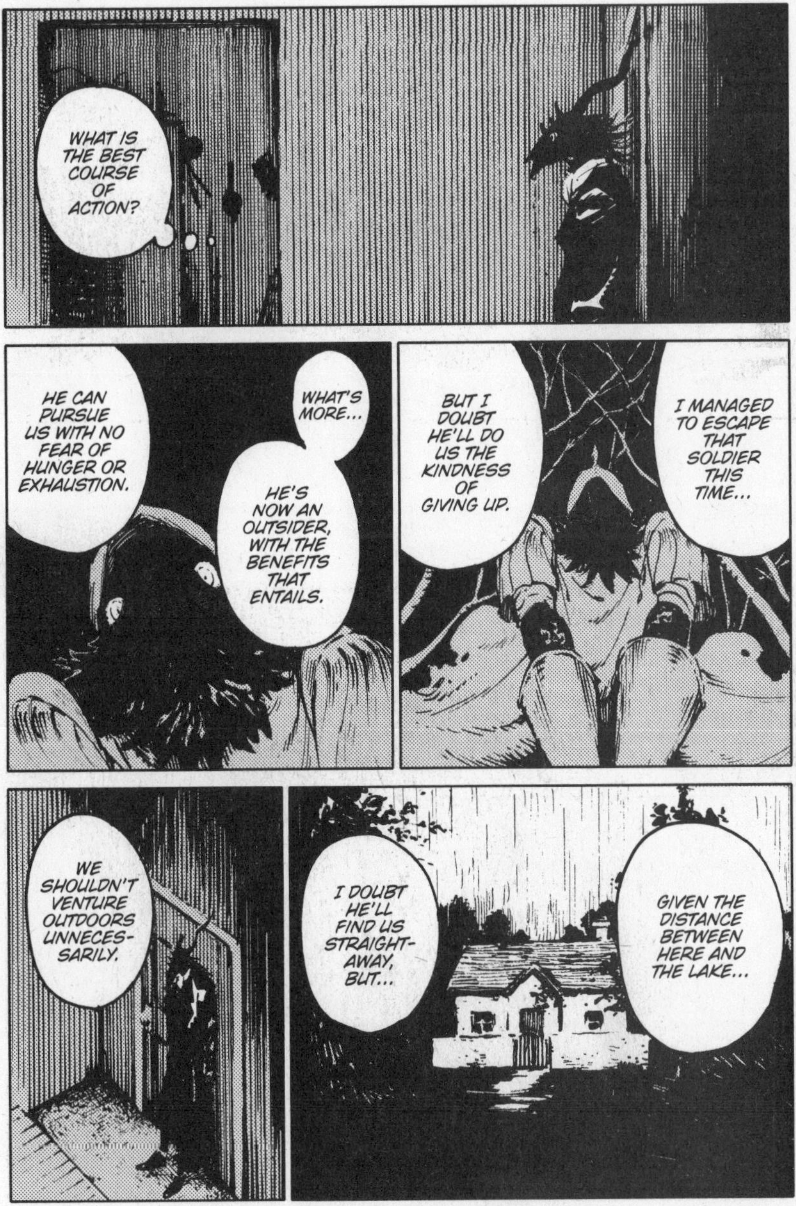
WHAT IS THE BEST COURSE OF ACTION?
I MANAGED TO ESCAPE THAT SOLDIER THIS TIME...
BUT I DOUBT HE'LL DO US THE KINDNESS OF GIVING UP.
WHAT'S MORE...
HE'S NOW AN OUTSIDER, WITH THE BENEFITS THAT ENTAILS.
HE CAN PURSUE US WITH NO FEAR OF HUNGER OR EXHAUSTION.
GIVEN THE DISTANCE BETWEEN HERE AND THE LAKE...
I DOUBT HE'LL FIND US STRAIGHT-AWAY, BUT...
WE SHOULDN'T VENTURE OUTDOORS UNNECES-SARILY.

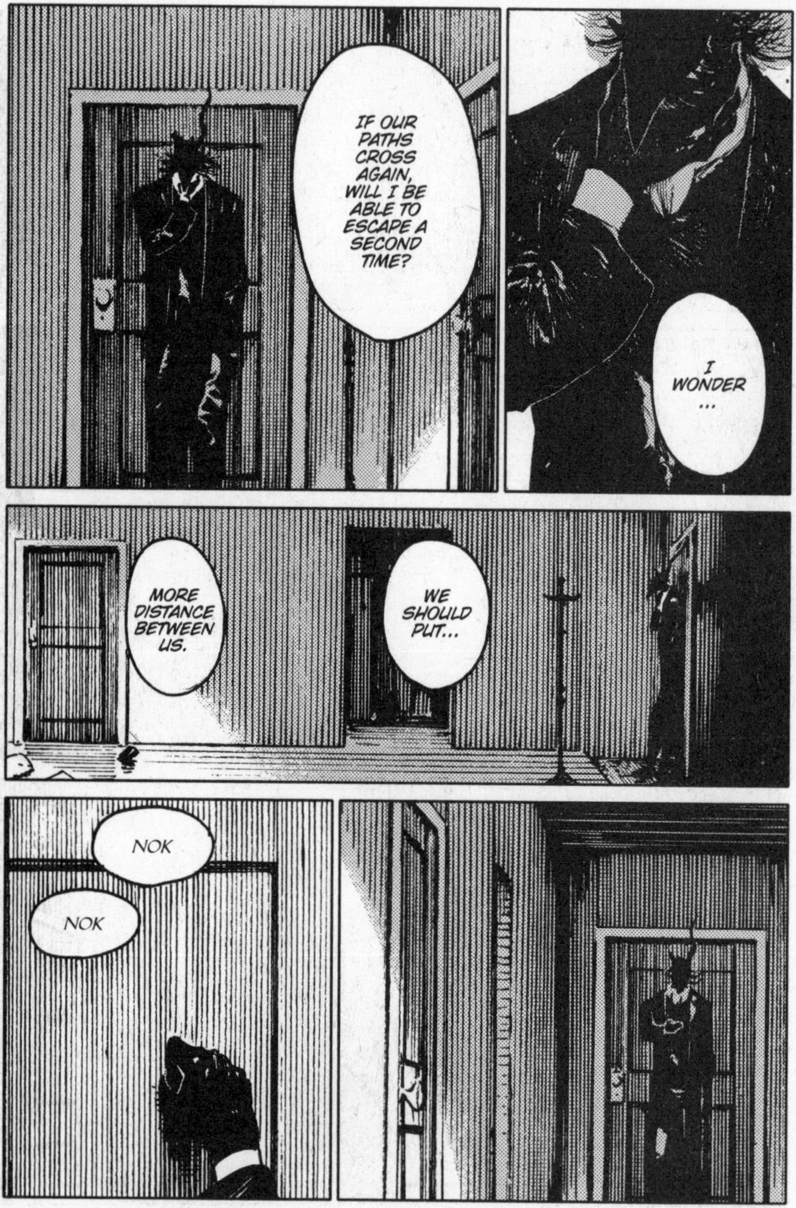
I WONDER ...
IF OUR PATHS CROSS AGAIN, WILL I BE ABLE TO ESCAPE A SECOND TIME?
WE SHOULD PUT...
MORE DISTANCE BETWEEN US.
NOK
NOK

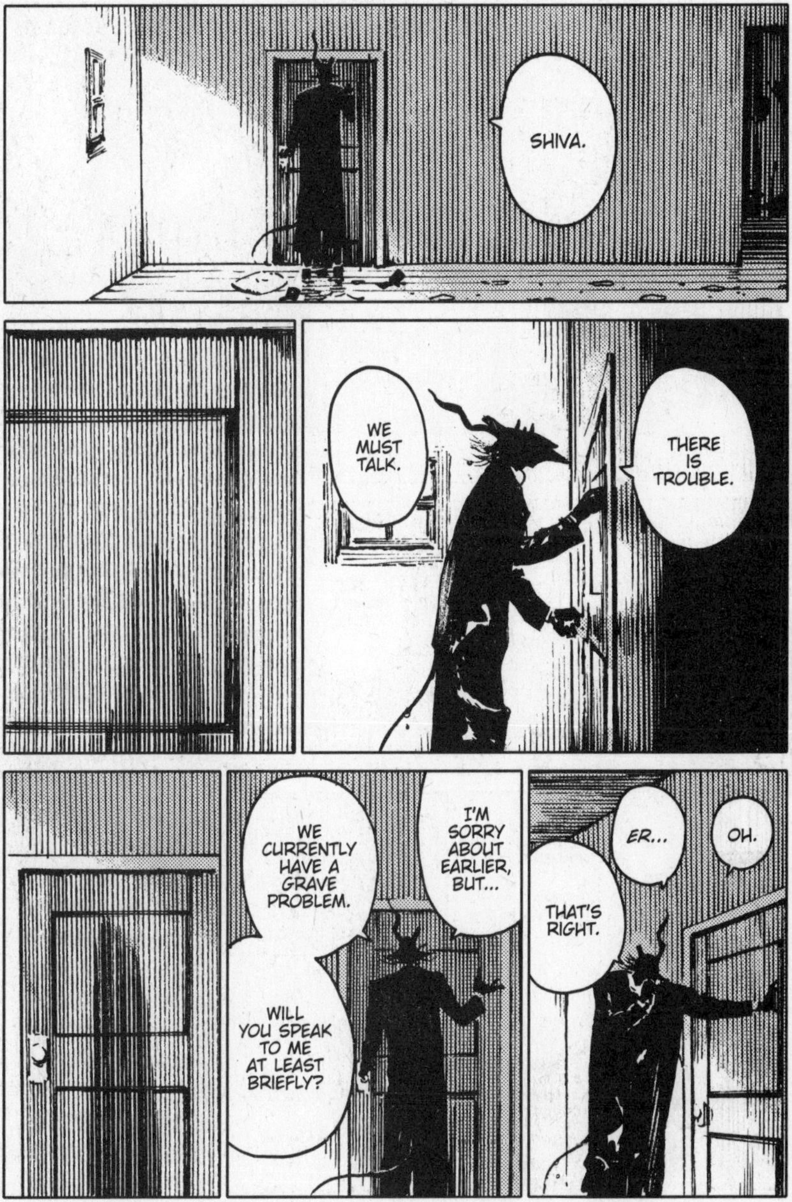
SHIVA.
THERE IS TROUBLE.
WE MUST TALK.
OH.
ER...
THAT'S RIGHT.
I'M SORRY ABOUT EARLIER, BUT...
WE CURRENTLY HAVE A GRAVE PROBLEM.
WILL YOU SPEAK TO ME AT LEAST BRIEFLY?

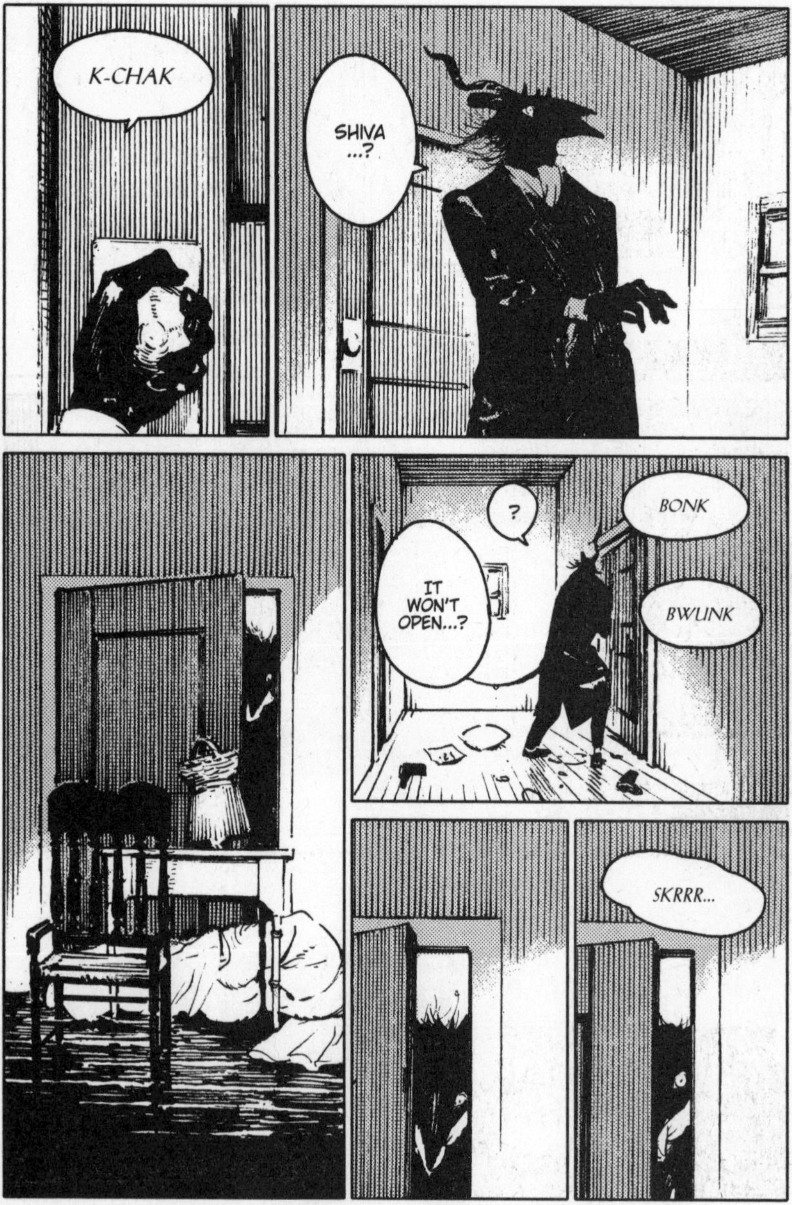
SHIVA ...?
K-CHAK
BONK
?
BWUNK
IT WON'T OPEN...?
SKRRR...

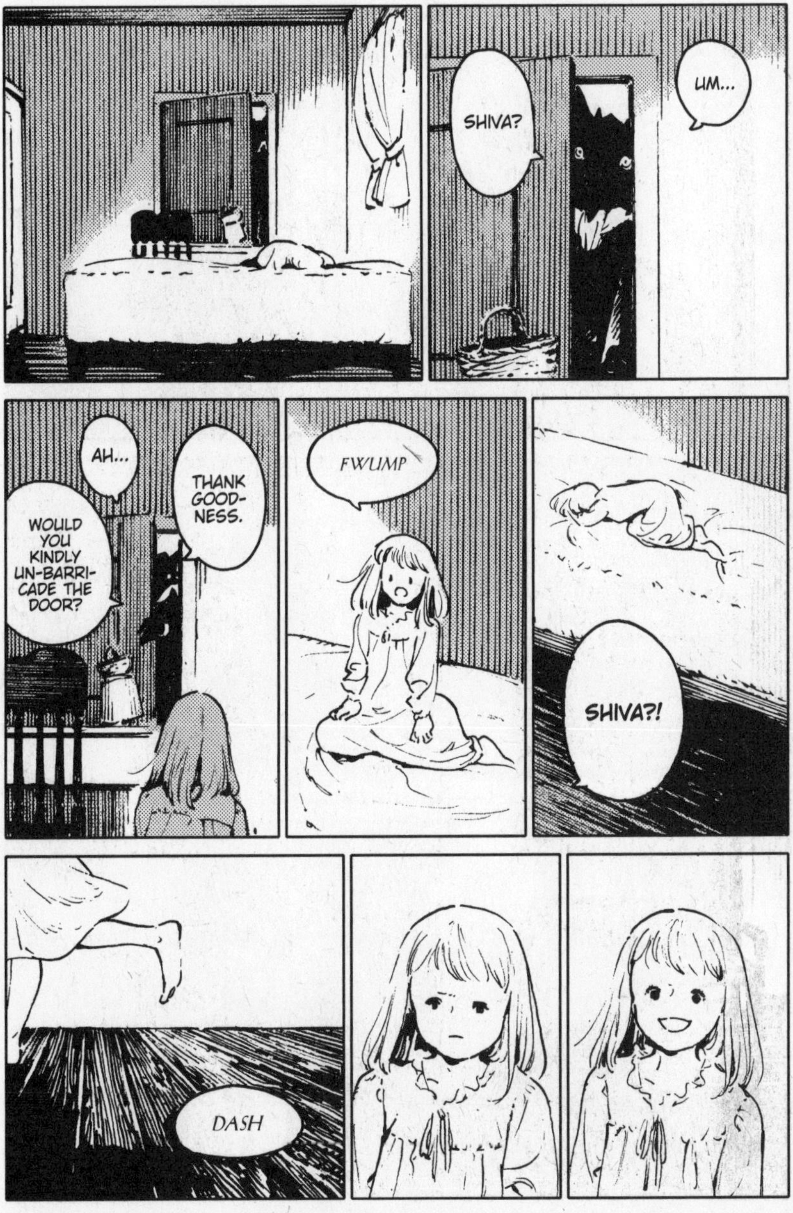
UM...
SHIVA?
THANK GOODNESS.
AH...
WOULD YOU KINDLY UN-BARRICADE THE DOOR?
SHIVA?!
FWUMP
DASH

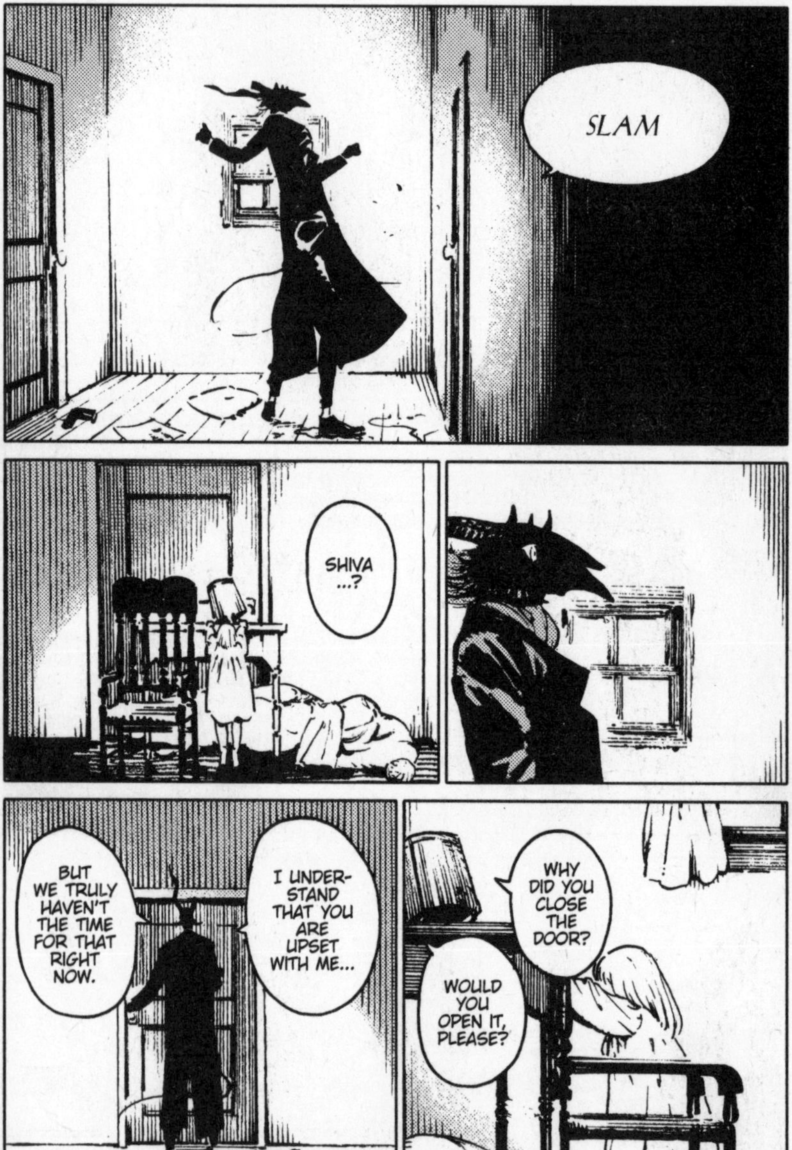
SLAM
SHIVA ...?
WHY DID YOU CLOSE THE DOOR?
WOULD YOU OPEN IT, PLEASE?
I UNDER-STAND THAT YOU ARE UPSET WITH ME...
BUT WE TRULY HAVEN'T THE TIME FOR THAT RIGHT NOW.

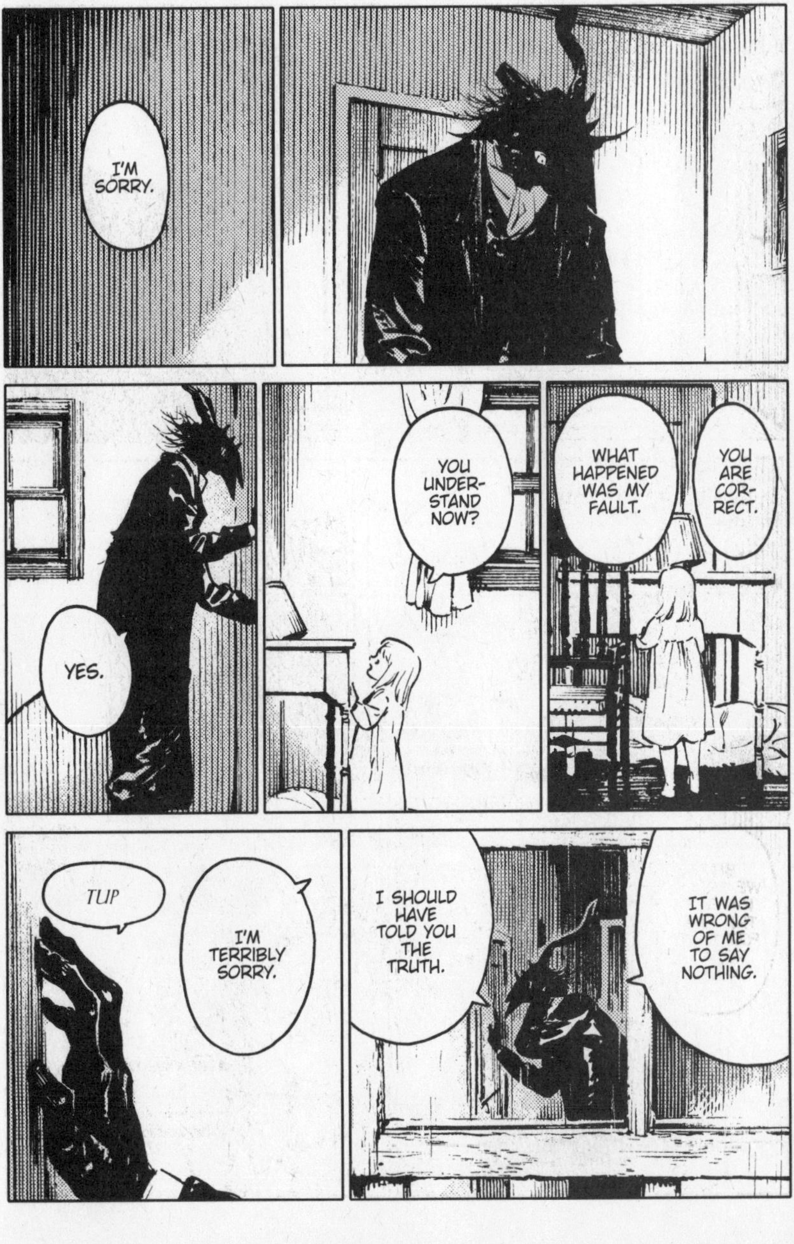
I'M SORRY.
YOU ARE COR-RECT.
WHAT HAPPENED WAS MY FAULT.
YOU UNDER-STAND NOW?
YES.
IT WAS WRONG OF ME TO SAY NOTHING.
I SHOULD HAVE TOLD YOU THE TRUTH.
I'M TERRIBLY SORRY.
TUP

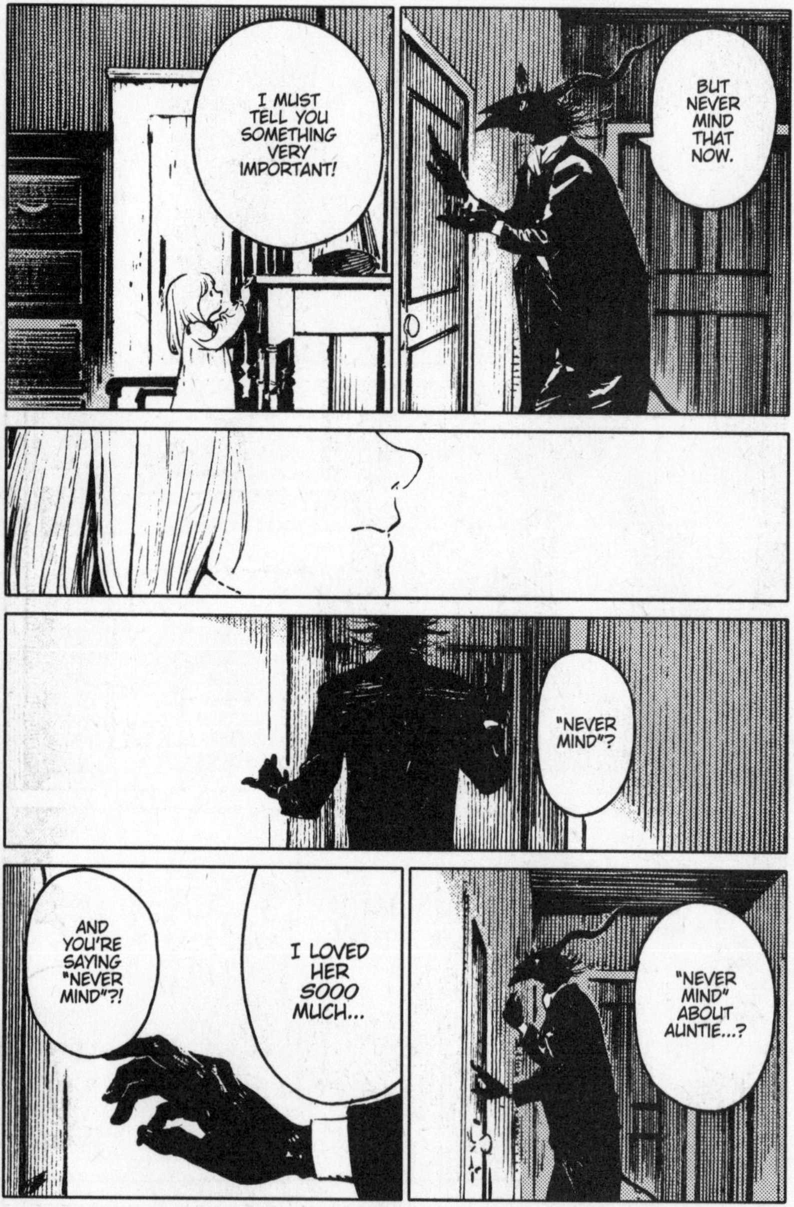
BUT NEVER MIND THAT NOW.
I MUST TELL YOU SOMETHING VERY IMPORTANT!
"NEVER MIND"?
"NEVER MIND" ABOUT AUNTIE...?
I LOVED HER *SOOO* MUCH...
AND YOU'RE SAYING "NEVER MIND"?!

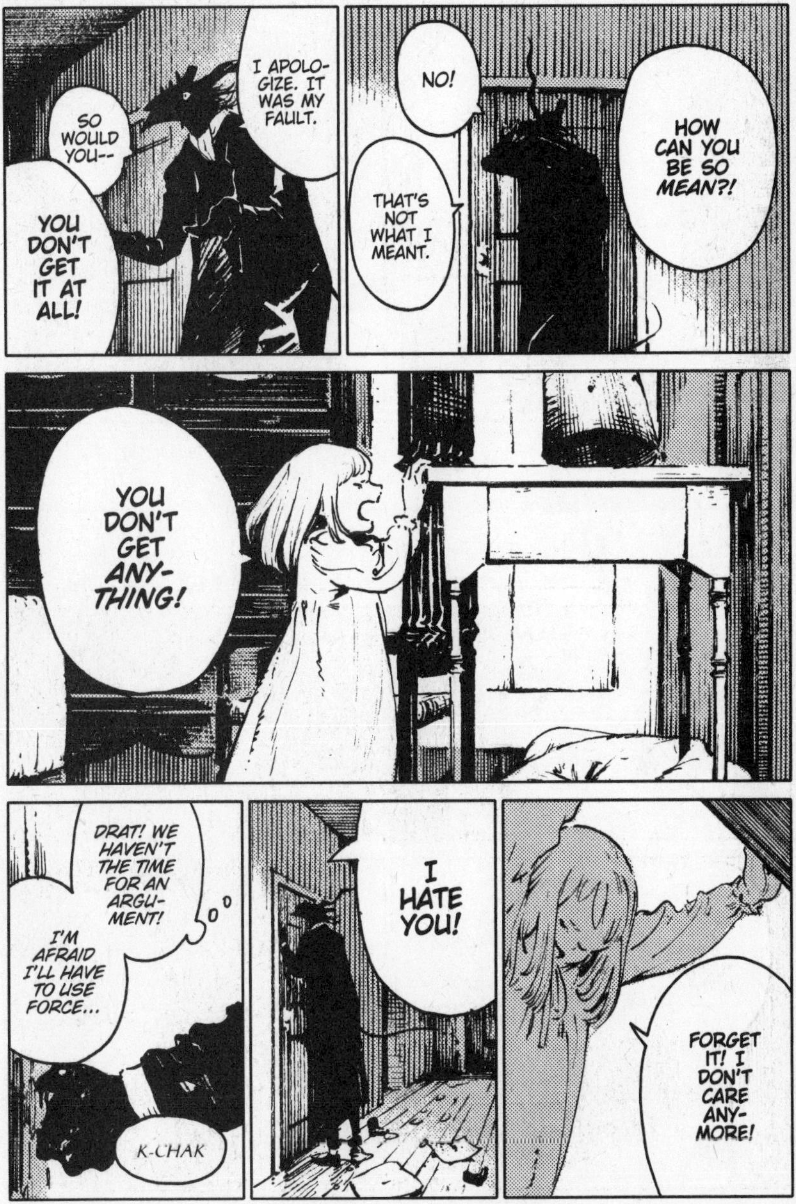
HOW CAN YOU BE SO MEAN?!
NO!
THAT'S NOT WHAT I MEANT.
I APOLOGIZE. IT WAS MY FAULT.
SO WOULD YOU--
YOU DON'T GET IT AT ALL!
YOU DON'T GET ANYTHING!
FORGET IT! I DON'T CARE ANYMORE!
I HATE YOU!
DRAT! WE HAVEN'T THE TIME FOR AN ARGUMENT!
I'M AFRAID I'LL HAVE TO USE FORCE...
K-CHAK

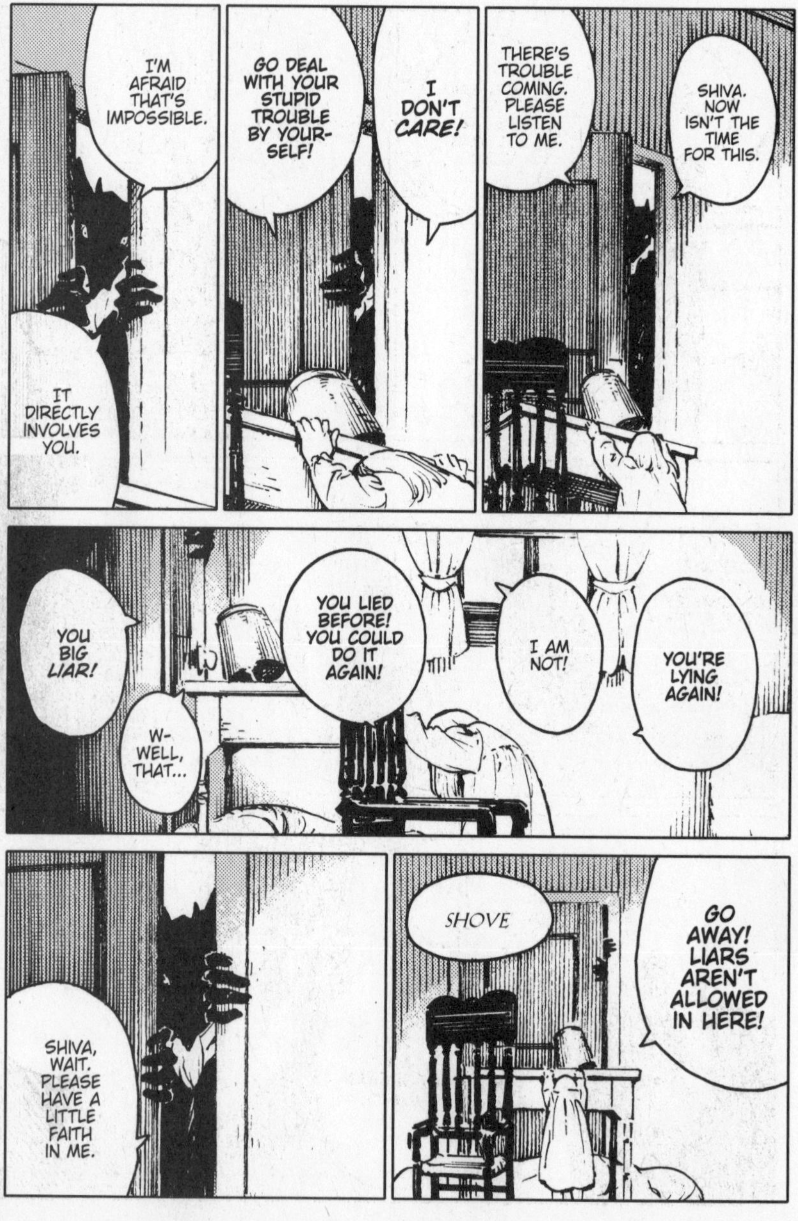
SHIVA. NOW ISN'T THE TIME FOR THIS.
THERE'S TROUBLE COMING. PLEASE LISTEN TO ME.
I DON'T *CARE!*
GO DEAL WITH YOUR STUPID TROUBLE BY YOURSELF!
I'M AFRAID THAT'S IMPOSSIBLE.
IT DIRECTLY INVOLVES YOU.
YOU'RE LYING AGAIN!
I AM NOT!
YOU LIED BEFORE! YOU COULD DO IT AGAIN!
YOU BIG *LIAR!*
W-WELL, THAT...
GO AWAY! LIARS AREN'T ALLOWED IN HERE!
SHOVE
SHIVA, WAIT. PLEASE HAVE A LITTLE FAITH IN ME.

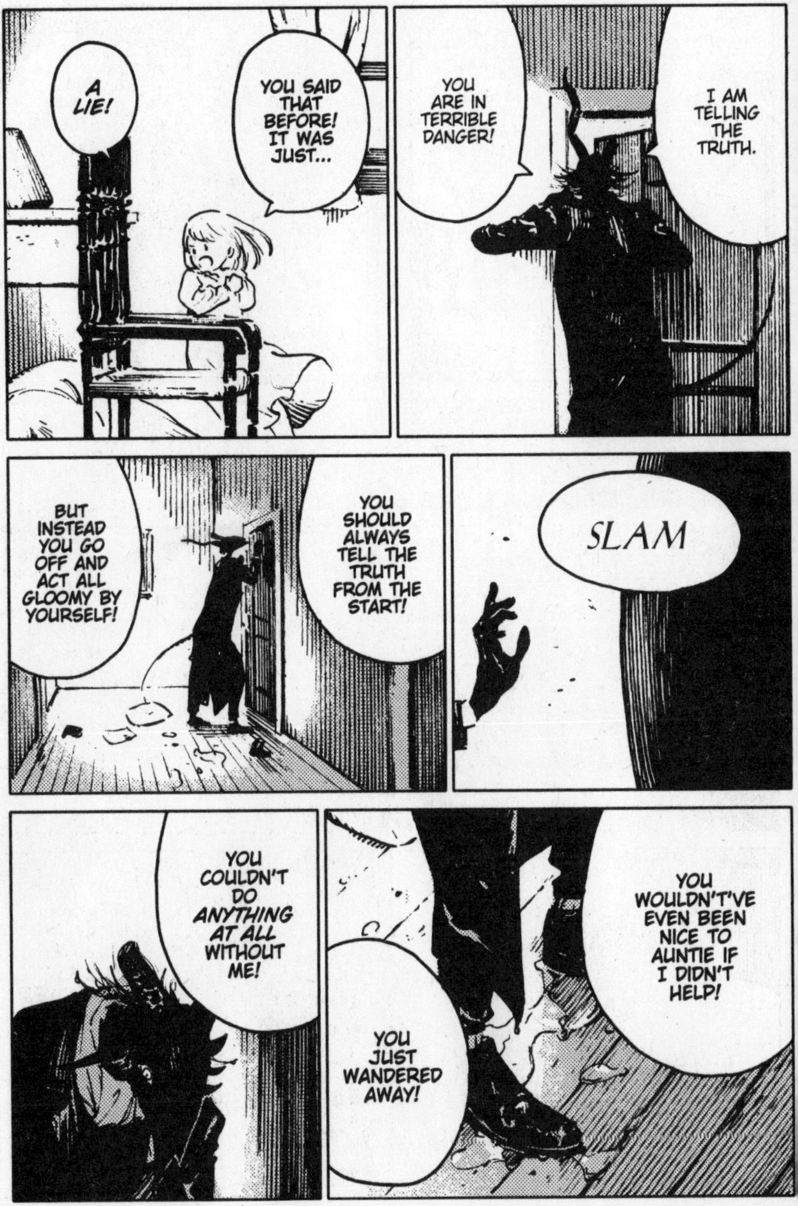
I AM TELLING THE TRUTH.
YOU ARE IN TERRIBLE DANGER!
YOU SAID THAT BEFORE! IT WAS JUST...
A LIE!
SLAM
YOU SHOULD ALWAYS TELL THE TRUTH FROM THE START!
BUT INSTEAD YOU GO OFF AND ACT ALL GLOOMY BY YOURSELF!
YOU WOULDN'T'VE EVEN BEEN NICE TO AUNTIE IF I DIDN'T HELP!
YOU JUST WANDERED AWAY!
YOU COULDN'T DO ANYTHING AT ALL WITHOUT ME!

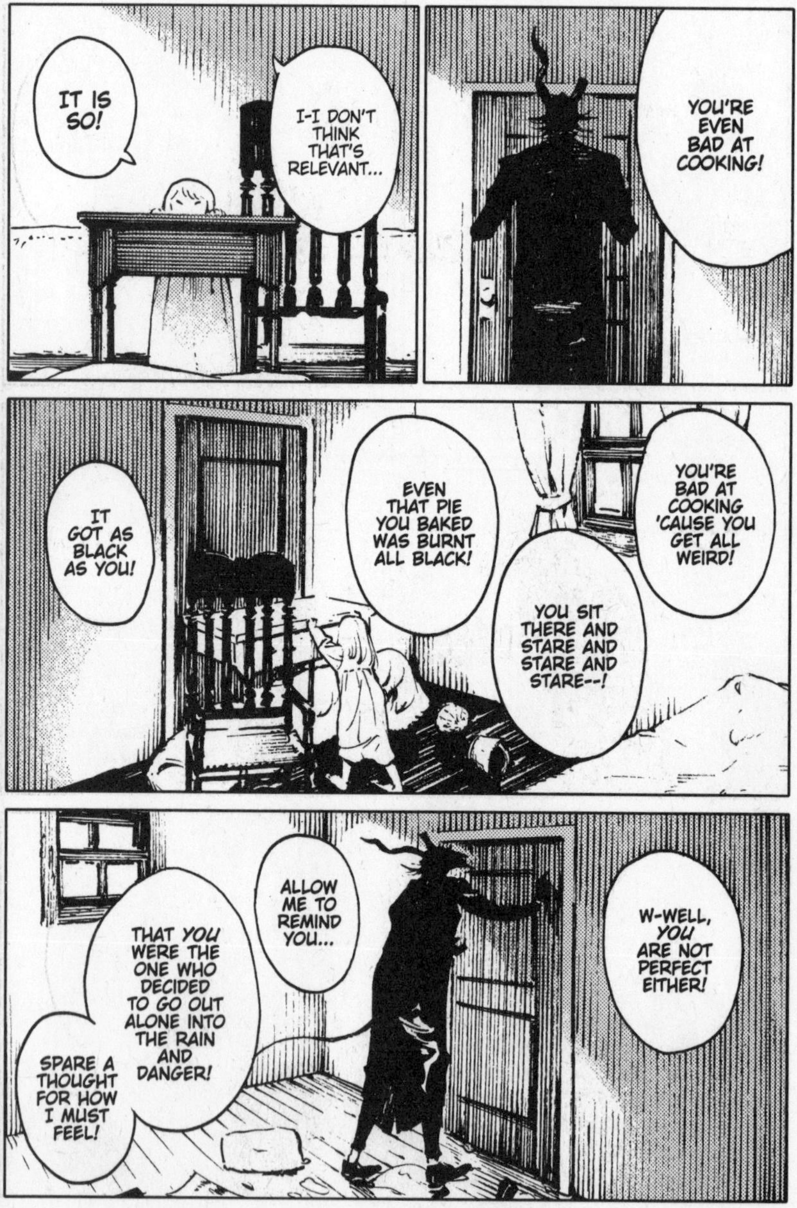
YOU'RE EVEN BAD AT COOKING!
I-I DON'T THINK THAT'S RELEVANT...
IT IS SO!
YOU'RE BAD AT COOKING 'CAUSE YOU GET ALL WEIRD!
YOU SIT THERE AND STARE AND STARE AND STARE--!
EVEN THAT PIE YOU BAKED WAS BURNT ALL BLACK!
IT GOT AS BLACK AS YOU!
W-WELL, *YOU* ARE NOT PERFECT EITHER!
ALLOW ME TO REMIND YOU...
THAT *YOU* WERE THE ONE WHO DECIDED TO GO OUT ALONE INTO THE RAIN AND DANGER!
SPARE A THOUGHT FOR HOW I MUST FEEL!

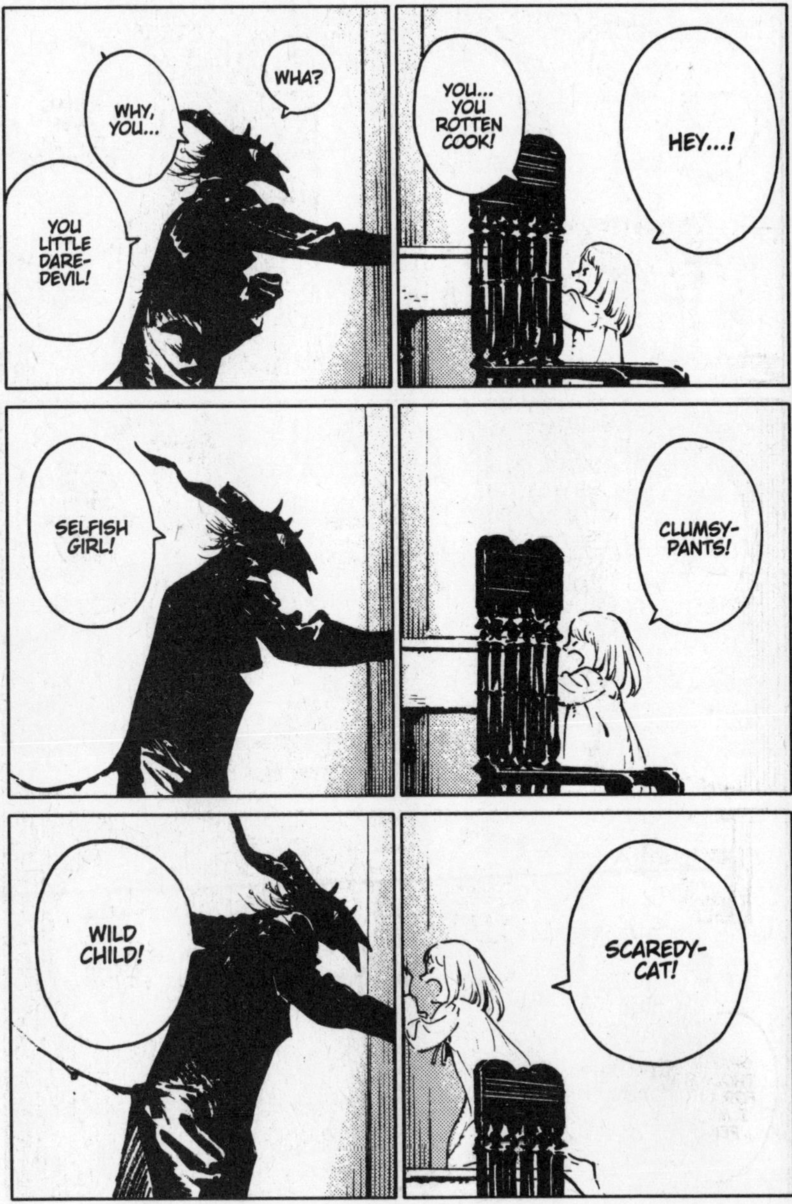
HEY...!
YOU... YOU ROTTEN COOK!
WHA?
WHY, YOU...
YOU LITTLE DARE-DEVIL!
CLUMSY-PANTS!
SELFISH GIRL!
SCAREDY-CAT!
WILD CHILD!

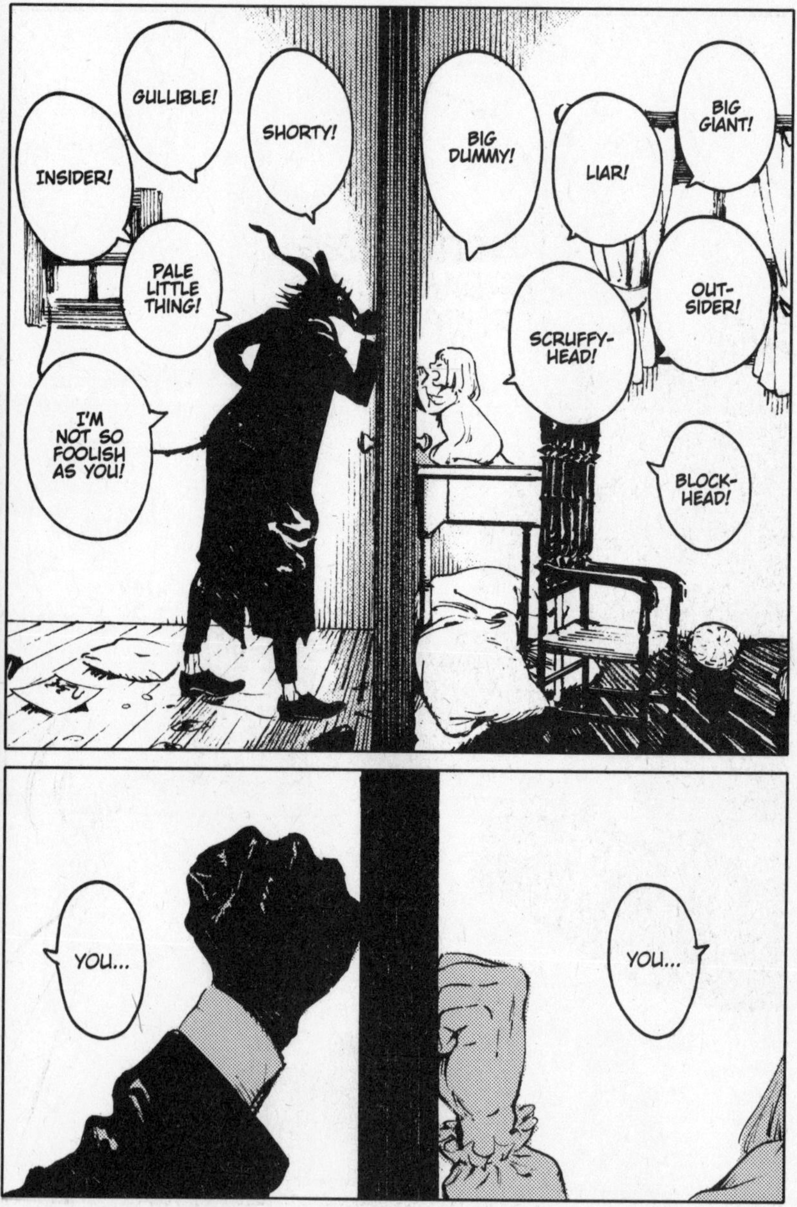
BIG GIANT!
LIAR!
BIG DUMMY!
OUT-SIDER!
SCRUFFY-HEAD!
BLOCK-HEAD!
SHORTY!
GULLIBLE!
INSIDER!
PALE LITTLE THING!
I'M NOT SO FOOLISH AS YOU!
YOU...
YOU...

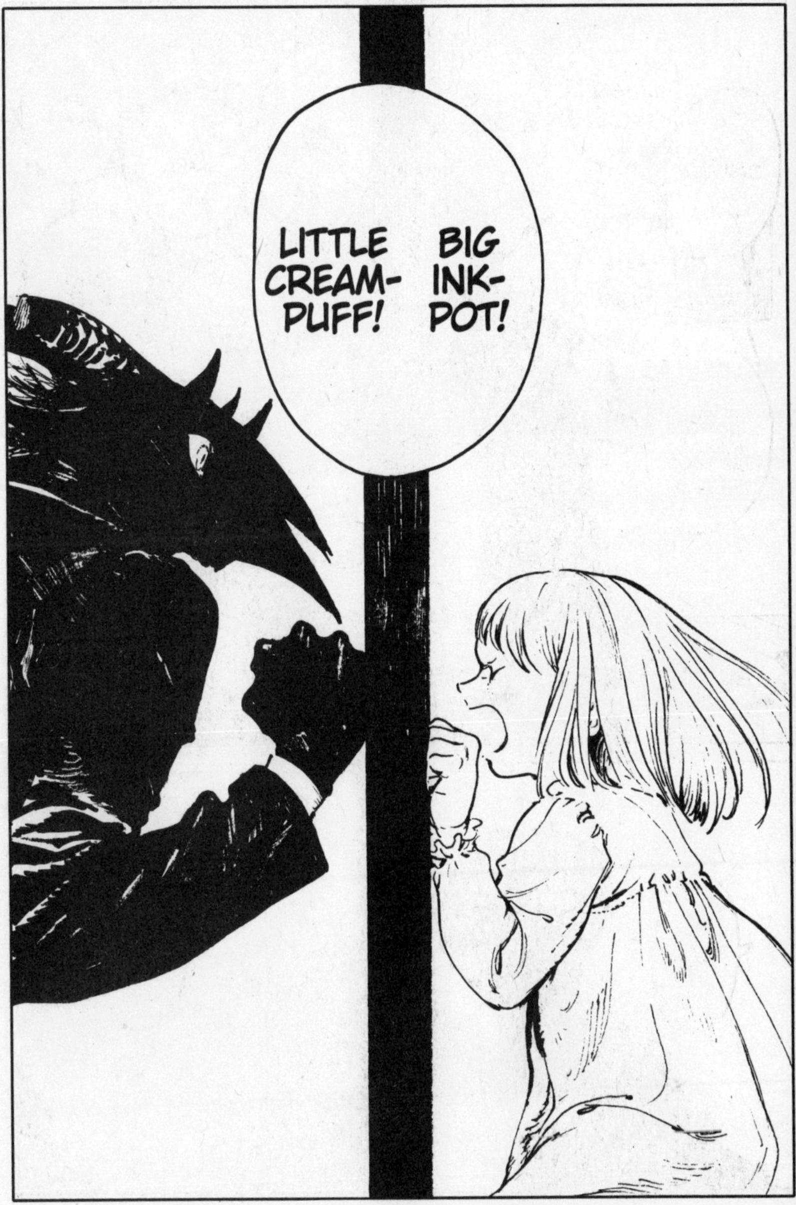
LITTLE CREAM-PUFF!
BIG INK-POT!

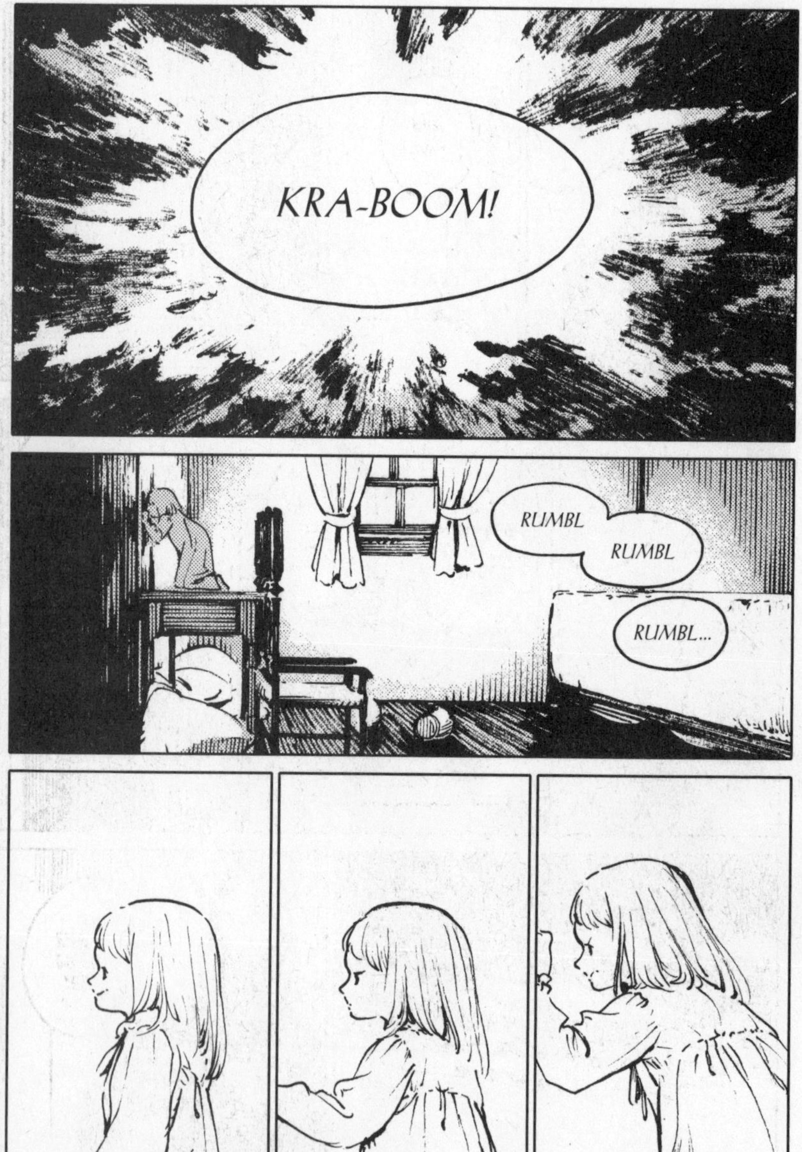
KRA-BOOM!
RUMBL
RUMBL
RUMBL...

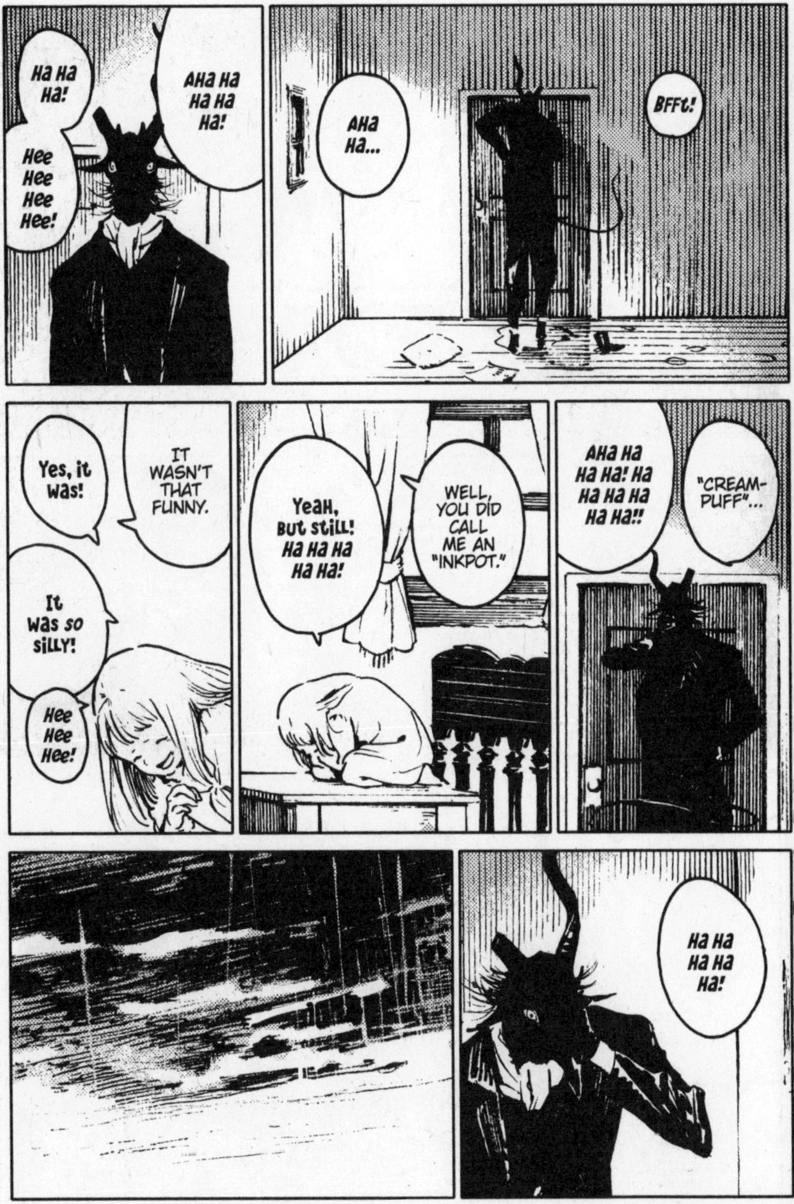
BFFt!
AHA HA...
AHA HA HA HA HA!
HA HA HA!
Hee Hee Hee Hee!
"CREAM-PUFF"...
AHA HA HA HA! HA HA HA HA HA HA!!
WELL, YOU DID CALL ME AN "INKPOT."
Yeah, But still! HA HA HA HA HA!
IT WASN'T THAT FUNNY.
Yes, it was!
It was so silly!
Hee Hee Hee!
HA HA HA HA HA!

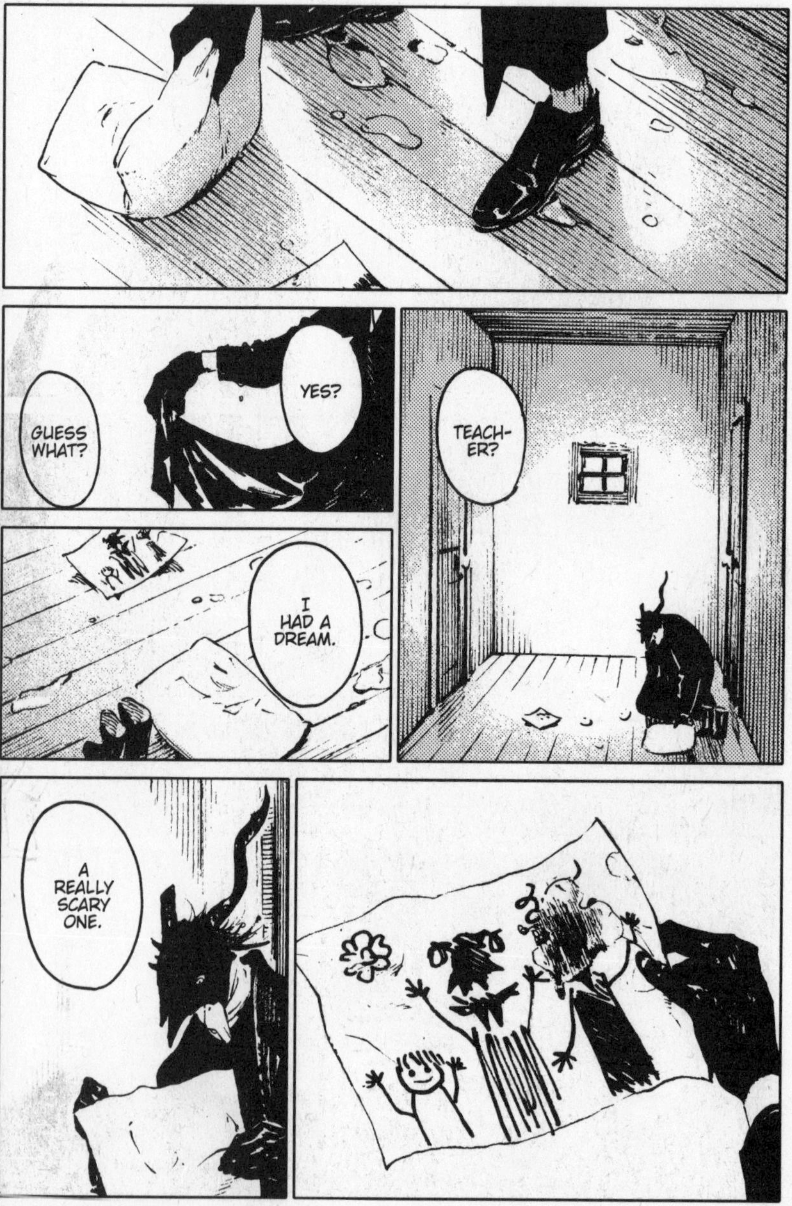
TEACHER?
YES?
GUESS WHAT?
I HAD A DREAM.
A REALLY SCARY ONE.

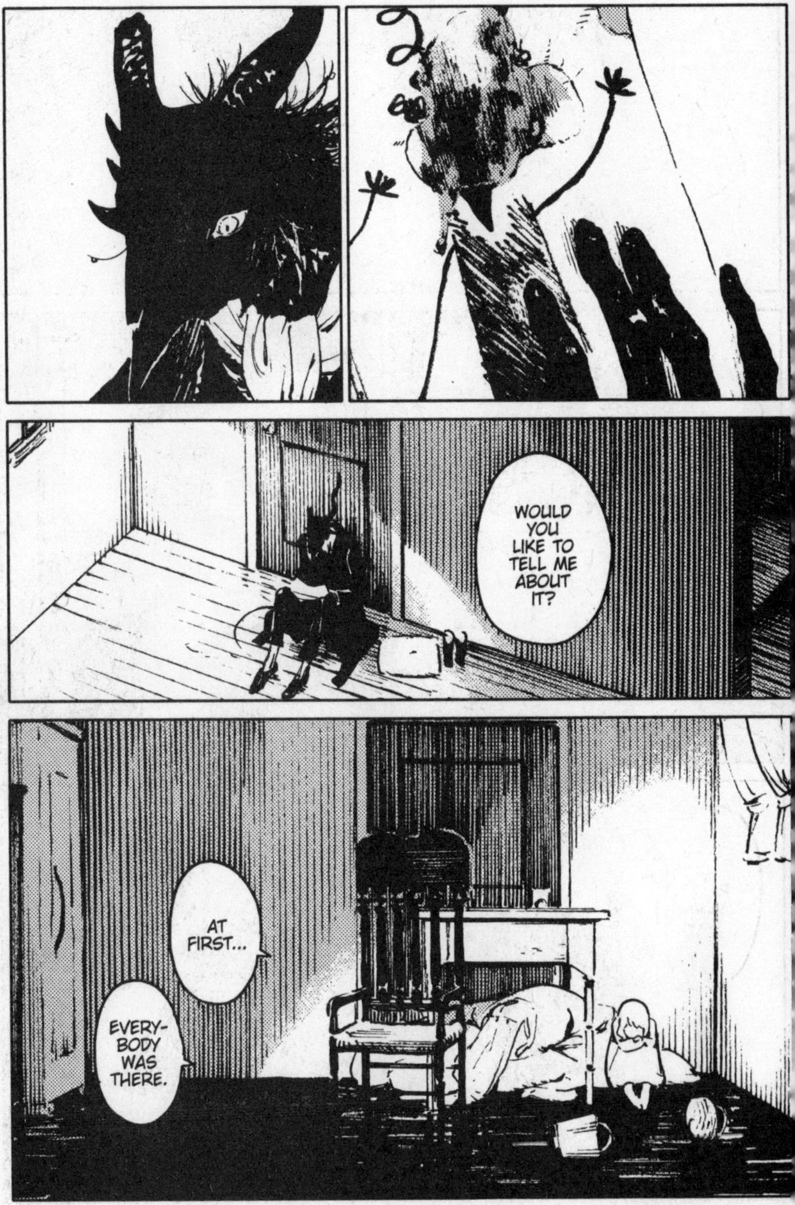
WOULD YOU LIKE TO TELL ME ABOUT IT?
AT FIRST...
EVERY-BODY WAS THERE.

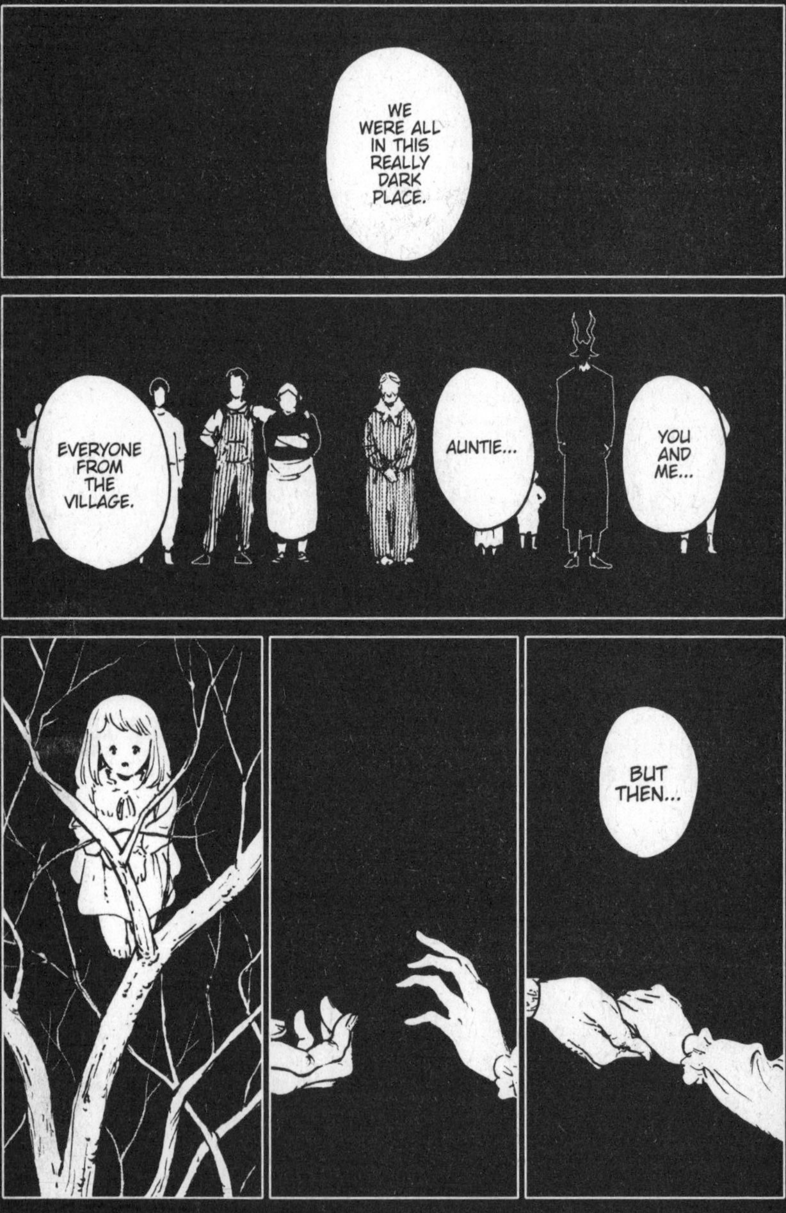
WE WERE ALL IN THIS REALLY DARK PLACE.
YOU AND ME...
AUNTIE...
EVERYONE FROM THE VILLAGE.
BUT THEN...

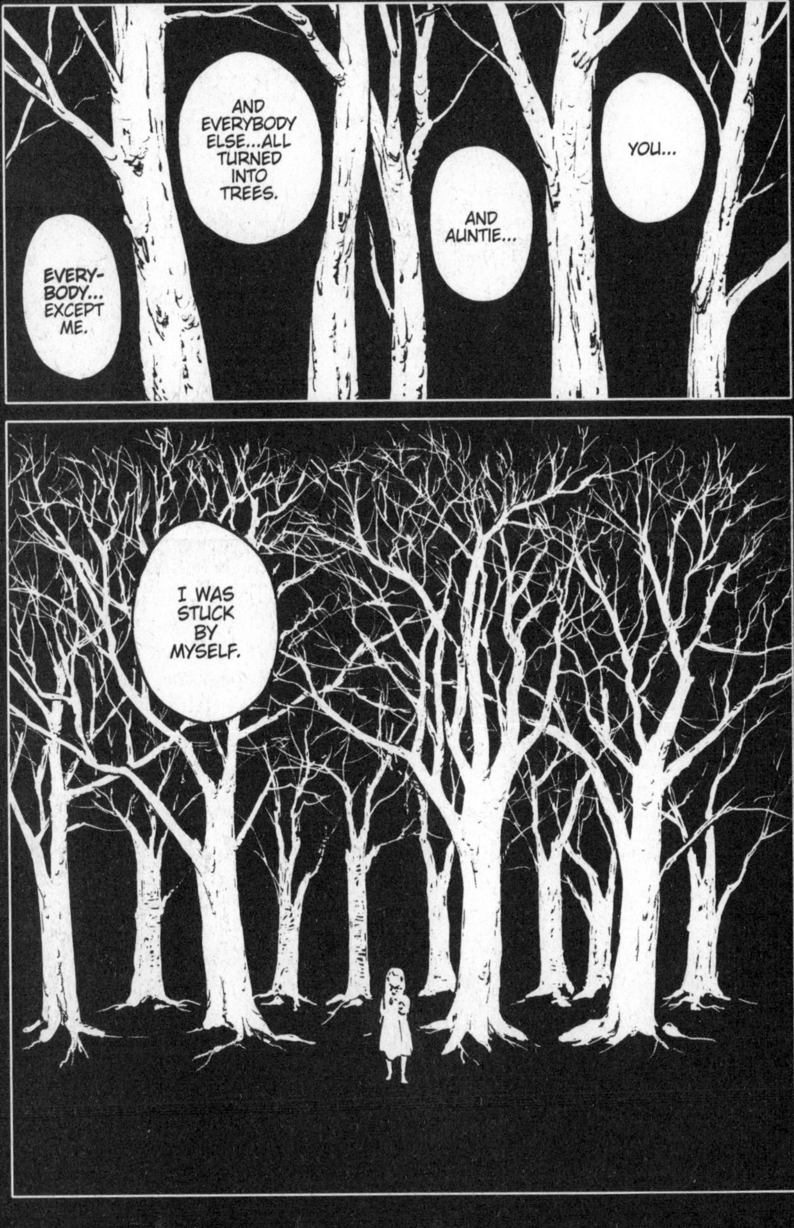
YOU...
AND AUNTIE...
AND EVERYBODY ELSE...ALL TURNED INTO TREES.
EVERY-BODY... EXCEPT ME.
I WAS STUCK BY MYSELF.

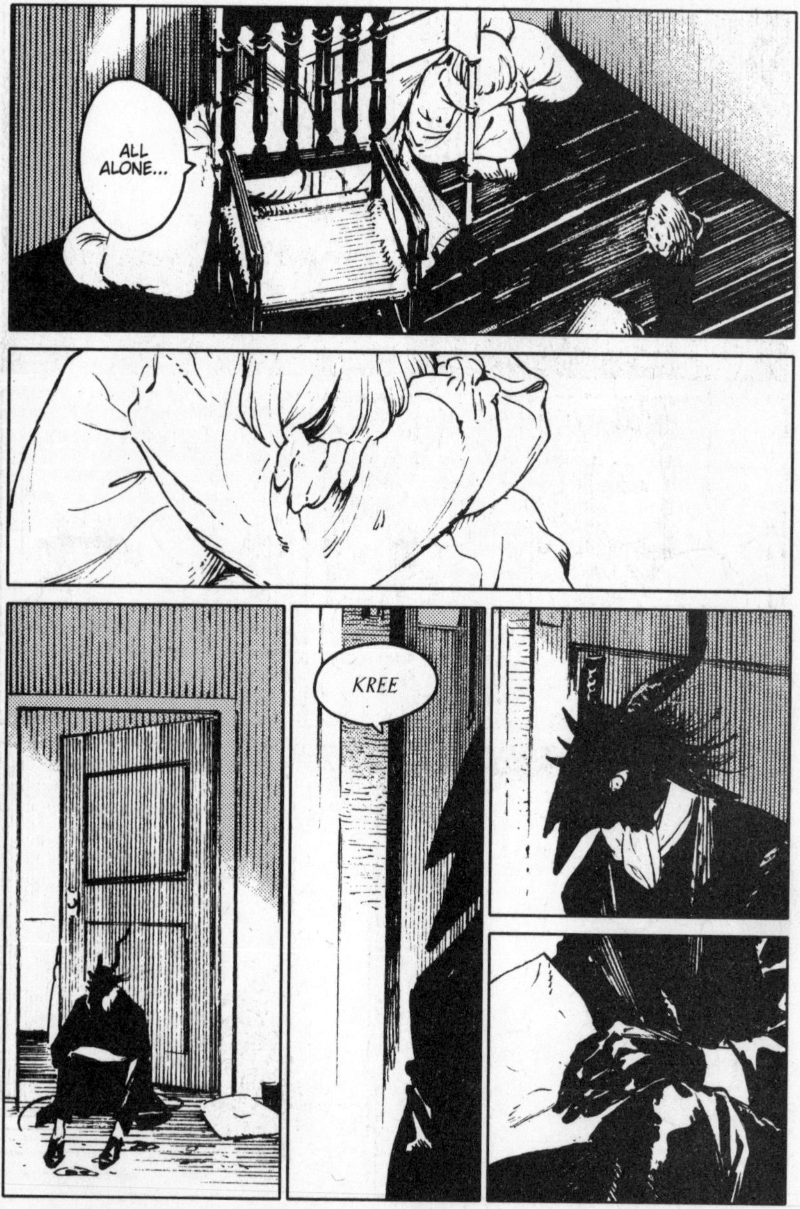
ALL ALONE...
KREE

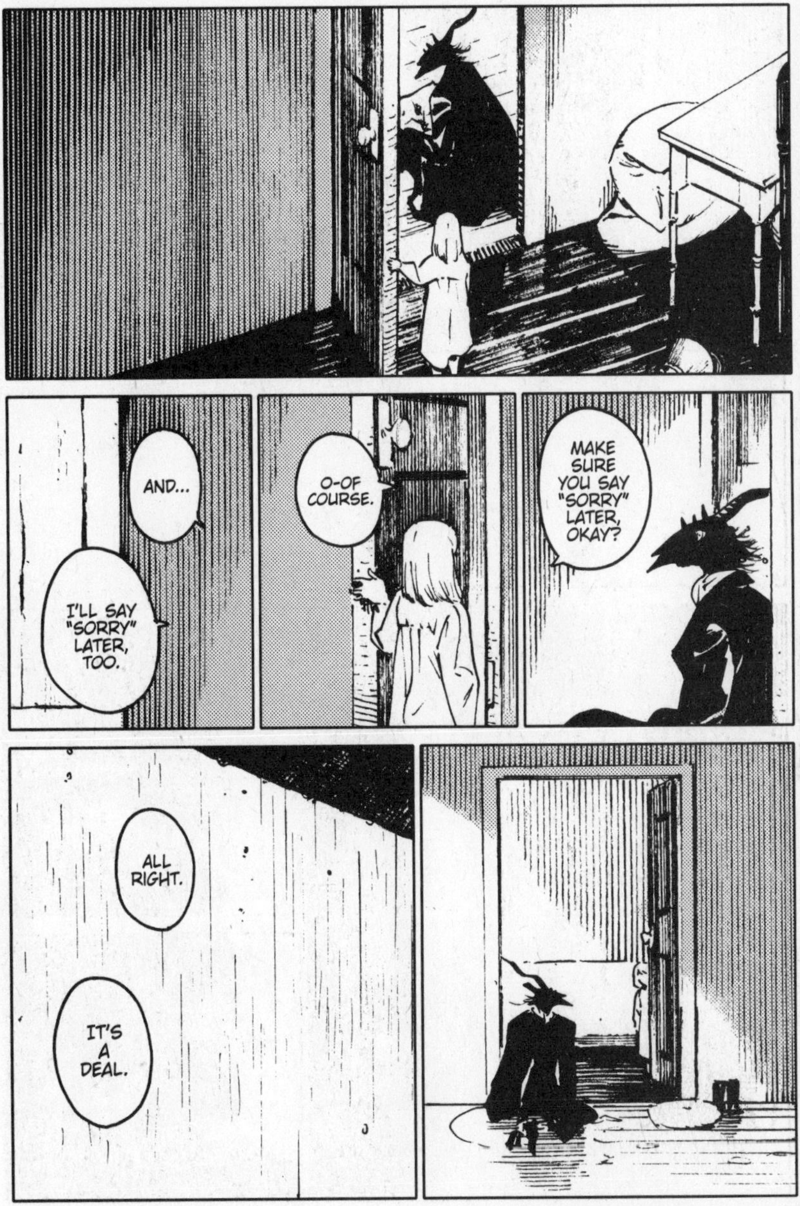
MAKE SURE YOU SAY "SORRY" LATER, OKAY?
O-OF COURSE.
AND...
I'LL SAY "SORRY" LATER, TOO.
ALL RIGHT.
IT'S A DEAL.

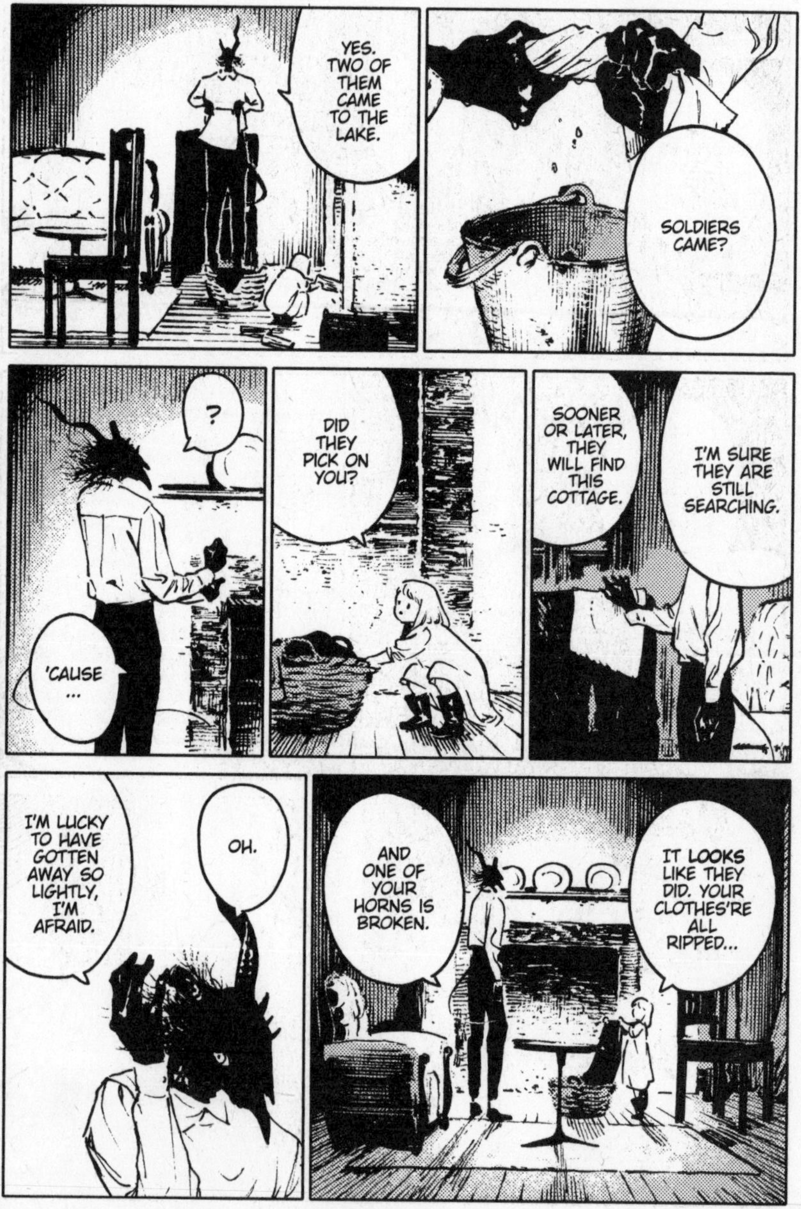
SOLDIERS CAME?
YES. TWO OF THEM CAME TO THE LAKE.
I'M SURE THEY ARE STILL SEARCHING.
SOONER OR LATER, THEY WILL FIND THIS COTTAGE.
DID THEY PICK ON YOU?
?
'CAUSE ...
IT LOOKS LIKE THEY DID. YOUR CLOTHES'RE ALL RIPPED...
AND ONE OF YOUR HORNS IS BROKEN.
OH.
I'M LUCKY TO HAVE GOTTEN AWAY SO LIGHTLY, I'M AFRAID.

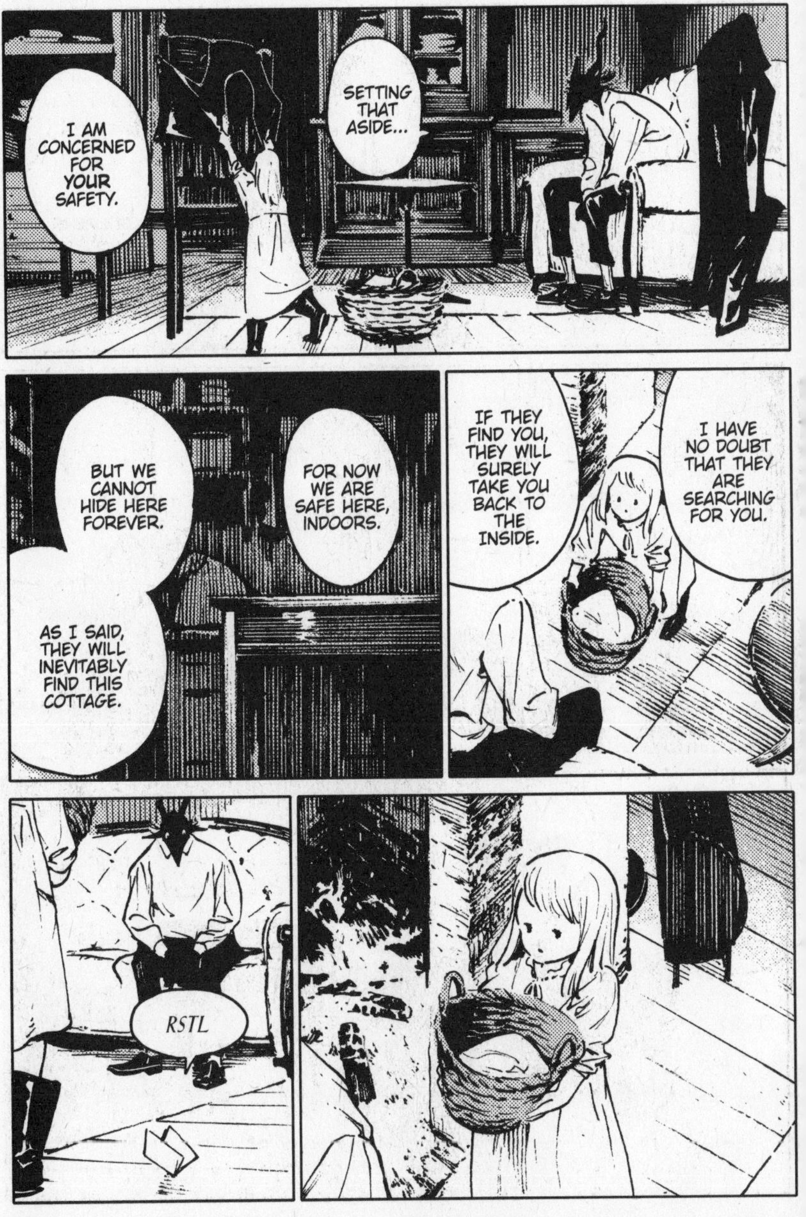
SETTING THAT ASIDE...
I AM CONCERNED FOR YOUR SAFETY.
I HAVE NO DOUBT THAT THEY ARE SEARCHING FOR YOU.
IF THEY FIND YOU, THEY WILL SURELY TAKE YOU BACK TO THE INSIDE.
FOR NOW WE ARE SAFE HERE, INDOORS.
BUT WE CANNOT HIDE HERE FOREVER.
AS I SAID, THEY WILL INEVITABLY FIND THIS COTTAGE.
RSTL

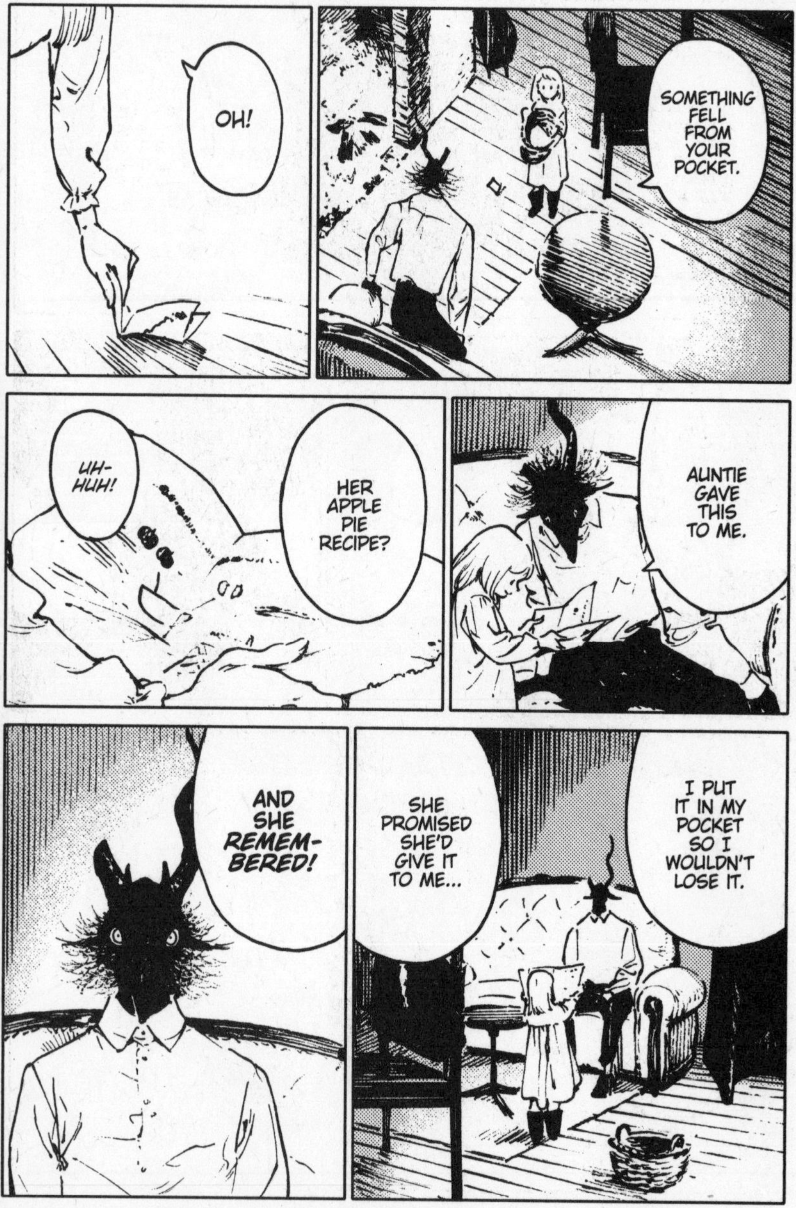
SOMETHING FELL FROM YOUR POCKET.
OH!
AUNTIE GAVE THIS TO ME.
HER APPLE PIE RECIPE?
UH-HUH!
I PUT IT IN MY POCKET SO I WOULDN'T LOSE IT.
SHE PROMISED SHE'D GIVE IT TO ME...
AND SHE *REMEMBERED!*

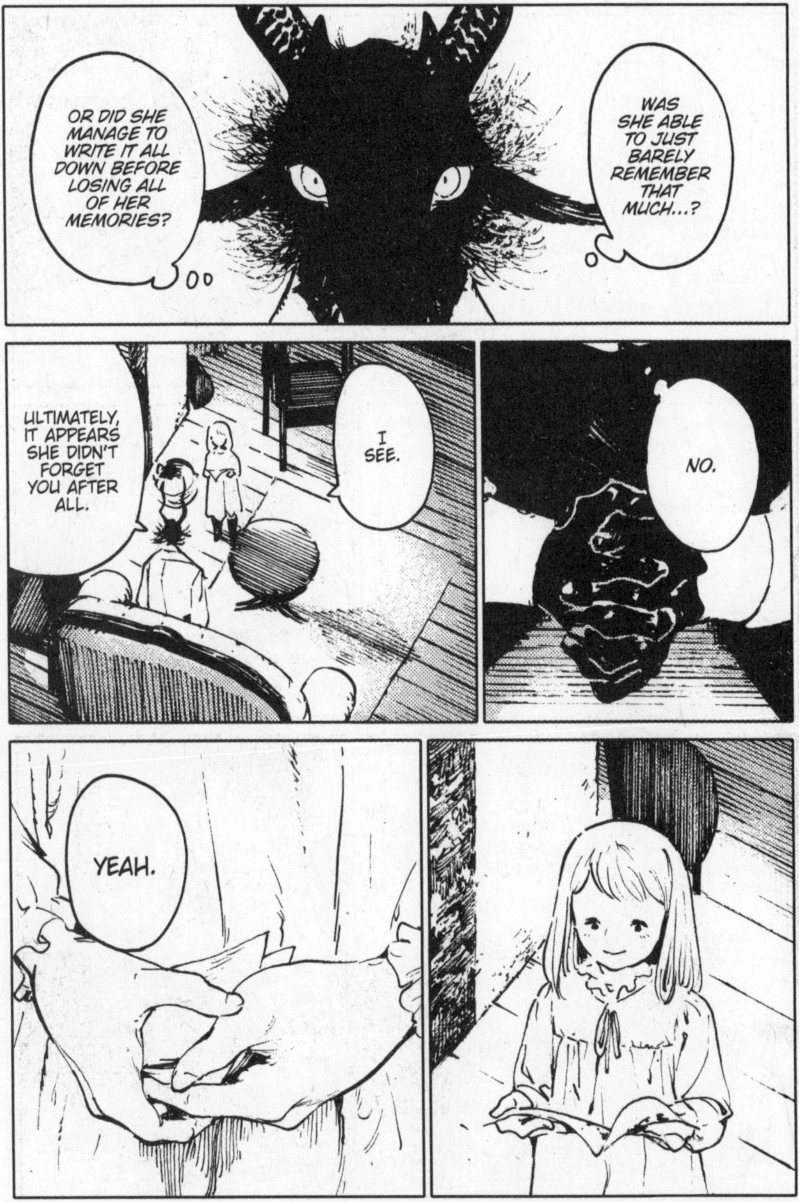
WAS SHE ABLE TO JUST BARELY REMEMBER THAT MUCH...?
OR DID SHE MANAGE TO WRITE IT ALL DOWN BEFORE LOSING ALL OF HER MEMORIES?
NO.
I SEE.
ULTIMATELY, IT APPEARS SHE DIDN'T FORGET YOU AFTER ALL.
YEAH.

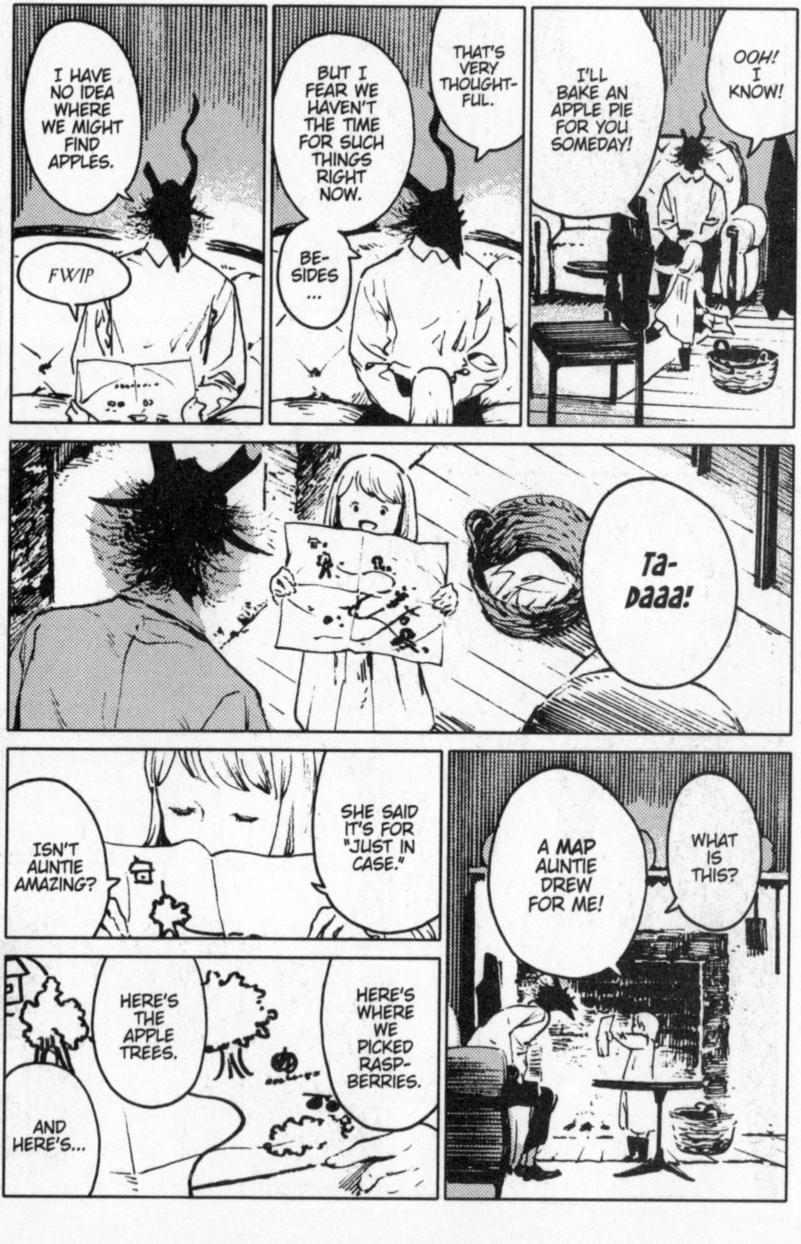
OOH! I KNOW!
I'LL BAKE AN APPLE PIE FOR YOU SOMEDAY!
THAT'S VERY THOUGHT-FUL.
BUT I FEAR WE HAVEN'T THE TIME FOR SUCH THINGS RIGHT NOW.
BE-SIDES ...
I HAVE NO IDEA WHERE WE MIGHT FIND APPLES.
FWIP
Ta-Daaa!
WHAT IS THIS?
A MAP AUNTIE DREW FOR ME!
SHE SAID IT'S FOR "JUST IN CASE."
ISN'T AUNTIE AMAZING?
HERE'S WHERE WE PICKED RASP-BERRIES.
HERE'S THE APPLE TREES.
AND HERE'S...

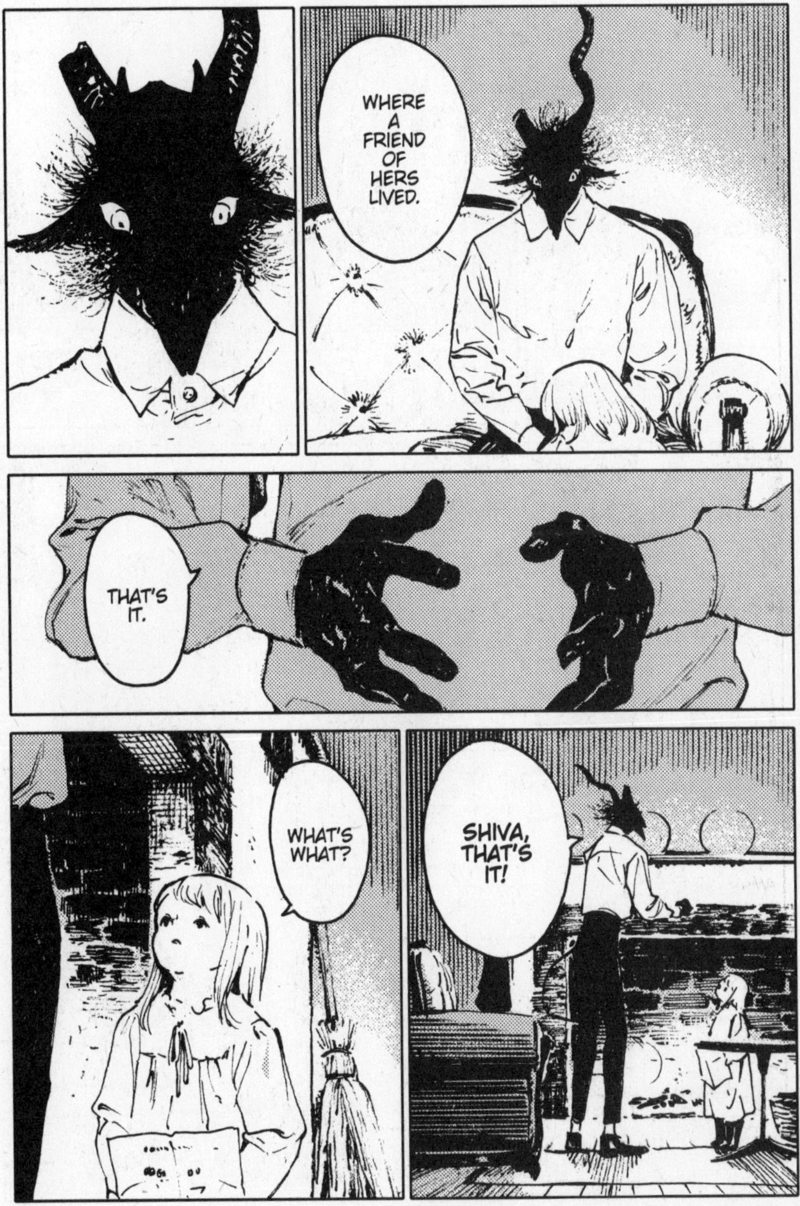
WHERE A FRIEND OF HERS LIVED.
THAT'S IT.
SHIVA, THAT'S IT!
WHAT'S WHAT?

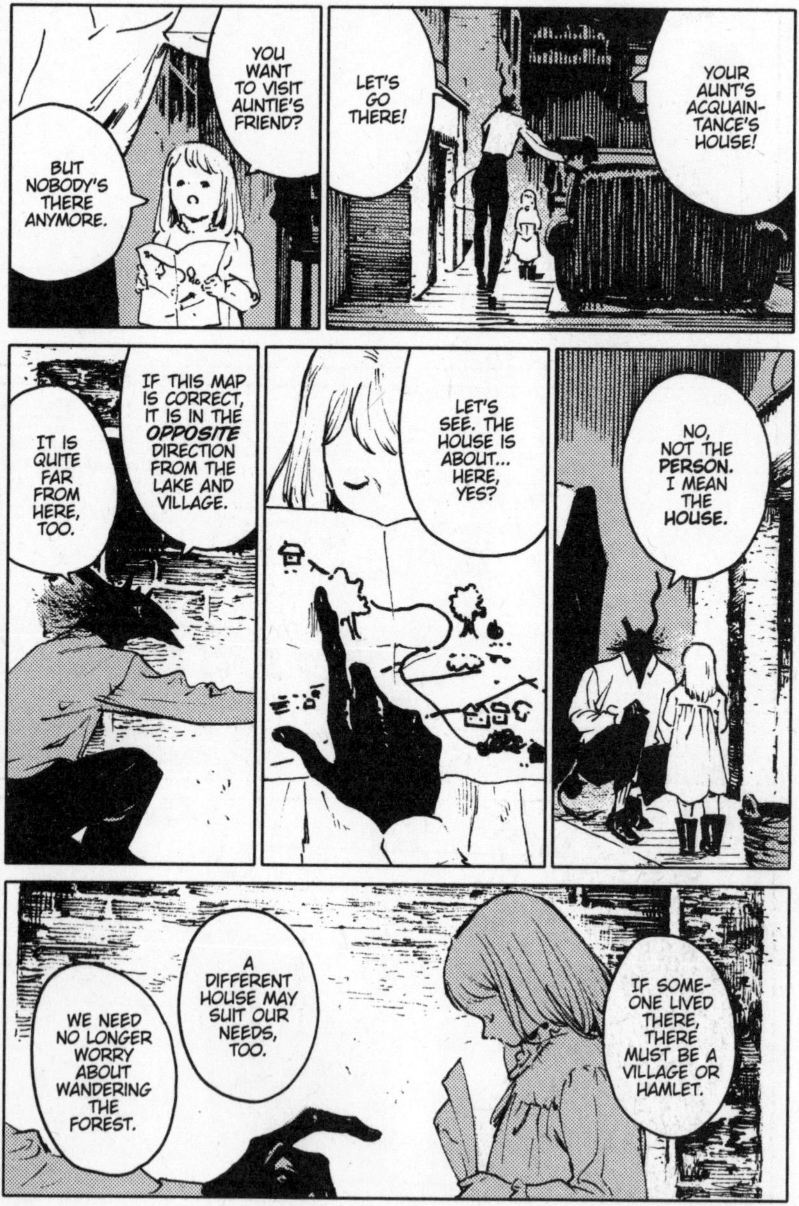
YOUR AUNT'S ACQUAIN-TANCE'S HOUSE!
LET'S GO THERE!
YOU WANT TO VISIT AUNTIE'S FRIEND?
BUT NOBODY'S THERE ANYMORE.
NO, NOT THE PERSON. I MEAN THE HOUSE.
LET'S SEE. THE HOUSE IS ABOUT... HERE, YES?
IF THIS MAP IS CORRECT, IT IS IN THE OPPOSITE DIRECTION FROM THE LAKE AND VILLAGE.
IT IS QUITE FAR FROM HERE, TOO.
IF SOME-ONE LIVED THERE, THERE MUST BE A VILLAGE OR HAMLET.
A DIFFERENT HOUSE MAY SUIT OUR NEEDS, TOO.
WE NEED NO LONGER WORRY ABOUT WANDERING THE FOREST.

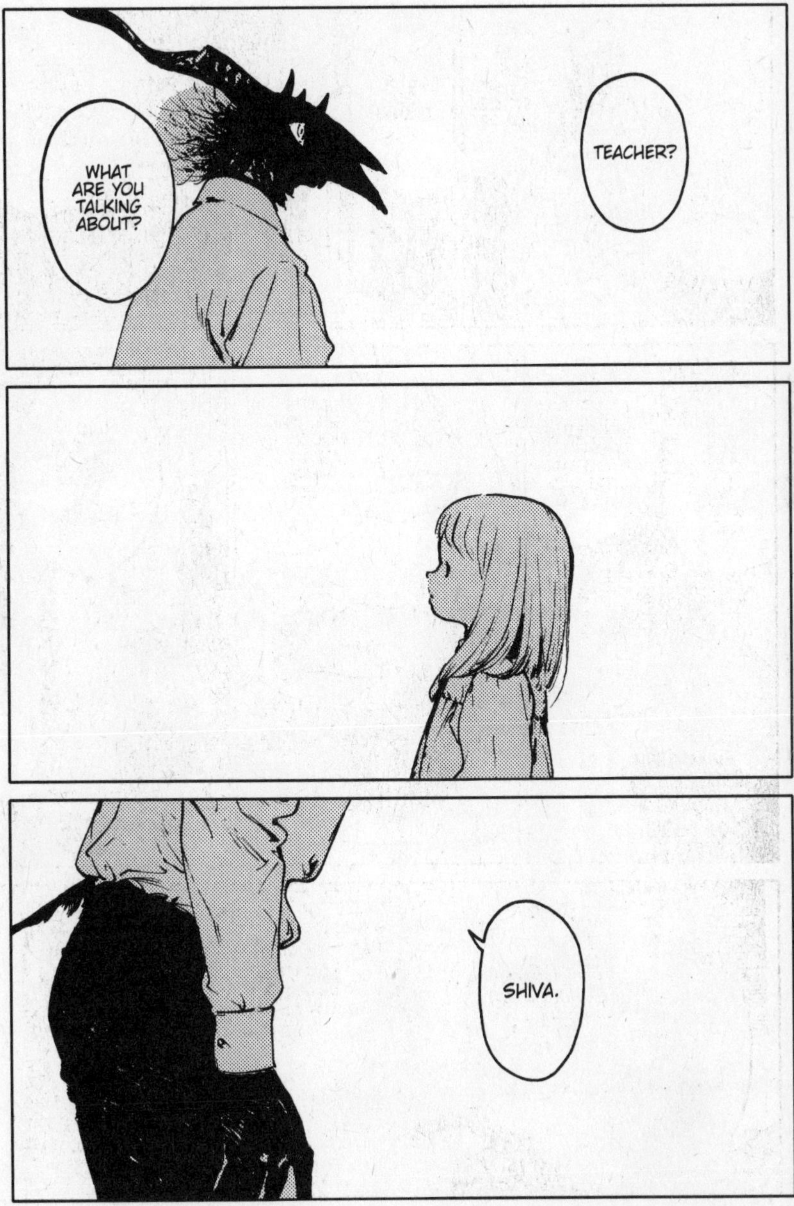
TEACHER?
WHAT ARE YOU TALKING ABOUT?
SHIVA.

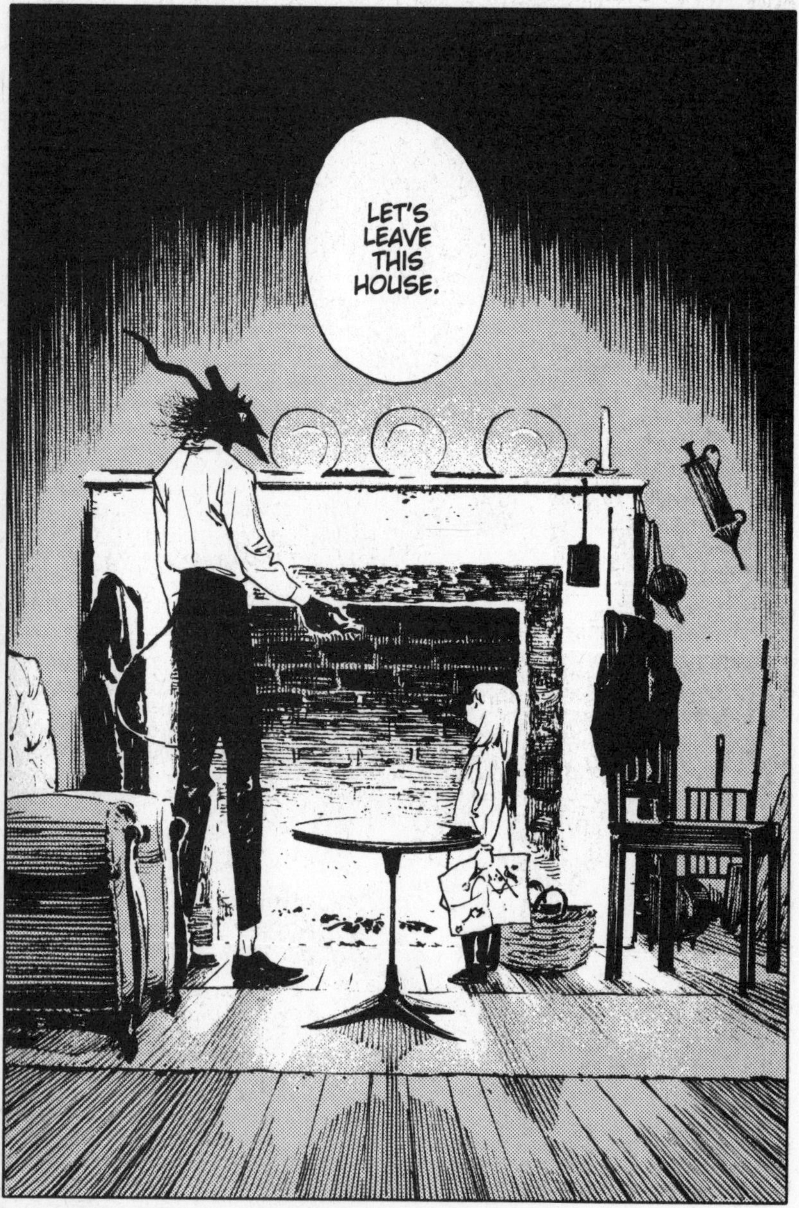
LET'S LEAVE THIS HOUSE.

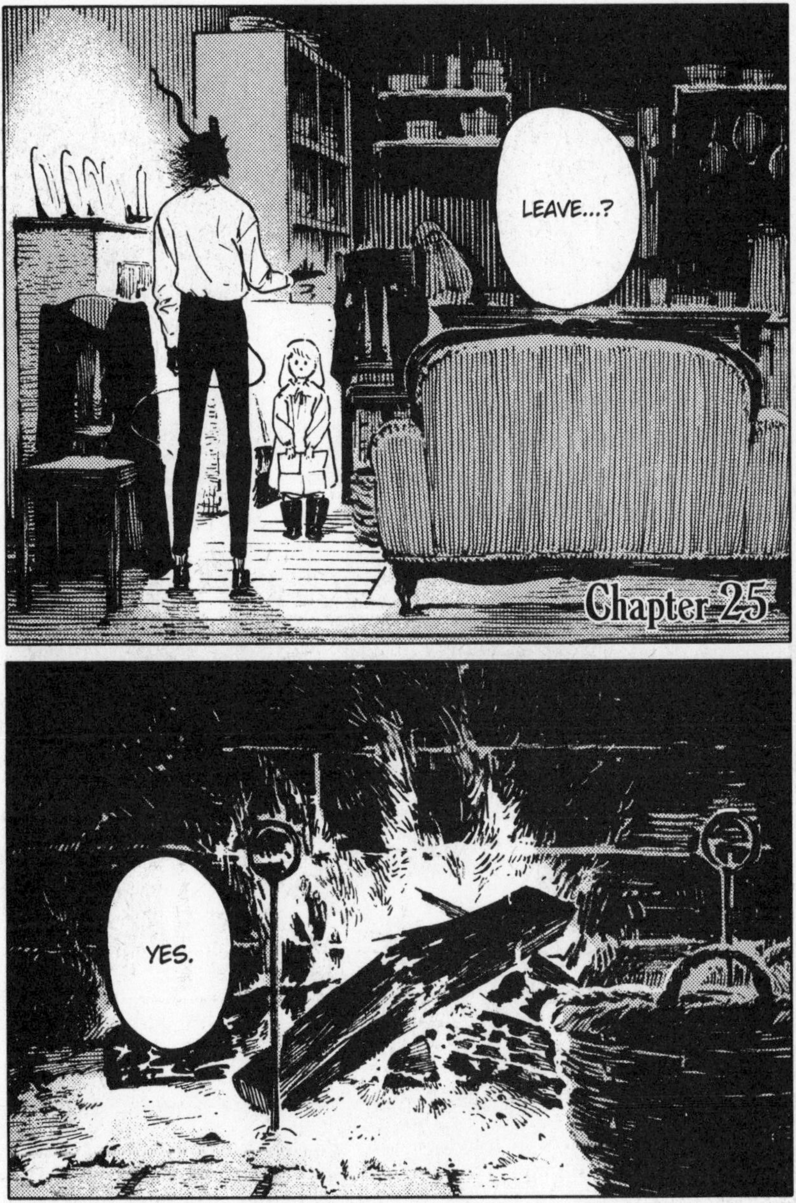
LEAVE...?
Chapter 25
YES.

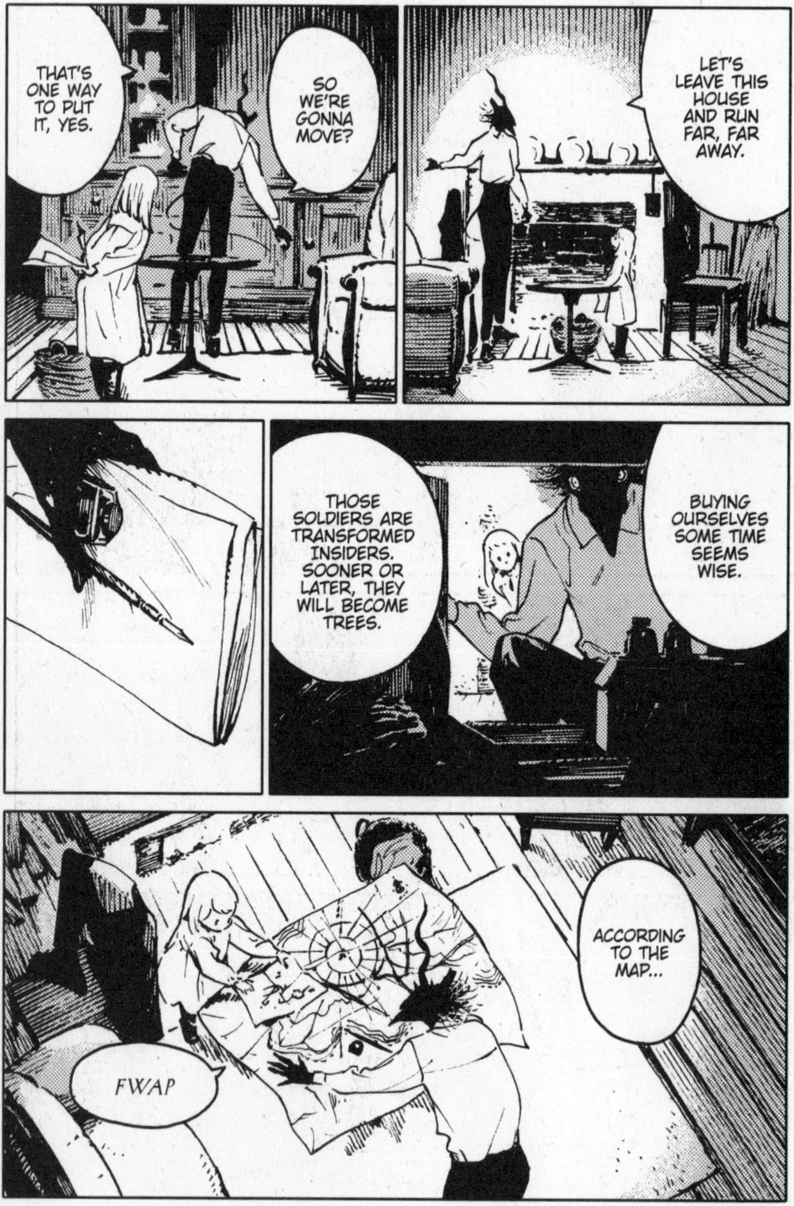
LET'S LEAVE THIS HOUSE AND RUN FAR, FAR AWAY.
SO WE'RE GONNA MOVE?
THAT'S ONE WAY TO PUT IT, YES.
BUYING OURSELVES SOME TIME SEEMS WISE.
THOSE SOLDIERS ARE TRANSFORMED INSIDERS. SOONER OR LATER, THEY WILL BECOME TREES.
ACCORDING TO THE MAP...
FWAP

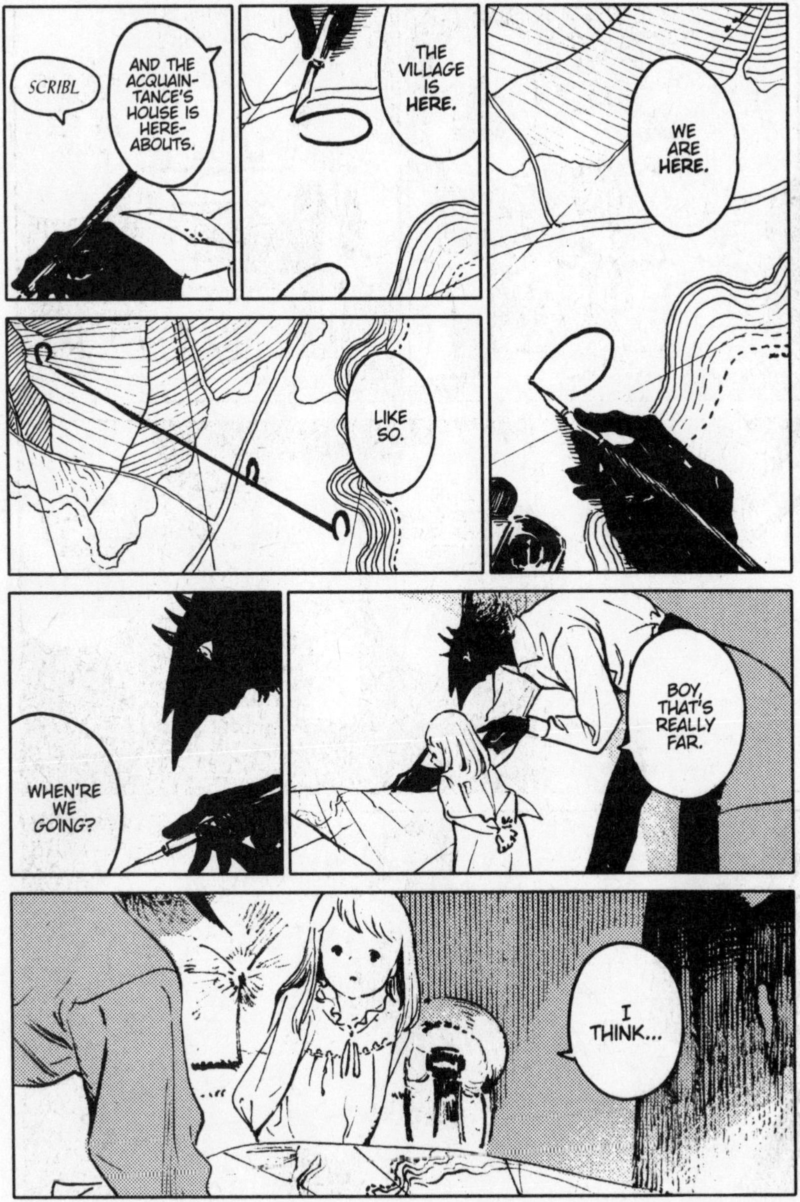
WE ARE HERE.
THE VILLAGE IS HERE.
AND THE ACQUAIN-TANCE'S HOUSE IS HERE-ABOUTS.
SCRIBL
LIKE SO.
BOY, THAT'S REALLY FAR.
WHEN'RE WE GOING?
I THINK...

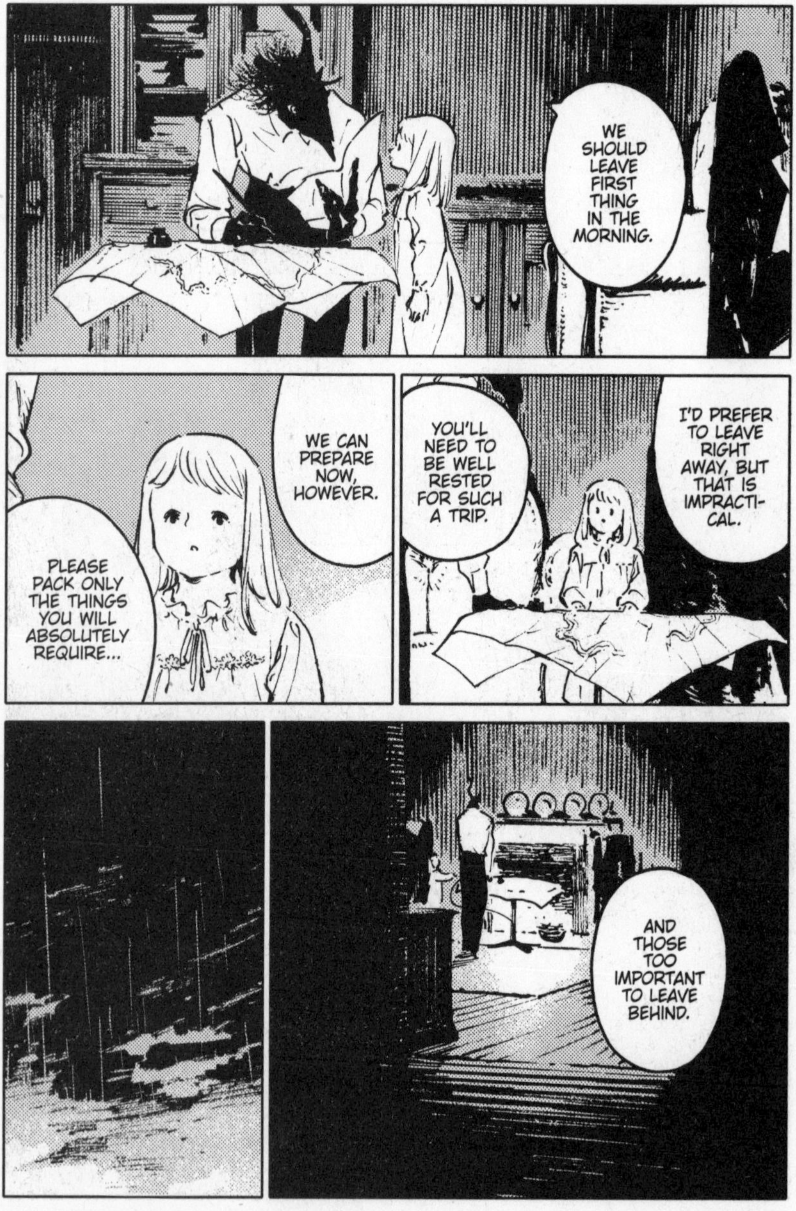
WE SHOULD LEAVE FIRST THING IN THE MORNING.
I'D PREFER TO LEAVE RIGHT AWAY, BUT THAT IS IMPRACTI-CAL.
YOU'LL NEED TO BE WELL RESTED FOR SUCH A TRIP.
WE CAN PREPARE NOW, HOWEVER.
PLEASE PACK ONLY THE THINGS YOU WILL ABSOLUTELY REQUIRE...
AND THOSE TOO IMPORTANT TO LEAVE BEHIND.

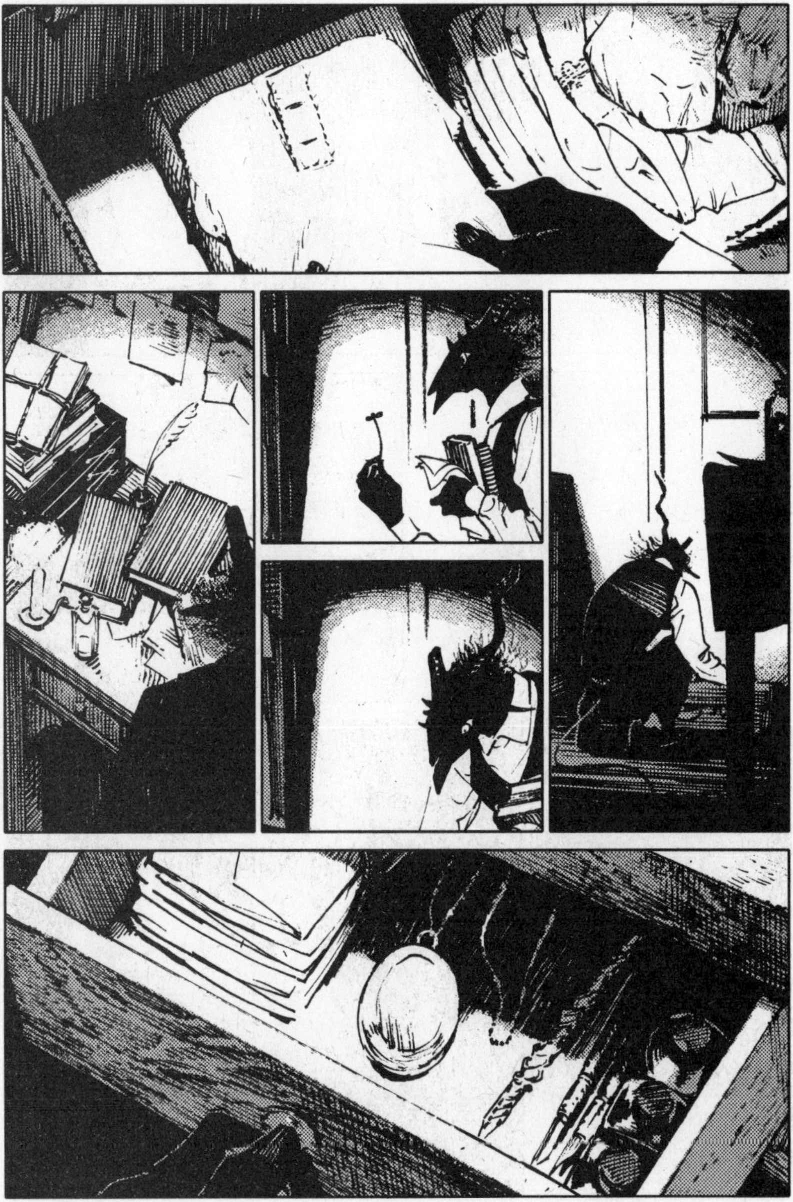

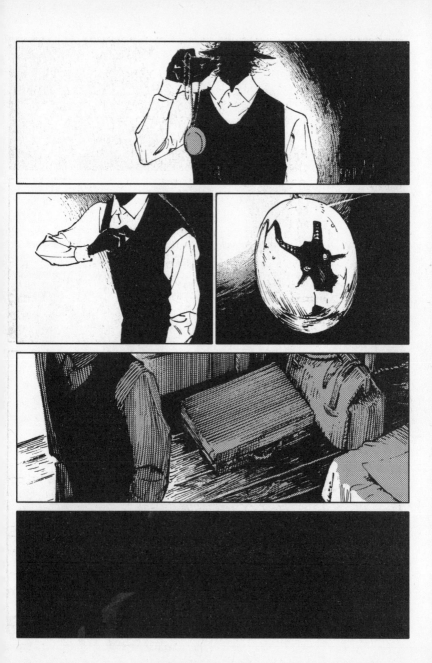

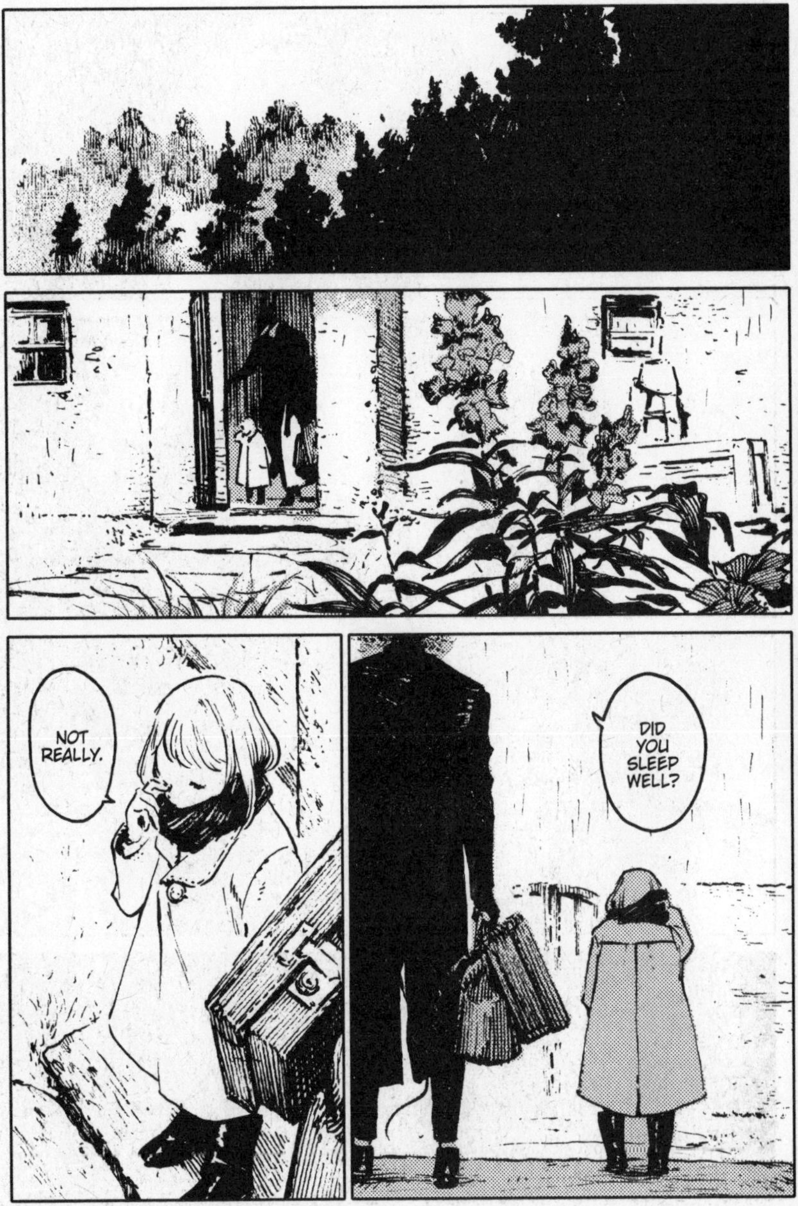
DID YOU SLEEP WELL?
NOT REALLY.

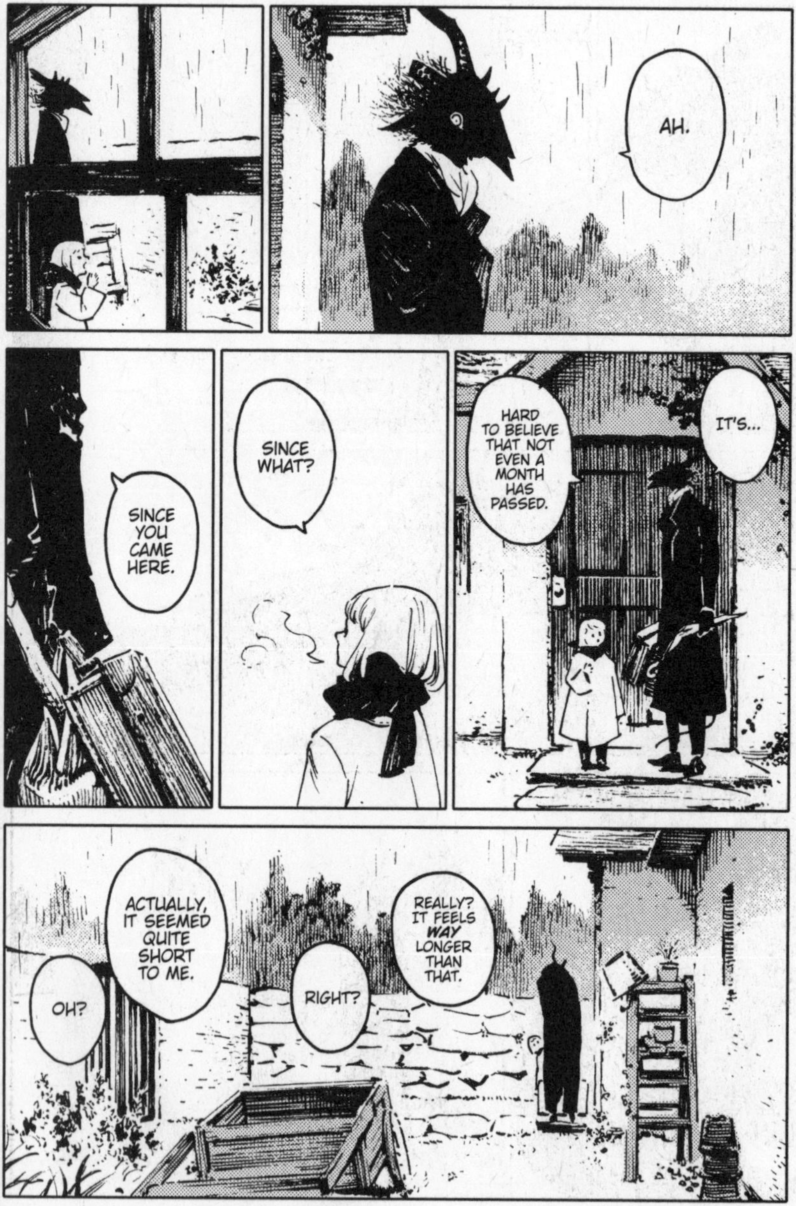
AH.
IT'S...
HARD TO BELIEVE THAT NOT EVEN A MONTH HAS PASSED.
SINCE WHAT?
SINCE YOU CAME HERE.
REALLY? IT FEELS *WAY* LONGER THAN THAT.
RIGHT?
ACTUALLY, IT SEEMED QUITE SHORT TO ME.
OH?

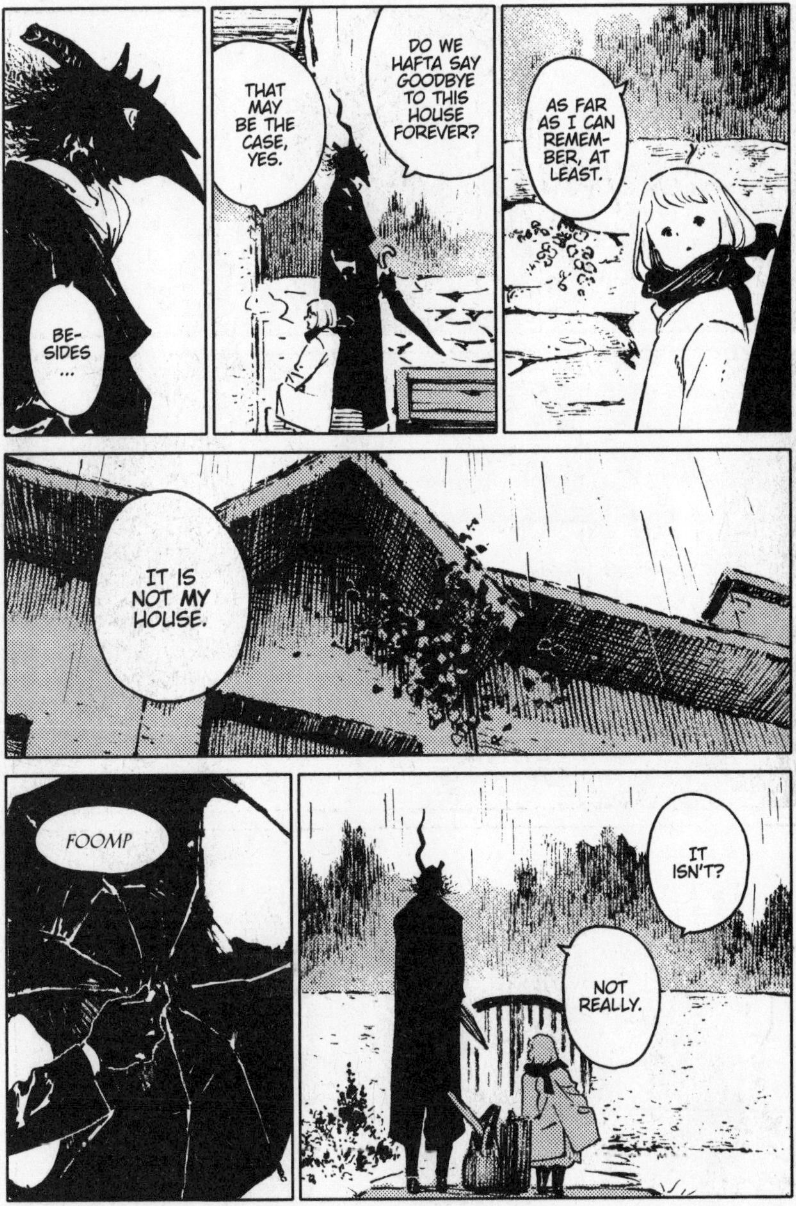
AS FAR AS I CAN REMEMBER, AT LEAST.
DO WE HAFTA SAY GOODBYE TO THIS HOUSE FOREVER?
THAT MAY BE THE CASE, YES.
BE-SIDES...
IT IS NOT MY HOUSE.
IT ISN'T?
NOT REALLY.
FOOMP

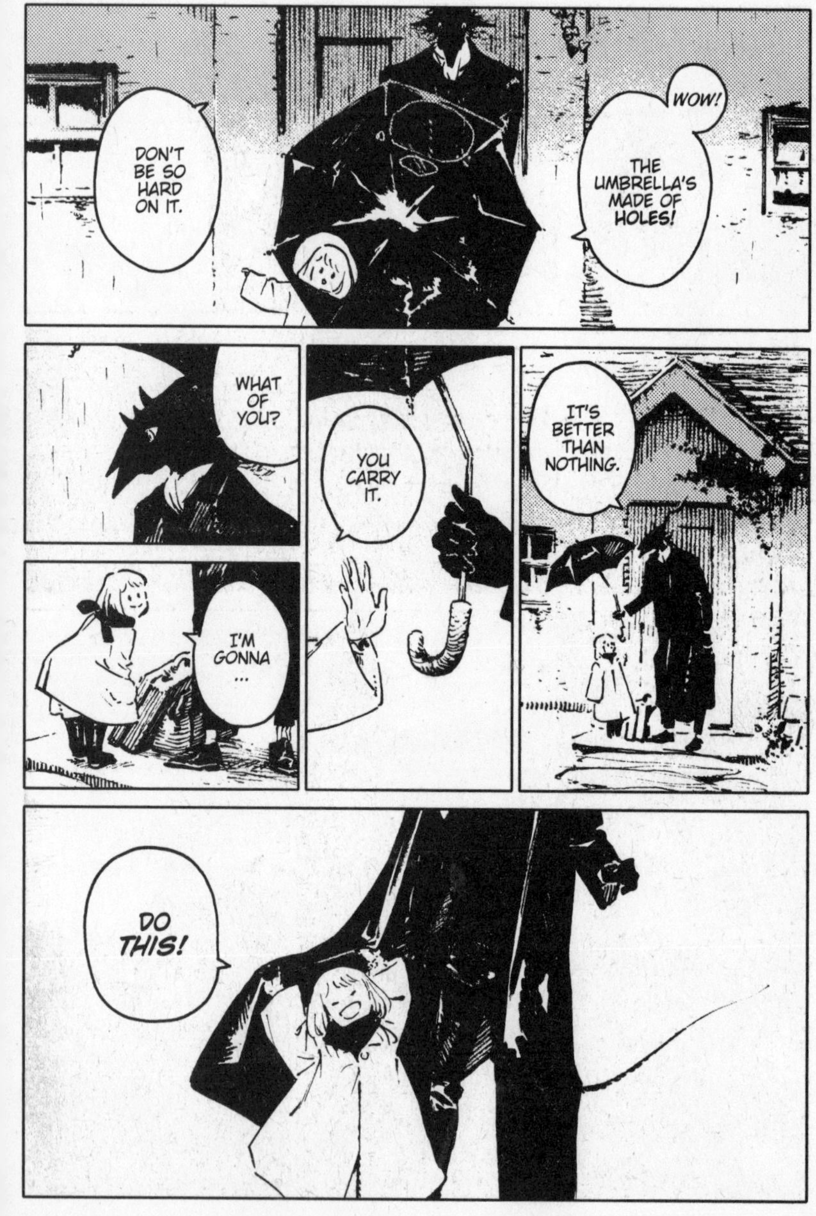
WOW!
THE UMBRELLA'S MADE OF HOLES!
DON'T BE SO HARD ON IT.
IT'S BETTER THAN NOTHING.
YOU CARRY IT.
WHAT OF YOU?
I'M GONNA ...
DO THIS!

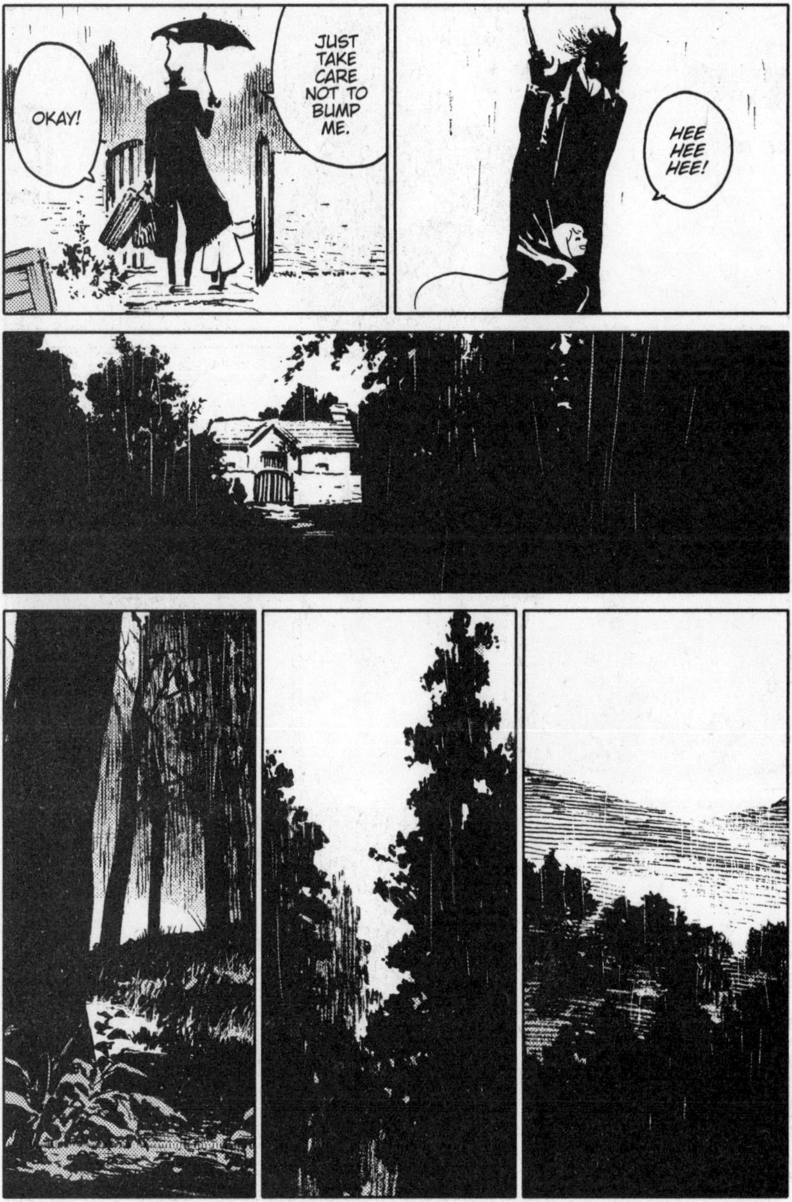
HEE HEE HEE!
JUST TAKE CARE NOT TO BUMP ME.
OKAY!

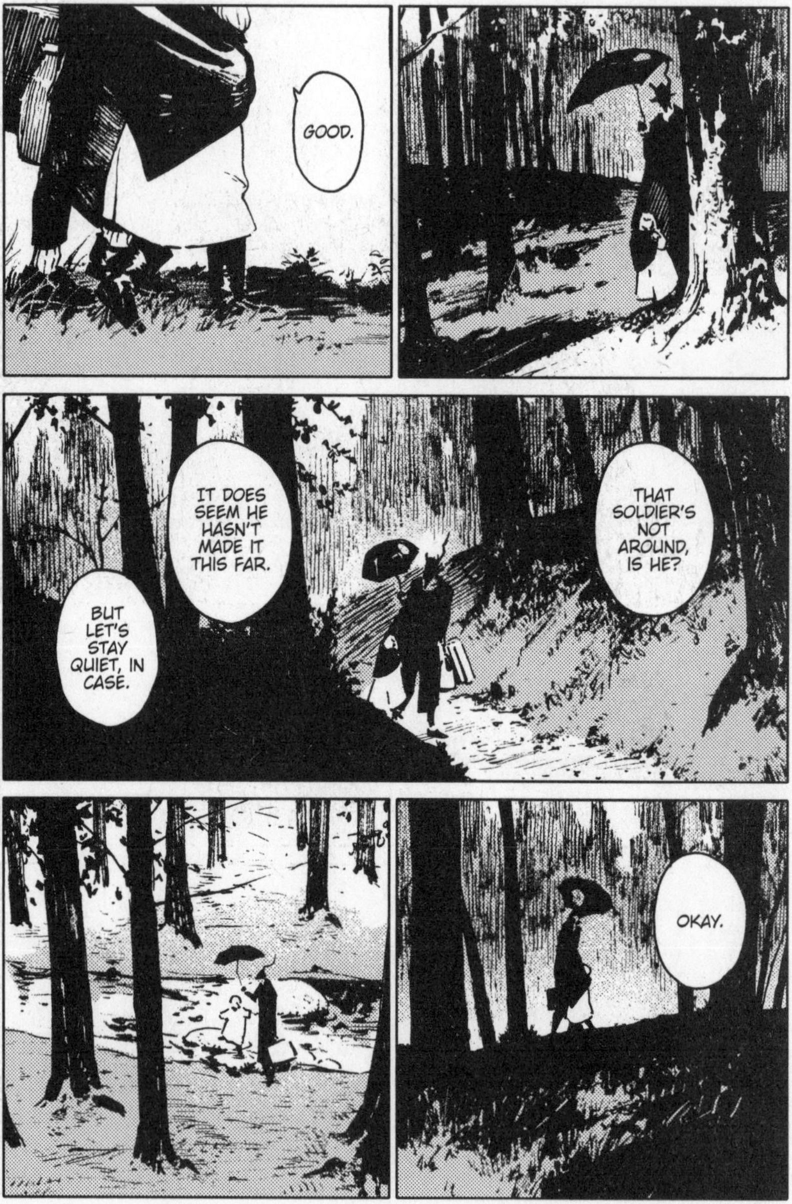
GOOD.
THAT SOLDIER'S NOT AROUND, IS HE?
IT DOES SEEM HE HASN'T MADE IT THIS FAR.
BUT LET'S STAY QUIET, IN CASE.
OKAY.

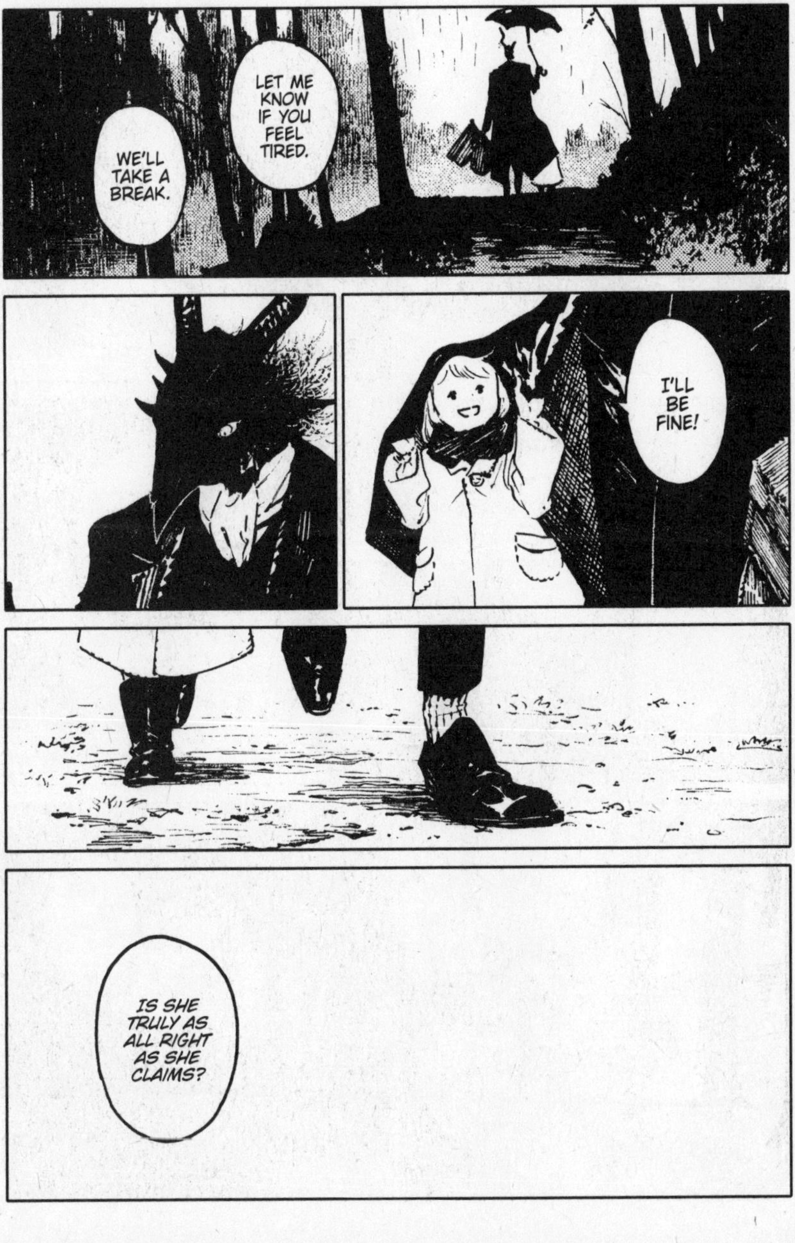
LET ME KNOW IF YOU FEEL TIRED.
WE'LL TAKE A BREAK.
I'LL BE FINE!
IS SHE TRULY AS ALL RIGHT AS SHE CLAIMS?

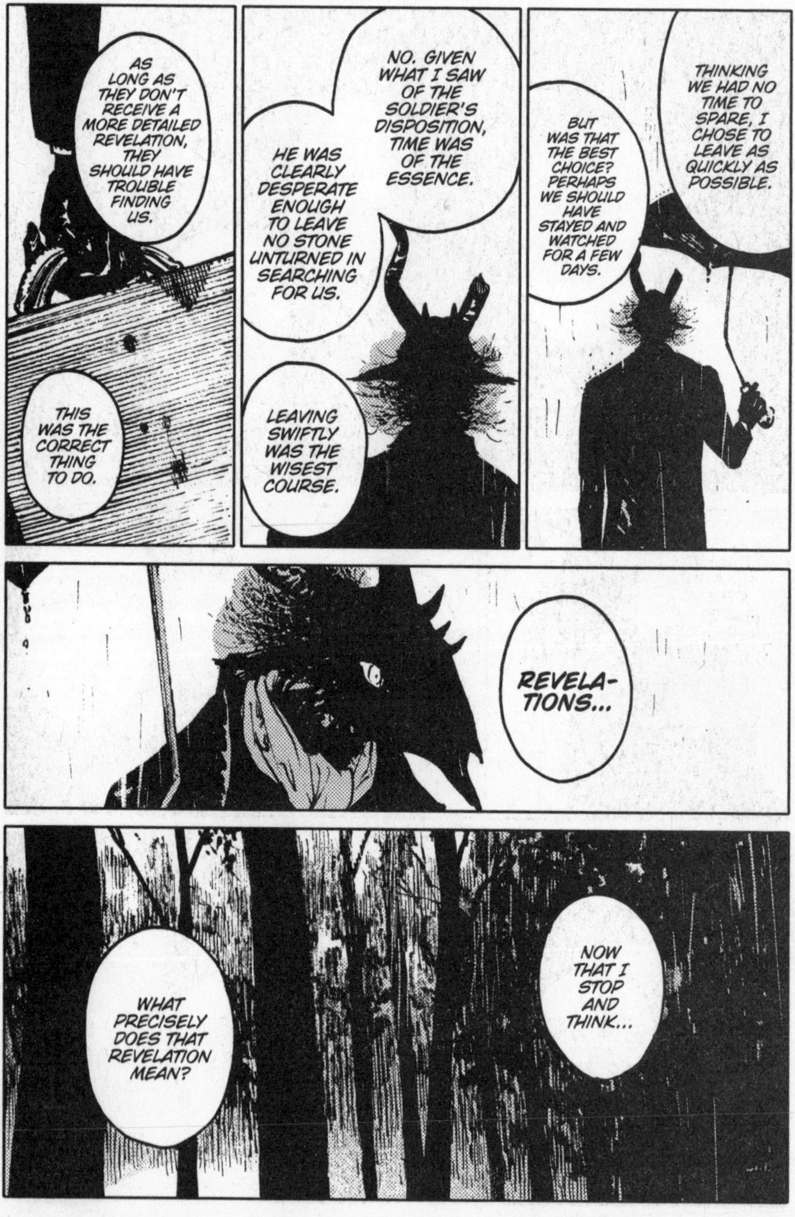
THINKING WE HAD NO TIME TO SPARE, I CHOSE TO LEAVE AS QUICKLY AS POSSIBLE.
BUT WAS THAT THE BEST CHOICE? PERHAPS WE SHOULD HAVE STAYED AND WATCHED FOR A FEW DAYS.
NO. GIVEN WHAT I SAW OF THE SOLDIER'S DISPOSITION, TIME WAS OF THE ESSENCE.
HE WAS CLEARLY DESPERATE ENOUGH TO LEAVE NO STONE UNTURNED IN SEARCHING FOR US.
LEAVING SWIFTLY WAS THE WISEST COURSE.
AS LONG AS THEY DON'T RECEIVE A MORE DETAILED REVELATION, THEY SHOULD HAVE TROUBLE FINDING US.
THIS WAS THE CORRECT THING TO DO.
REVELATIONS...
NOW THAT I STOP AND THINK...
WHAT PRECISELY DOES THAT REVELATION MEAN?

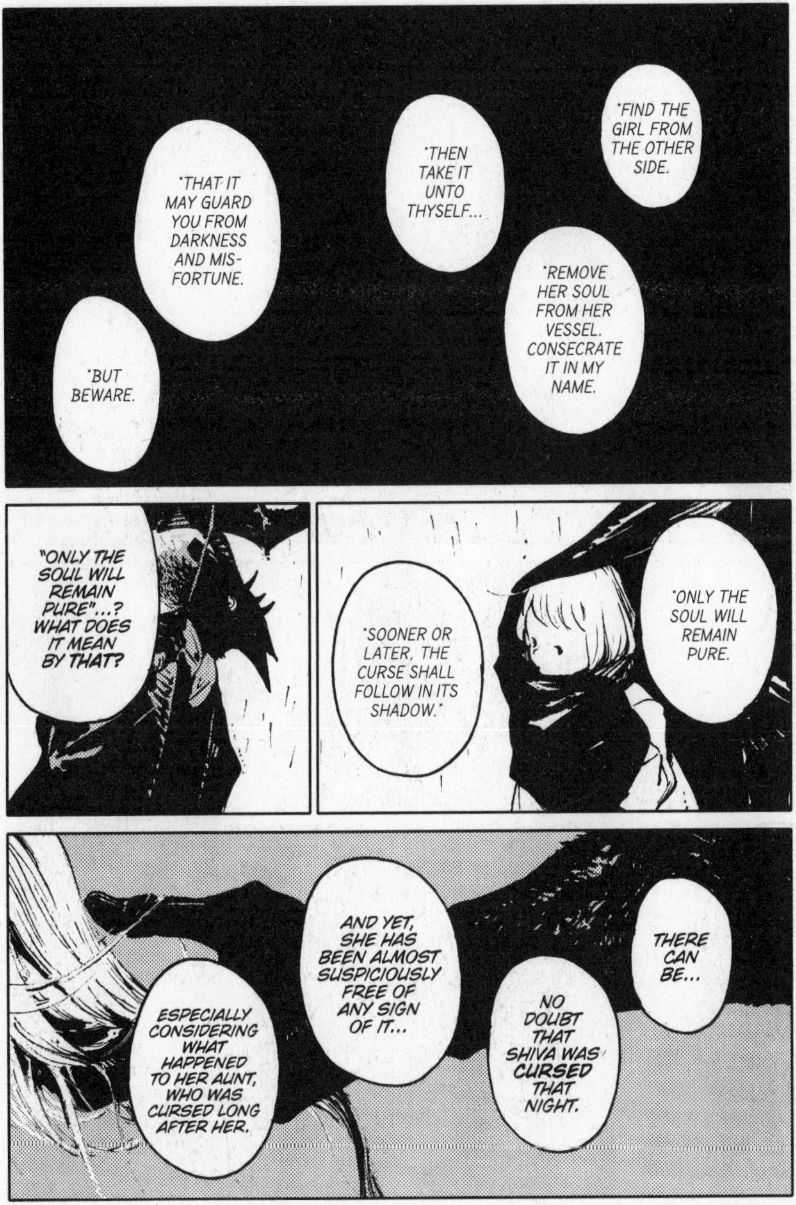
"FIND THE GIRL FROM THE OTHER SIDE.
"REMOVE HER SOUL FROM HER VESSEL. CONSECRATE IT IN MY NAME.
"THEN TAKE IT UNTO THYSELF...
"THAT IT MAY GUARD YOU FROM DARKNESS AND MIS-FORTUNE.
"BUT BEWARE.
"ONLY THE SOUL WILL REMAIN PURE.
"SOONER OR LATER, THE CURSE SHALL FOLLOW IN ITS SHADOW."
"ONLY THE SOUL WILL REMAIN PURE"...? WHAT DOES IT MEAN BY THAT?
THERE CAN BE...
NO DOUBT THAT SHIVA WAS CURSED THAT NIGHT.
AND YET, SHE HAS BEEN ALMOST SUSPICIOUSLY FREE OF ANY SIGN OF IT...
ESPECIALLY CONSIDERING WHAT HAPPENED TO HER AUNT, WHO WAS CURSED LONG AFTER HER.

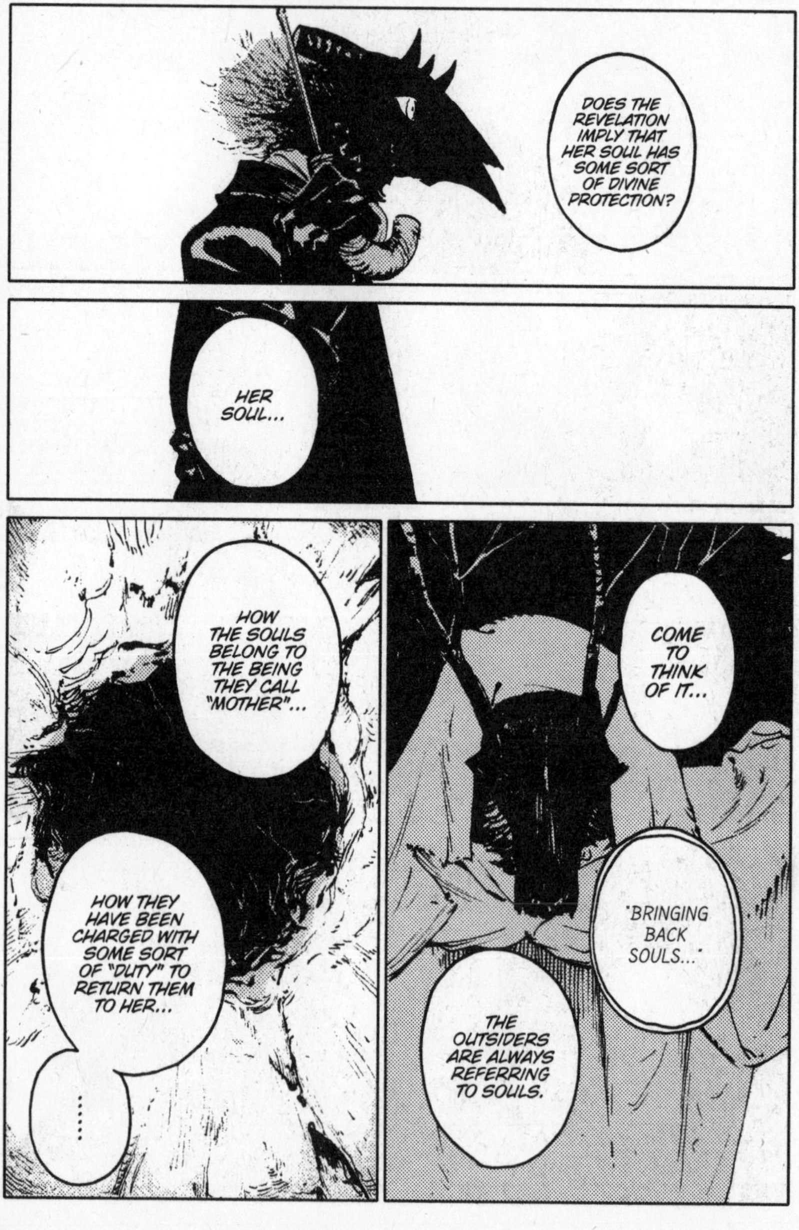
DOES THE REVELATION IMPLY THAT HER SOUL HAS SOME SORT OF DIVINE PROTECTION?
HER SOUL...
COME TO THINK OF IT...
"BRINGING BACK SOULS..."
THE OUTSIDERS ARE ALWAYS REFERRING TO SOULS.
HOW THE SOULS BELONG TO THE BEING THEY CALL "MOTHER"...
HOW THEY HAVE BEEN CHARGED WITH SOME SORT OF "DUTY" TO RETURN THEM TO HER...
......

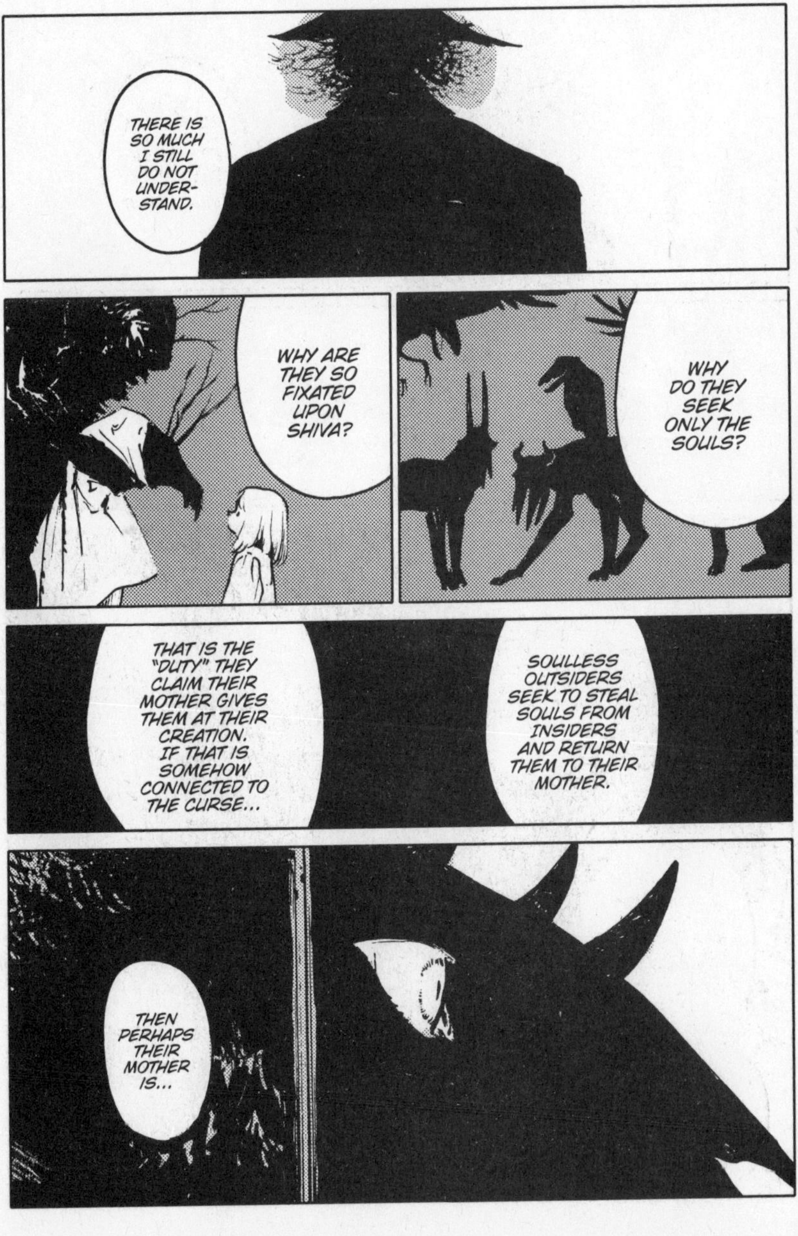
THERE IS SO MUCH I STILL DO NOT UNDER-STAND.
WHY DO THEY SEEK ONLY THE SOULS?
WHY ARE THEY SO FIXATED UPON SHIVA?
SOULLESS OUTSIDERS SEEK TO STEAL SOULS FROM INSIDERS AND RETURN THEM TO THEIR MOTHER.
THAT IS THE "DUTY" THEY CLAIM THEIR MOTHER GIVES THEM AT THEIR CREATION. IF THAT IS SOMEHOW CONNECTED TO THE CURSE...
THEN PERHAPS THEIR MOTHER IS...

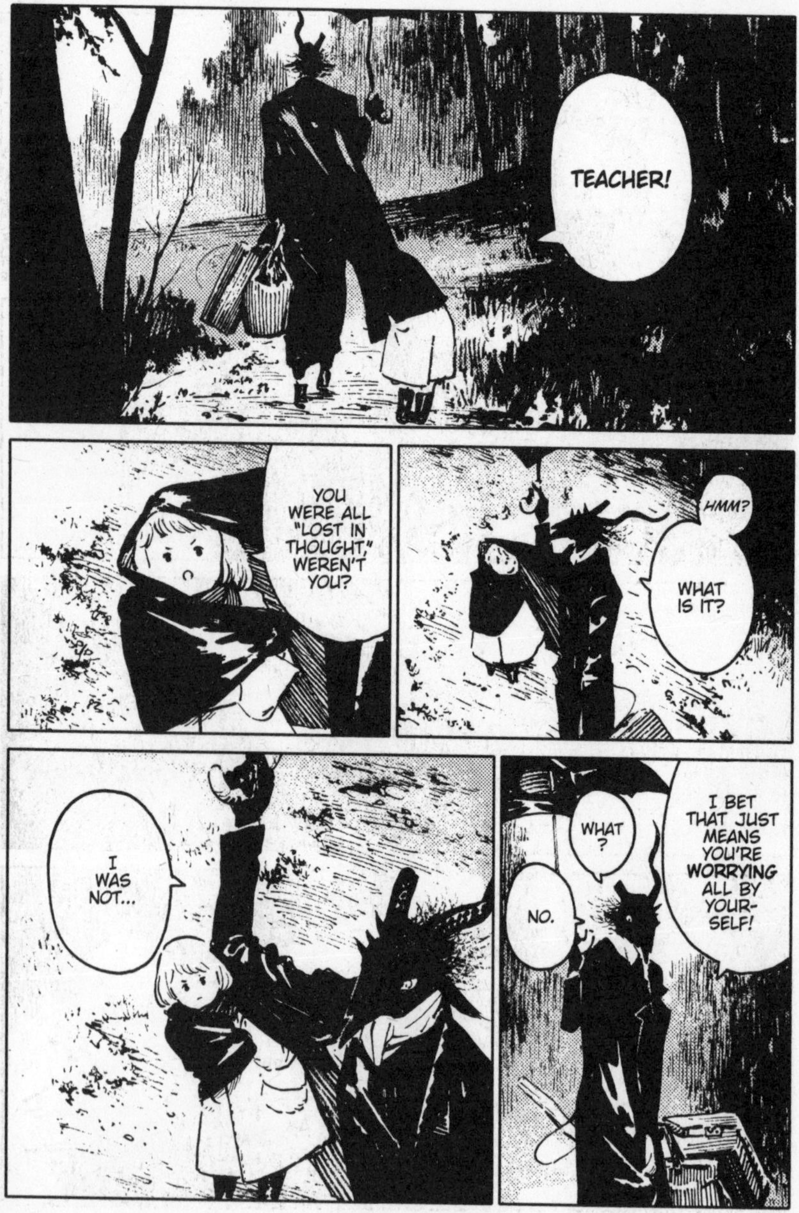
TEACHER!
HMM?
WHAT IS IT?
YOU WERE ALL "LOST IN THOUGHT," WEREN'T YOU?
I BET THAT JUST MEANS YOU'RE WORRYING ALL BY YOUR-SELF!
WHAT?
NO.
I WAS NOT...

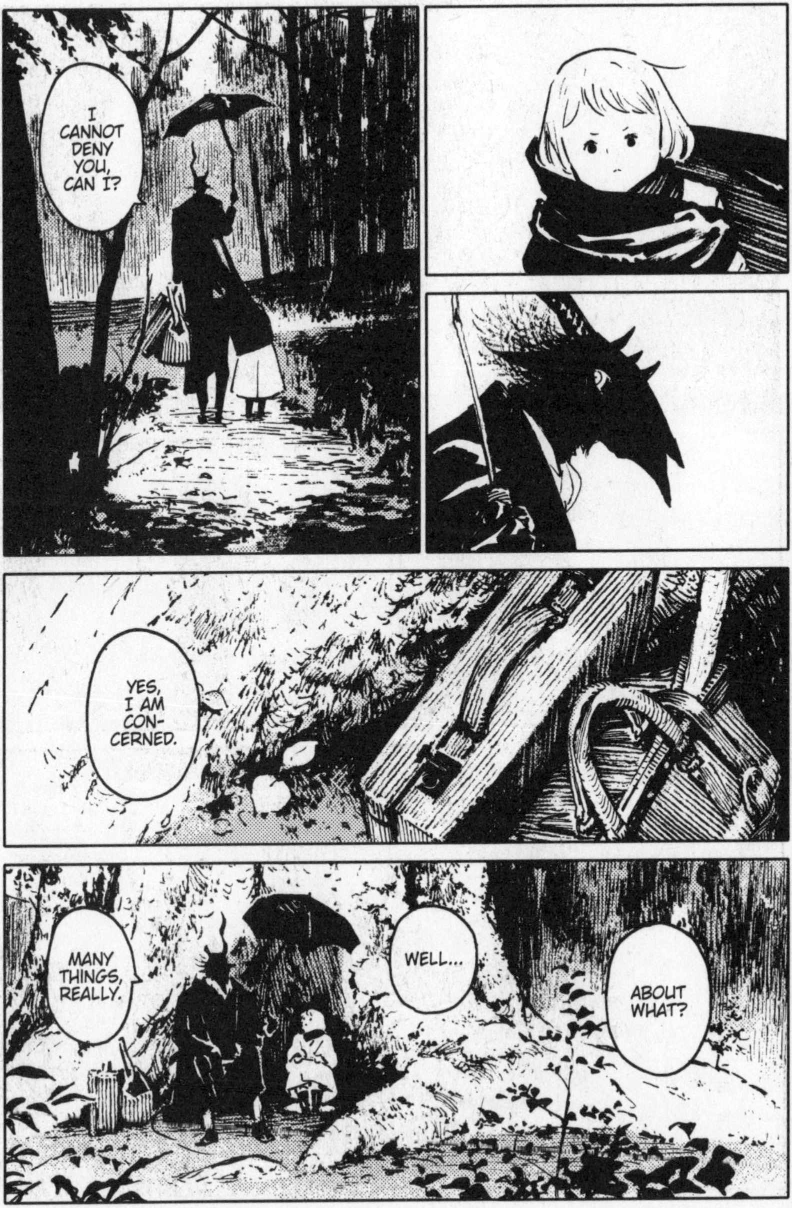
I CANNOT DENY YOU, CAN I?
YES, I AM CON-CERNED.
ABOUT WHAT?
WELL...
MANY THINGS, REALLY.

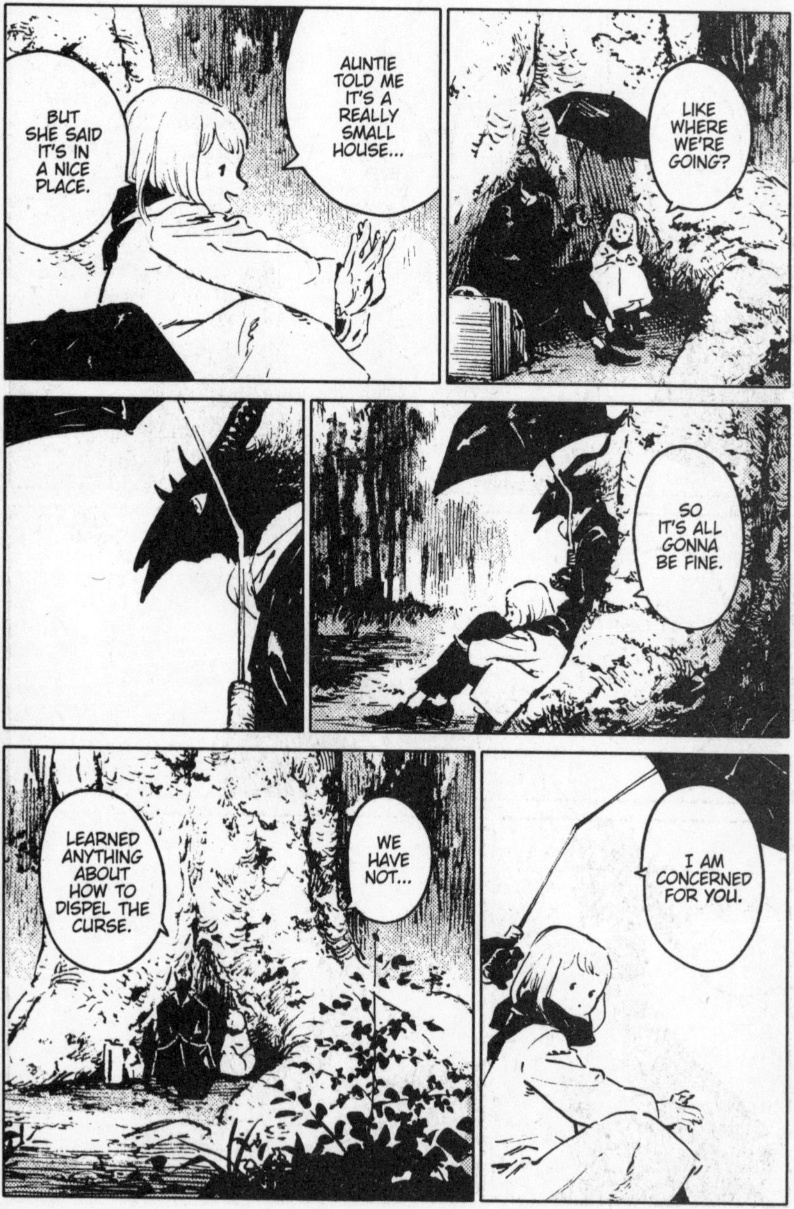
LIKE WHERE WE'RE GOING?
AUNTIE TOLD ME IT'S A REALLY SMALL HOUSE...
BUT SHE SAID IT'S IN A NICE PLACE.
SO IT'S ALL GONNA BE FINE.
I AM CONCERNED FOR YOU.
WE HAVE NOT...
LEARNED ANYTHING ABOUT HOW TO DISPEL THE CURSE.

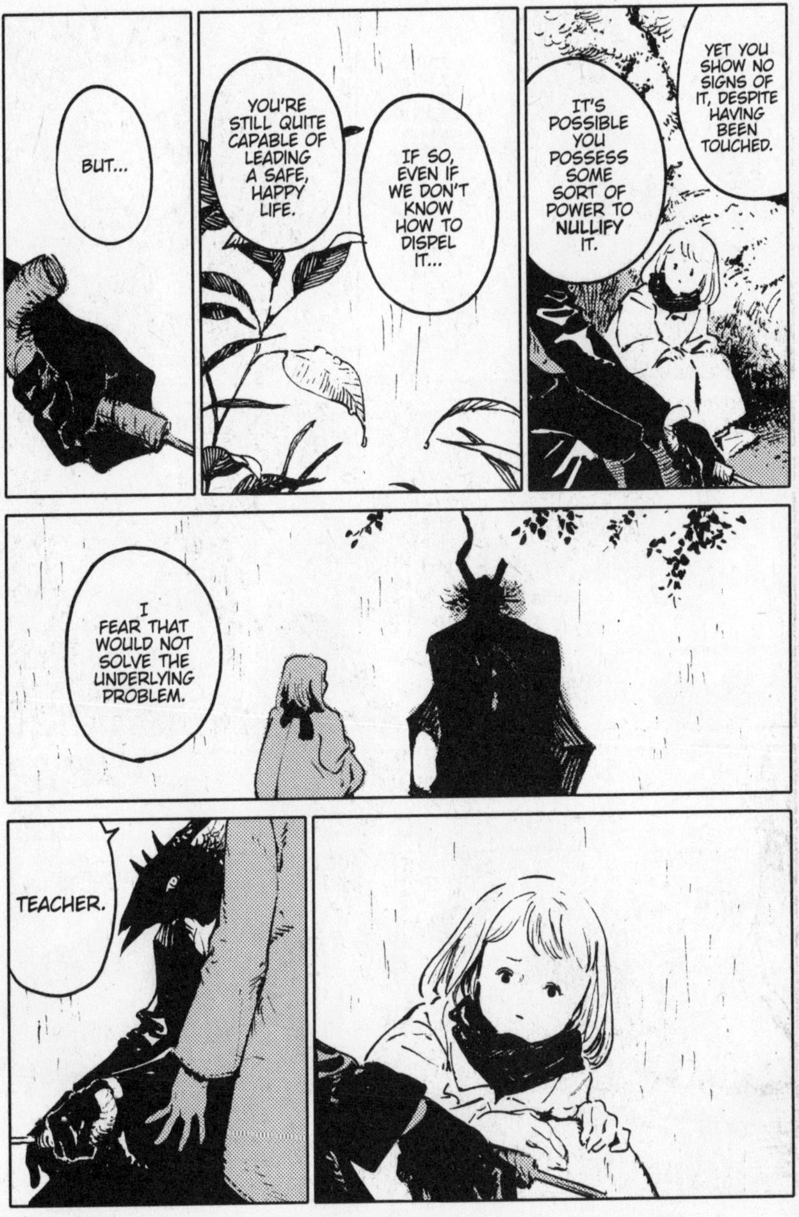
YET YOU SHOW NO SIGNS OF IT, DESPITE HAVING BEEN TOUCHED.
IT'S POSSIBLE YOU POSSESS SOME SORT OF POWER TO **NULLIFY** IT.
IF SO, EVEN IF WE DON'T KNOW HOW TO DISPEL IT...
YOU'RE STILL QUITE CAPABLE OF LEADING A SAFE, HAPPY LIFE.
BUT...
I FEAR THAT WOULD NOT SOLVE THE UNDERLYING PROBLEM.
TEACHER.

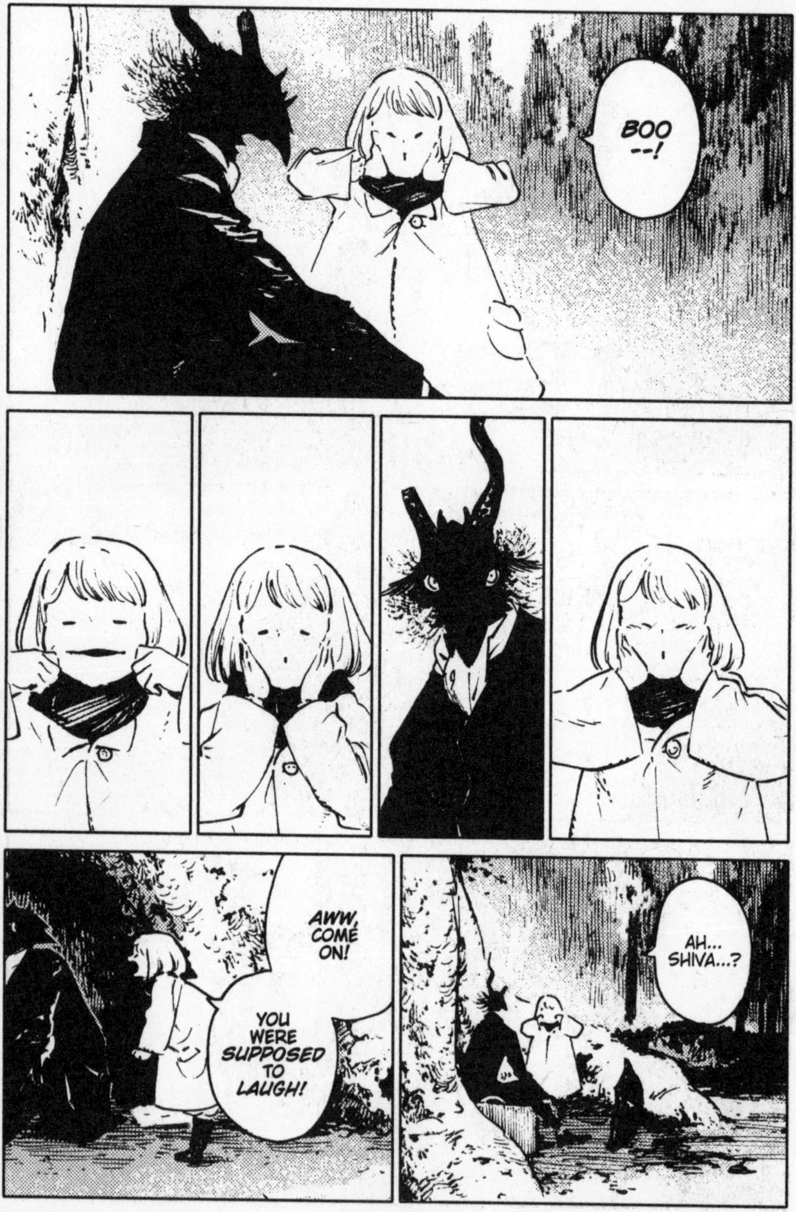
BOO--!
AH... SHIVA...?
AWW, COME ON!
YOU WERE SUPPOSED TO LAUGH!

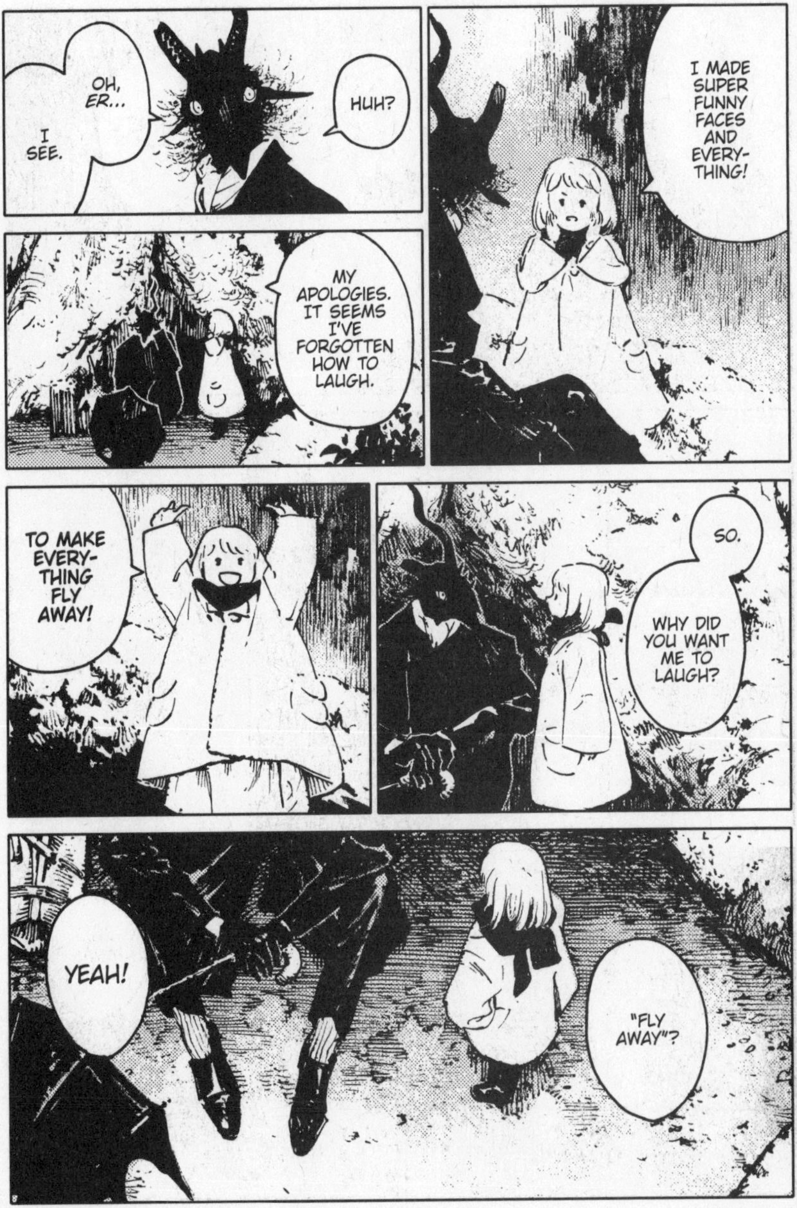
I MADE SUPER FUNNY FACES AND EVERY-THING!
HUH?
OH, ER...
I SEE.
MY APOLOGIES. IT SEEMS I'VE FORGOTTEN HOW TO LAUGH.
SO.
WHY DID YOU WANT ME TO LAUGH?
TO MAKE EVERY-THING FLY AWAY!
"FLY AWAY"?
YEAH!

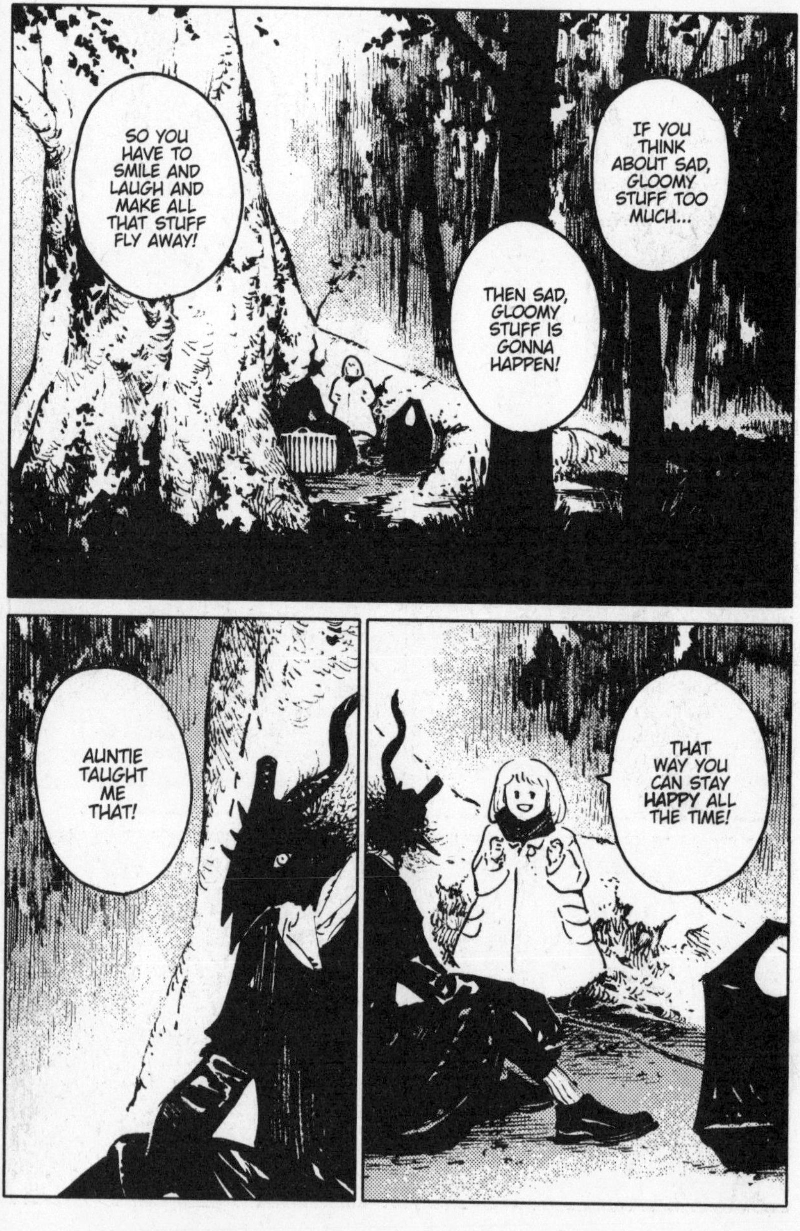
IF YOU THINK ABOUT SAD, GLOOMY STUFF TOO MUCH...
THEN SAD, GLOOMY STUFF IS GONNA HAPPEN!
SO YOU HAVE TO SMILE AND LAUGH AND MAKE ALL THAT STUFF FLY AWAY!
THAT WAY YOU CAN STAY HAPPY ALL THE TIME!
AUNTIE TAUGHT ME THAT!

. . . .

TEACH-ERRRR...!

REMIND ME, HOW DOES ONE SMILE...?

I'M SORRY.

SO SMILE, OKAY?

GOOD.

WHEN WE REACH OUR NEW HOME, I WILL PRACTICE.

GUESS WHAT?

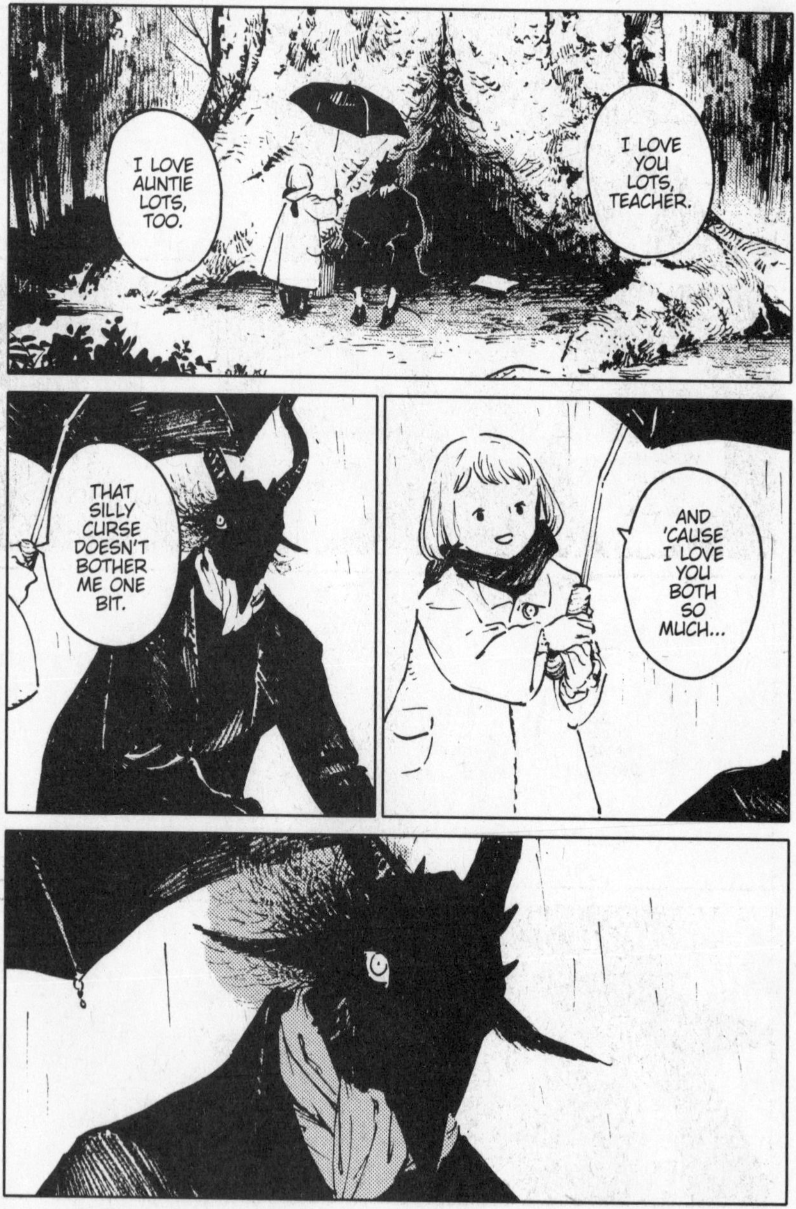
I LOVE YOU LOTS, TEACHER.
I LOVE AUNTIE LOTS, TOO.
AND 'CAUSE I LOVE YOU BOTH SO MUCH...
THAT SILLY CURSE DOESN'T BOTHER ME ONE BIT.

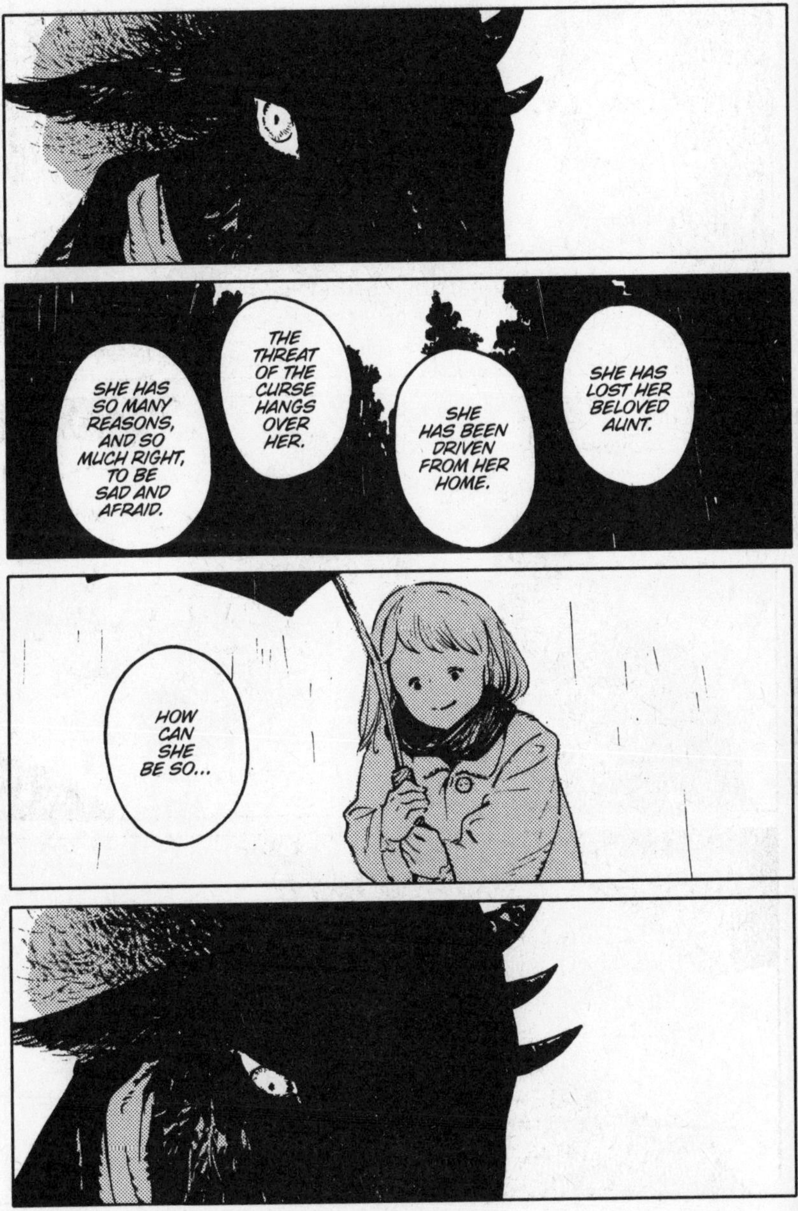
SHE HAS LOST HER BELOVED AUNT.
SHE HAS BEEN DRIVEN FROM HER HOME.
THE THREAT OF THE CURSE HANGS OVER HER.
SHE HAS SO MANY REASONS, AND SO MUCH RIGHT, TO BE SAD AND AFRAID.
HOW CAN SHE BE SO...

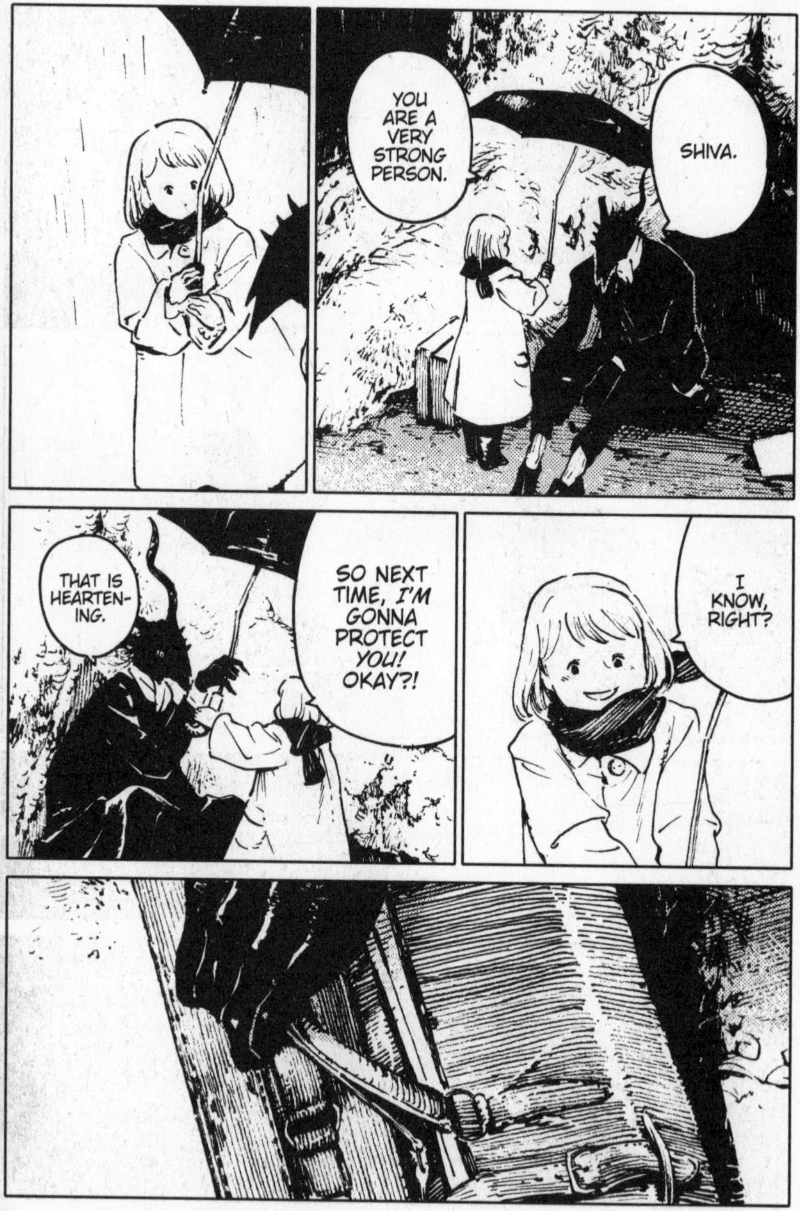
SHIVA.
YOU ARE A VERY STRONG PERSON.
I KNOW, RIGHT?
SO NEXT TIME, *I'M* GONNA PROTECT *YOU!* OKAY?!
THAT IS HEARTEN-ING.

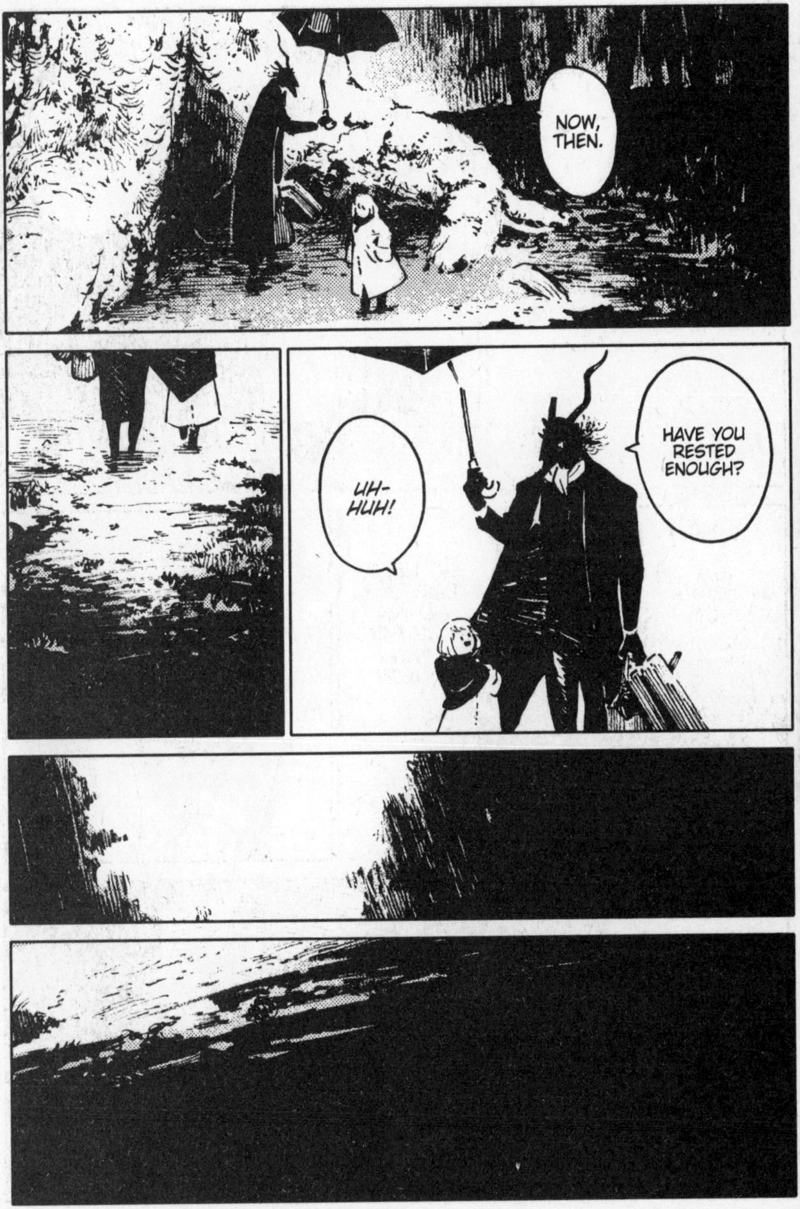
NOW, THEN.
HAVE YOU RESTED ENOUGH?
UH-HUH!

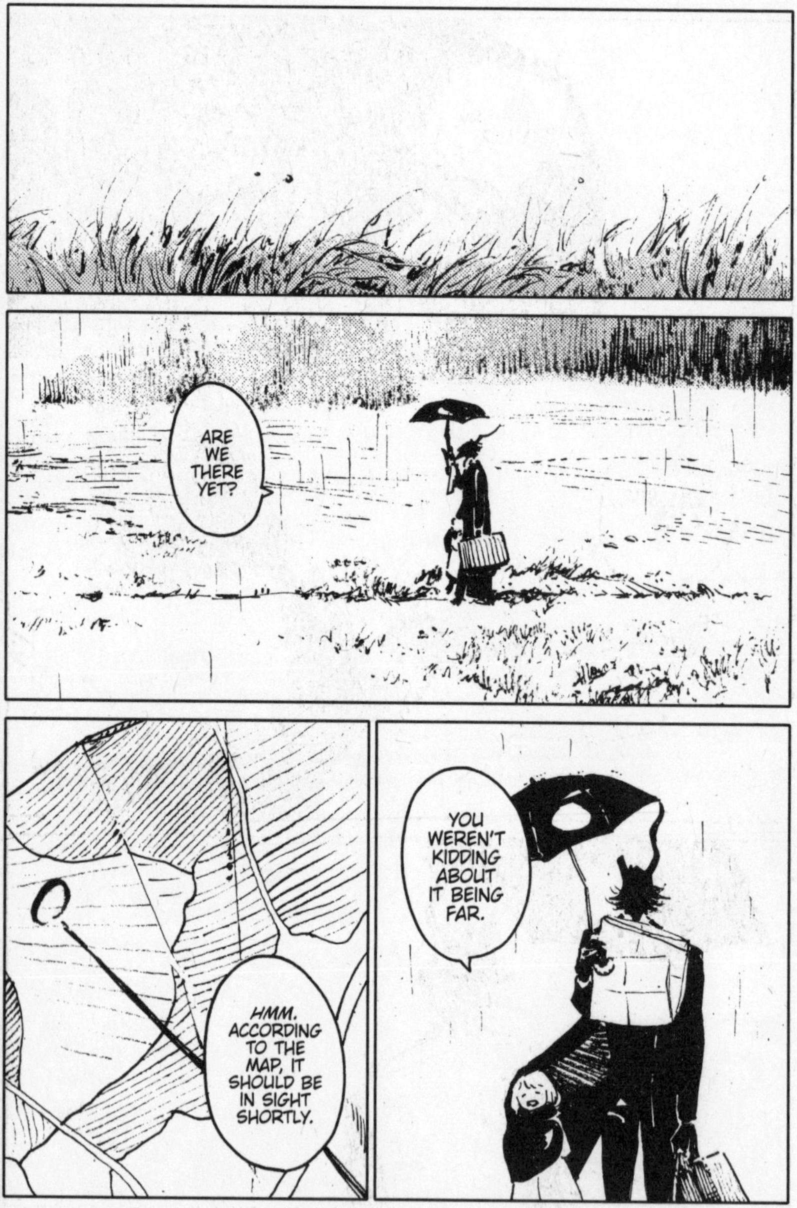
ARE WE THERE YET?
YOU WEREN'T KIDDING ABOUT IT BEING FAR.
HMM. ACCORDING TO THE MAP, IT SHOULD BE IN SIGHT SHORTLY.

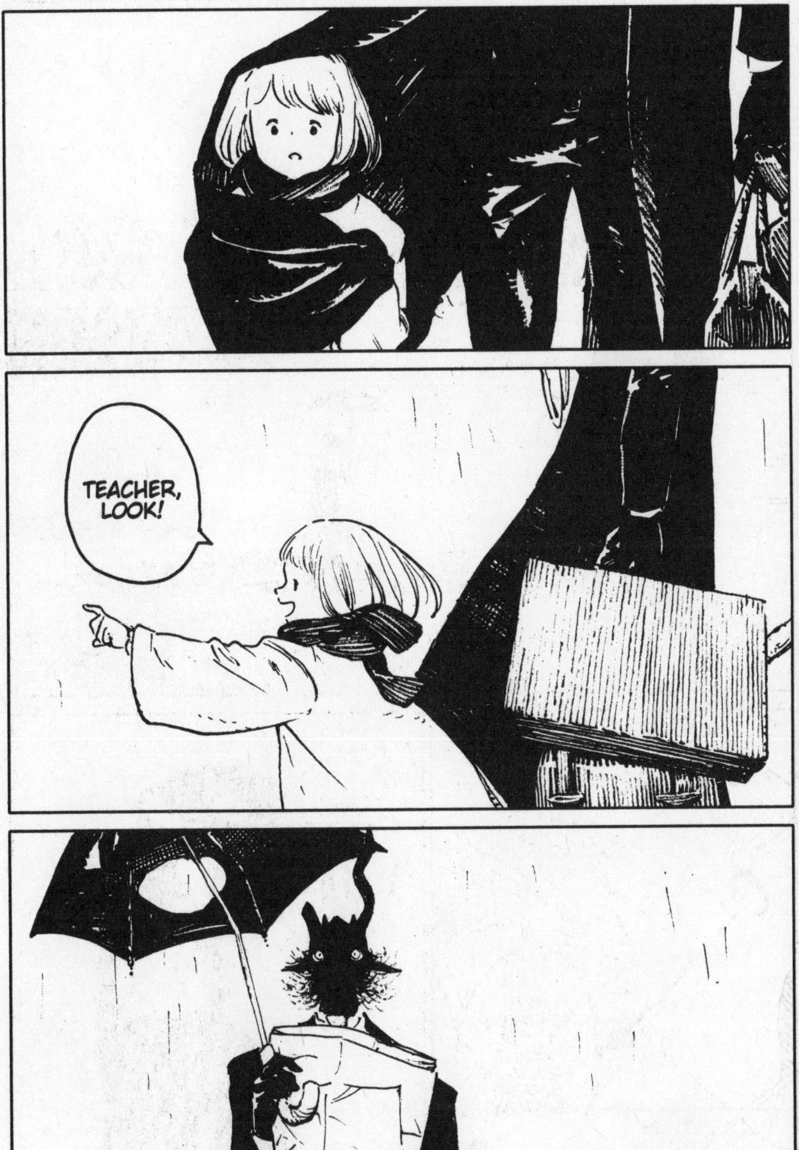
TEACHER, LOOK!

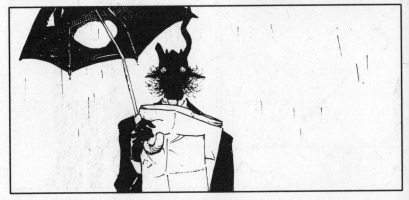

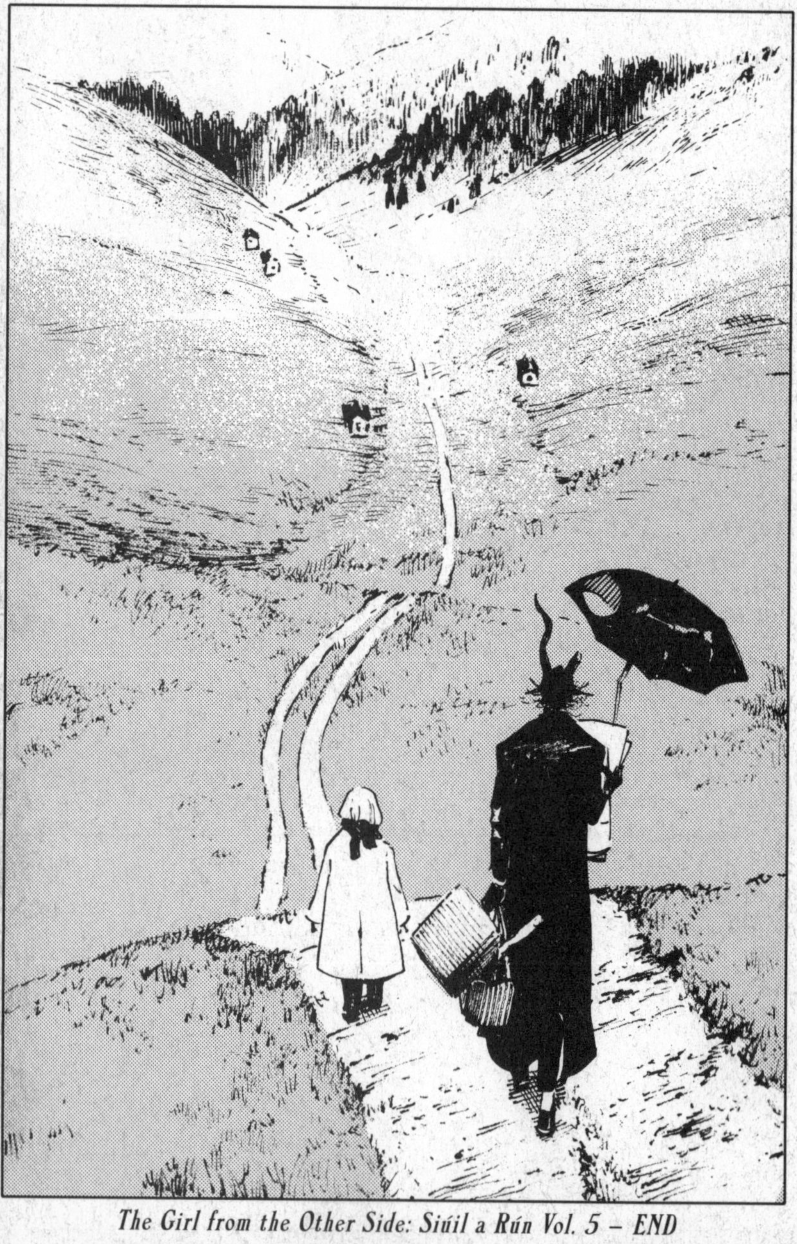

The Girl from the Other Side: Siúil a Rún Vol. 5 – END

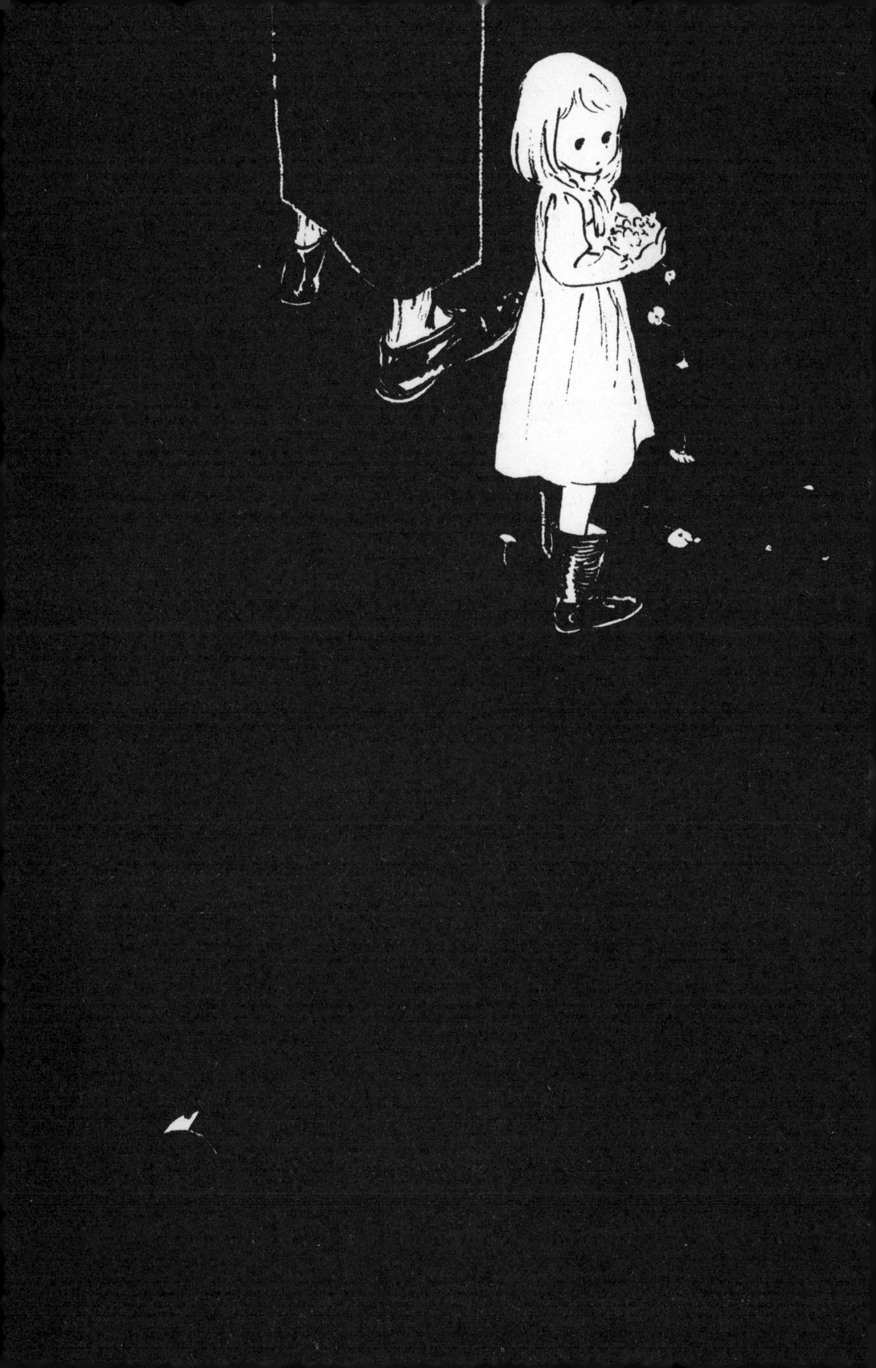

A Bonus from the Other Side

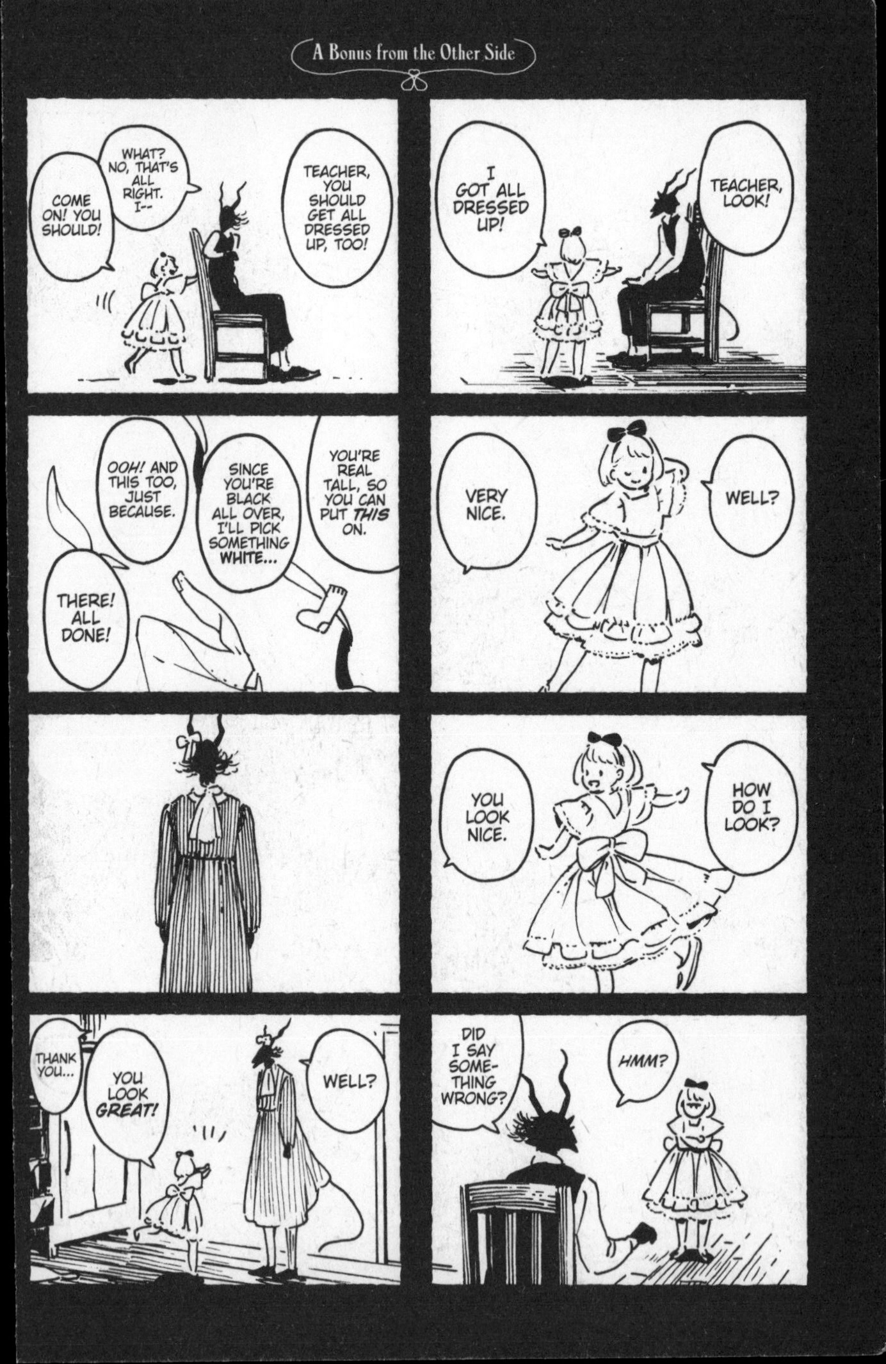
TEACHER, LOOK!
I GOT ALL DRESSED UP!
TEACHER, YOU SHOULD GET ALL DRESSED UP, TOO!
WHAT? NO, THAT'S ALL RIGHT. I--
COME ON! YOU SHOULD!
WELL?
VERY NICE.
YOU'RE REAL TALL, SO YOU CAN PUT *THIS* ON.
SINCE YOU'RE BLACK ALL OVER, I'LL PICK SOMETHING **WHITE...**
OOH! AND THIS TOO, JUST BECAUSE.
THERE! ALL DONE!
HOW DO I LOOK?
YOU LOOK NICE.
HMM?
DID I SAY SOME-THING WRONG?
WELL?
YOU LOOK *GREAT!*
THANK YOU...

A Bonus from the Outside

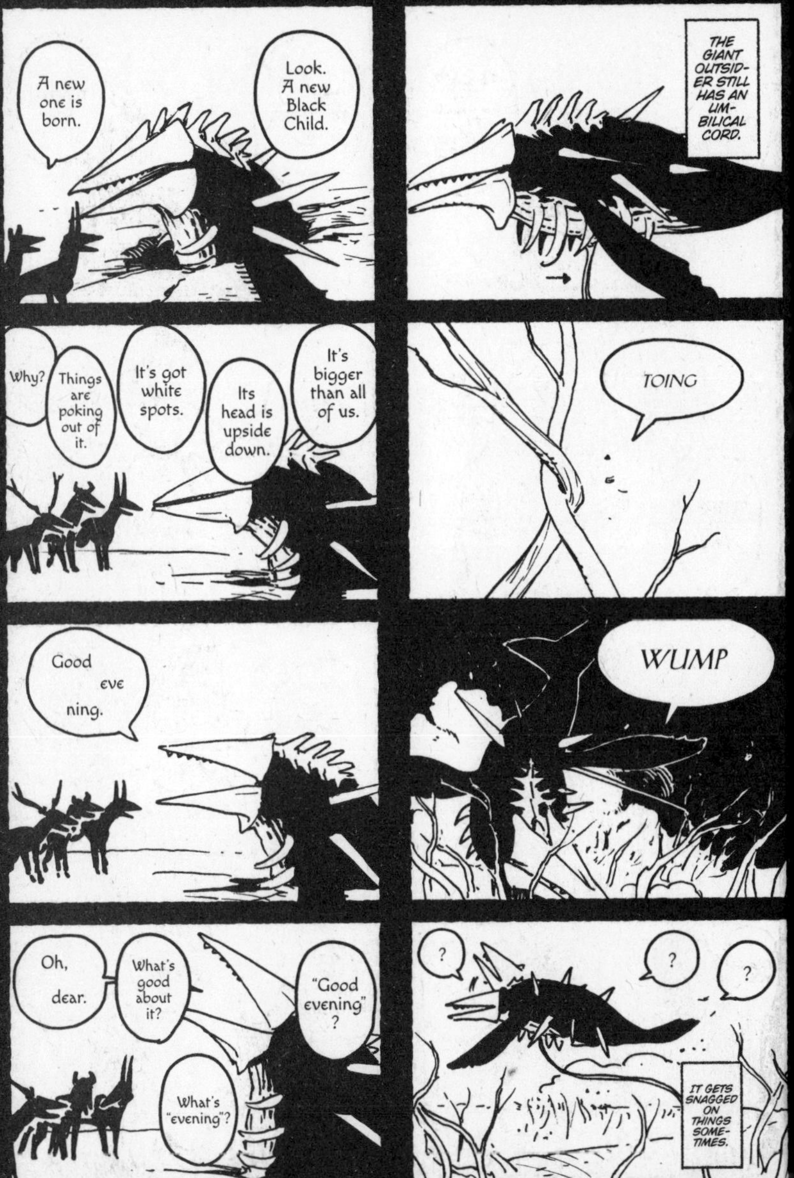

THE GIANT OUTSIDER STILL HAS AN UMBILICAL CORD.
Look. A new Black Child.
A new one is born.
TOING
It's bigger than all of us.
Its head is upside down.
It's got white spots.
Things are poking out of it.
Why?
WUMP
Good evening.
?
?
?
IT GETS SNAGGED ON THINGS SOMETIMES.
"Good evening"?
What's good about it?
What's "evening"?
Oh, dear.

SEVEN SEAS ENTERTAINMENT PRESENTS

Siúil, a Rún
The Girl from the Other Side

story and art by **NAGABE** vol. 5

TRANSLATION
Adrienne Beck

ADAPTATION
Ysabet MacFarlane

LETTERING AND RETOUCH
Lys Blakeslee

LOGO DESIGN
Karis Page

COVER DESIGN
Nicky Lim

PROOFREADER
Kurestin Armada
Cae Hawksmoor

ASSISTANT EDITOR
J.P. Sullivan

PRODUCTION ASSISTANT
CK Russell

PRODUCTION MANAGER
Lissa Pattillo

EDITOR-IN-CHIEF
Adam Arnold

PUBLISHER
Jason DeAngelis

THE GIRL FROM THE OTHER SIDE: SIUIL, A RUN VOL. 5

Originally published in Japan in 2018 by MAG Garden Corporation, Tokyo.
English translation rights arranged through TOHAN CORPORATION, Tokyo.

ISBN: 978-1-626928-47-3

Printed in Canada

First Printing: September 2018

10 9 8 7 6 5 4 3 2 1

FOLLOW US ONLINE: ***www.sevenseasentertainment.com***

READING DIRECTIONS

This book reads from ***right to left***, Japanese style. If this is your first time reading manga, you start reading from the top right panel on each page and take it from there. If you get lost, just follow the numbered diagram here. It may seem backwards at first, but you'll get the hang of it! Have fun!!

1
2
3
4
5
6
7
8
9

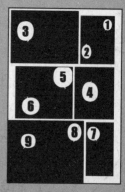